HACKNEY DOWNS

Also available from Cassell:

Dick Atkinson: *Radical Urban Solutions*
Dick Atkinson: *Cities of Pride*
Michael Barber: *Education in the Capital*
Michael Barber: *Education and the Teacher Unions*
Dave Hill and Mike Cole: *Promoting Equality in Secondary Schools*
Ian Lawrence: *Power and Politics at the Department of Education and Science*
Peter Ribbins and Brian Sherratt: *Radical Education Policies and Conservative Secretaries of State*
John Sayer: *The General Teaching Council*

Hackney Downs

The School that Dared to Fight

Maureen O'Connor, Elizabeth Hales,
Jeff Davies and Sally Tomlinson

CASSELL
London and New York

Cassell

Wellington House
125 Strand
London WC2R 0BB

370 Lexington Avenue
New York
NY 10017-6550

© Maureen O'Connor, Elizabeth Hales, Jeff Davies and
  Sally Tomlinson 1999

First published 1999

British Library Cataloguing in Publication Data
A catalogue record for this book is available from the British Library

ISBN   0-304-70710-4

Typeset by Kenneth Burnley, Wirral, Cheshire
Printed and bound in Great Britain by Redwood Books,
Trowbridge, Wiltshire

Contents

Acknowledgements

There were too many players in the final stages of this story for them all to be mentioned by name. The children, parents and staff of Hackney Downs in its closing days would like to thank all of those who sent or gave their support during that most difficult of times. They know who they are, and they can be satisfied that they did not bend with the wind.

This is the story of a community, of children betrayed in the interests of expediency, of parents who possessed a strength and will they hadn't realized they had, and of a staff who to their eternal credit and at the risk of their professional lives, stayed with those children until the end.

Especial thanks to Chris Gardiner, who looked, saw for himself, was convinced, and remained a steadfast friend.

Betty Hales and Jeff Davies would like personally to thank Daphne for her wisdom, Ken for sharing with them his love for the school and the kids, and Maureen Thurlow for being the 'heart' of Hackney Downs.

Thanks also to Lesley Douglas for helping to collect together and organize much of the original documentation on which the book is based.

Foreword

This extraordinary story of Hackney Downs School could also have been written about a number of other city schools and not exclusively in London. Each story would provide variations on a theme and, of course, Hackney Downs shows that when something can go wrong, Murphy's Law applies and almost everything else goes wrong at the same time. And the last chapter of the book shows there are many lessons to be learned from the experience if it is not always to be the poor that get the blame. Make no mistake about it, the real losers in this story are the pupils and their families unfortunate enough to be caught in a mess not of their own making.

To change the prospects for those youngsters, and others like them, we need five things to happen. Most of them need to occur long before secondary school starts.

First, for example, there needs to be not a 'Sure Start' that the new Labour government proposes, but rather a 'Flying Start' with a network of paraprofessionals skilled in language and behaviour development who pick up where the Health Visitor leaves off. Then there would be a high quality service for first-time parents and those with large young families who live in densely populated areas without a partner and/or on benefit. As a result their children would have an emotional foundation that is sufficiently stable to take full advantage of the time when their brain is growing, so that in late infancy and early childhood they would be able to make the most of the environmental factors which make it the most propitious time for learning.

Second, following early experience in voluntary groups and nursery experience, the growing infant and then the child must be in a school sufficiently well and stably staffed with learning assistants (who will give security) and teachers (who will provide expertly organized learning experiences) so that we can catch their flood of optimism and identify that special talent each child needs to believe they have. This will be nurtured not just in their primary school, which will be linked to another in similar circumstances in a common endeavour geared towards school improvement, but also in a network of Children's University extra learning opportunities at the weekends, after school and in the holidays.

Third, inter-agency and multidisciplinary working is essential if the small amount of time – only nine minutes of every waking hour – which a youngster spends in statutory schooling, is to have full impact. Whilst this is important for families with children in infancy and early childhood, especially if they are in social housing and in poverty, it is also important for adolescents when youngsters need an adult whom they can trust and who is interested and reliable enough to act as guide through the jungle of distractions and dangers that can be fellow travellers to the urban adolescent. We have only just begun to scratch the surface of the ways in which health, housing, education, leisure and the police need to work together if the Hackney Downs sagas are not to be repeated, because the task they face is so formidable for want of earlier intervention and simultaneous external-to-the-school support.

Fourth – and in a way it is connected to the last point relating to inter-agency and multidisciplinary work – there are huge gaps in our network of support in urban areas. We are loath to admit it, but we actually lose children between the cracks of frequent home moves and even between primary and secondary schools. Unique pupil identifiers, which are now being pioneered by the government, will help, but real continuity will come from curriculum modules which start in the last three weeks of every primary school and finish in the first three of their chosen secondary school. If we could insist on a prescriptive National Curriculum at points of transfer, we could dispense with most of the prescription in the rest.

Fifth, secondary education should, from the pupil's point of view, be seen as belonging to a secondary school plus something else. In Birmingham we have called the something else The University of the First Age. This provides enriched curriculum experiences during those early years of impressionable adolescence when the youngster needs the invigorating and confidence-building taste of early accredited success, at least in some aspect of their learning. The University of the First Age has established accelerated early learning through mixed-age intensive and interest-led courses. We have only just begun to harness the promise of information communication technology, which provides the tantalizing prospect of enabling the city pedagogues to make the breakthrough which their energy and skill, not to mention their single-minded commitment, deserve.

And all these five pre-conditions before we even begin to look at the lessons of Hackney Downs! Indeed, to fail on any one of them is to stack the odds against the secondary schools which the authors of this book so accurately describe as 'at the wrong end of the pecking order'. The real issue therefore is the impact of market forces and in particular the exercise of parental preference, or choice as it is sometimes misleadingly called – on the quality of secondary schooling for those pupils who are often from the less articulate, motivated and supportive families. When, almost unnoticed and unremarked, 'parental preference' and the first publication of school prospectuses were introduced in 1980, the dice were damagingly cast in favour of market forces. True, per-pupil funding of schools and a common national curriculum and set of test and examination results, which enabled each school's position to be charted in the league tables, appeared about a decade later, but the exercise of loosely regulated parental preferences has been the innovation which has caused the most damage.

As you read this tragic story, feel pity for the participants. The teachers – and the instability of staff and leadership did not help Hackney Downs, as it does not any hard-pressed urban school, especially in London – give energy, skill and commitment, but they burn themselves out in the 'time and energy trap' which is the story of the last years of Hackney Downs. Anger there is aplenty, as good faith and straight dealing go out of the window. Decisions are taken on out-of-date information. Apparently decent people, who in other circumstances are known to be honourable, behave out of character in these situations. So why?

The explanation, at least in part, lies in the market virus, of which parental preference is the most insidious ingredient. Until that is addressed, even if birth-to-5 provision is reformed and all the other measures advocated above for primary schools are implemented, there will be more stories like Hackney Downs. Unbridled rein to parental preference contributes to the chaos within which Hackney Downs operated, as some commentary within this book reveals. Left to their own devices, parents have a habit of preferring single-sex for their girls and co-educational schools for their boys, and where preference is real, as is the case in urban areas, that can lead to dangerously damaging imbalances of boys to girls in co-educational schools. It can also lead to many, in effect secondary modern boys' schools, struggling to survive. Allowing separate admission authorities – and in London that is a number of small LEAs, hundreds of aided and foundation schools – to operate separately rather than through a single clearing house, is to leave parents with many first choices, schools choosing parents rather than vice versa, and an accelerator to the pecking order system that makes some schools like Hackney Downs desperate to admit any pupil, however awkward, who is excluded from another school, to 'keep our numbers up'. This means of course that short-term they need the money that comes with the pupil: hence within this book the story of the children within the school awaiting Statements and therefore more money per pupil.

Whenever there is a new government it is always interesting to try to spot the apparently small things that happen that will have a long-term defining impact undetected at the time. For Mrs Thatcher in 1979, it was the 1980 Act. For Mr Blair and more probably Mr Blunkett perhaps it is the admission code flowing from the School Standards and Framework Act. Certainly it looks as though there is to be a rude awakening for those aided and foundation schools, who used to choose their pupils, once a dispute is called under the admissions arrangements code and an 'adjudicator' is called into action. Reforms to 'fair funding' may also allow more inclusive and less exclusive practices to be created. The targeting of resources to inner cities through the 'Excellence in Cities' programme also represents the arrival of the cavalry.

As you read this sad and gripping tale of Hackney Downs, however, you cannot help feeling that, for those who played their painful parts in the unfolding story, such measures must seem ironically too late. And so they are, for them as for their pupils and families, but they, along with the other pre-conditions set out earlier, represent a real chance to ensure their experiences have not been in vain. The authors deserve the thanks of all those who work in inner cities for telling this cautionary tale.

PROFESSOR TIM BRIGHOUSE
Chief Education Officer
Birmingham LEA

Introduction

This book tells a long story of educational neglect and betrayal which left a small group of teachers and families in one of the poorest neighbourhoods of one of the country's poorest boroughs with a burning sense of injustice. It calls into question policies pursued in the 1990s of labelling schools as 'failing'.

The story of the last two years of Hackney Downs School's existence was, for those involved, an emotional, professional and political roller-coaster which raises serious questions about acceptable methods of school improvement in Britain.

On 14 October 1994 a faxed message arrived at Hackney Downs to say that at a meeting the previous evening one of the borough's education sub-committees had proposed to consult on the closure of the school which had, since the previous August, been designated by Ofsted as 'in need of special measures'. For the intervening two months the Director of Education, colleagues and councillors had been supporting the school's recovery plans both verbally and in writing. Only days before the confidential meeting at which closure was raised, the school's governors had been told that the Director would lead 'a drive for recovery'.

On 28 June the following year, a long and energetic campaign by councillors, parents, governors, staff and pupils at Hackney Downs, succeeded in reversing Hackney Council's decision to close the school. The Council pledged financial as well as moral support to keep the school open and to continue to build on improvements which had by now been recognized by HMI. The school was at this stage halfway through the two-year period in which Ofsted normally expects schools on special measures to turn themselves round.

On 4 July the school was told, in response to an inquiry, that the

Secretary of State, to whom the closure proposal had already been referred, no longer had 'an interest in the matter of Hackney Downs School'. But on 13 July, just nine days later, another faxed message reached the school informing the head that the Secretary of State 'was minded' to set up an Education Association to take over the running of Hackney Downs from the LEA and the governors. The sense of *déjà vu* was overwhelming. Having dared to fight and win, Hackney Downs was once more under threat. The staff could see no other reason for the EA's appointment but to look for fresh reasons to close them down.

This time the school faced the might of a Conservative government which had long proclaimed its determination to be tough on failure in education. It had been advised on policies such as the closure and reopening of failing schools, as is the present government, by Professor Michael Barber, a former Chair of Education in Hackney and subsequently to be appointed a member of this first Education Association; or, as the popular Press more succinctly put it, 'hit squad'. Hackney Downs, euphoric but war-wounded, looked like a sitting target.

After much discussion and soul-searching, the governors, management and the whole staff of Hackney Downs agreed to co-operate with the EA. They hoped that, given the legal remit of the Association under the Education Act 1993, there might be a way forward for Hackney Downs, with aid and support and perhaps even extra resources under the new regime.

On 31 October 1995, just half a term later, the senior management of the school were informed that the EA had decided to recommend that the school should close on 31 December. They were asked to pass on the reasons for this decision to the staff and pupils.

This book is written from the point of view of all those who dared to fight for a future for Hackney Downs School. The account of events is the authors' interpretation of what happened to a school which was held at the time, by some of the popular Press, to be 'the worst school in Britain'. This dubious accolade had previously been bestowed on a neighbouring Hackney secondary school and has since been inherited by a handful of other schools which have had the misfortune to be found wanting, not only by Her Majesty's

Inspectors or by the Office for Standards in Education, but also by the media.

It might be thought that pupils, parents and staff who have suffered the experience of being associated with a 'failing school' would be happy to draw a veil over the events which led to its closure. In Hackney, one of the poorest boroughs in England, this is not the case. Very many of those involved still feel a sense of injustice about what happened at Hackney Downs in 1995, and have warmly supported this attempt to clarify what went wrong at a school which had been, during its history, both a highly regarded grammar school and a flourishing comprehensive.

This is a story of many strands: of market forces and their inevitable creation of 'sink' schools; of harsh cuts in educational spending in a deeply impoverished borough; of teacher militancy and unprofessionalism on one hand and of dedication and determination on the other; of political vacillation and opportunism; of neglect and incompetence; of accusations of bad faith; and of a community in desperate poverty which found the strength to fight for what it valued.

Anyone looking for a single person or institution to blame for the loss of Hackney Downs School will be disappointed by this book. A Conservative government and two Labour education authorities played their roles, some teachers, governors, parents and pupils behaved badly, and politicians of all shades frequently took advantage of the school's difficulties. Some sections of the media, at the end, were immensely supportive, while others tried to crucify the school, its staff and, most disgracefully, its pupils.

In the light of the controversy which still surrounds the death of Hackney Downs, one thing has to be made abundantly clear. There are on the political Left, which is where the authors stand, two views on the education of working-class children. There is the view that because most children from poor homes will remain for their whole lives at the bottom of the heap, educating them for unemployment or the worst-paid jobs in a capitalist society is essentially a betrayal. This was the view taken by the teachers at William Tyndale School in London in the 1970s and rejected firmly – and we believe rightly – by the Labour-controlled Inner London Education Authority.

The alternative view is that it is only through providing working-class children with a first-class education that they stand any chance of making their way in the world and living fulfilled lives both as individuals and as active members of society. In our experience this is the view of most teachers working in the inner cities. The authors of this book give way to no one in their conviction that the children of Hackney deserved, and continue to deserve, a first-class education.

Hackney Downs fought for those children and that education. This book puts its struggle into context. The death of the school raises many important questions about how an excellent education can be achieved for some of the most difficult children in one of the most impoverished areas of the United Kingdom. The authors hope that it will point to some lessons to be learned for the future in the 'failing' schools debate.

Maureen O'Connor is an educational journalist; **Betty Hales** was Headteacher, and **Jeff Davies** was Deputy Headteacher, of Hackney Downs School; **Professor Sally Tomlinson** works at the Department of Educational Studies at the University of Oxford.

Chronology

1876   The school is founded by The Worshipful Company of Grocers to provide a practical rather than a classical education for local boys.

1906   The school is transferred to the control of the London County Council.

1969   The school staff vote to switch from grammar to comprehensive status under the Inner London Education Authority. Hackney Downs takes its first comprehensive intake in September.

1980   Hackney secondary schools reduced from fifteen to ten, leaving Hackney Downs undisturbed, but without the generous staffing and funding of the amalgamated schools.

1985   The school roll begins to fall and includes far fewer Band 1 (high ability) boys. An ILEA inspection commends the school's strengths but warns that academic standards are too low.

1987   After industrial action over teachers' pay, the school is further disrupted when asbestos has to be removed from the building, leading to partial closure.

1989   Some black staff and parents form 'action groups'. Gus John is appointed as Hackney's first Director of Education, with Michael Barber as Chair of the Education Committee. The long-serving headteacher retires.

1990   The school is transferred to the new London Borough of Hackney education authority following the abolition of the ILEA. The school is transferred as one of eight 'giving cause for concern'.

1991   Internal disputes over the role of the Black Staff and Parents' Group intensify.

1992   LEA inspectors put school on 'at risk' register. School roll rises slightly. Headteacher seconded to other duties at the end of the year.

1993   New headteacher seconded to become acting head with Daphne Gould as consultant head on a two-year contract. Review of Secondary Provision in Hackney argues that the borough will need all its secondary places in future but proposes that Hackney Downs becomes a co-educational school. The LEA recommends a bar on Year 7 recruitment in 1994 to allow for refurbishment and preparation for co-education. Acting head leaves at the end of the year.

1994   New acting headteacher appointed, but goes on sick leave after two weeks. He is replaced by Betty Hales. In February, the increasingly bitter dispute between the school and some black teachers results in a public campaign against the school in the local community.

In March, the DfE rejects the co-educational proposal. The LEA reaffirms its commitment to the school's future. The LEA persists in its refusal to allow the school to recruit a Year 7, in spite of the governors' requests and DfE guidance to the contrary.

In May the school is inspected by Ofsted.

In July, the Ofsted report designates the school as 'needing special measures', whilst praising progress made in recent months.

In August and September, the school prepares its action plan and argues further for a Year 7 intake. The school roll falls to just over 300 due to the lack of Year 7 and the effects of the Black Group campaign.

In October the school and the LEA submit their action plans to the DfE. Almost immediately the LEA decides to move to consultation on the closure of the school, using arguments which appear to contradict its own secondary review of 1993.

Two abortive attempts are made to appoint a permanent headteacher in July and October.

In November, financial delegation of the school budget is removed by the LEA and additional LEA governors are appointed. The governors vote to oppose the closure proposal.

1995   A fierce community campaign develops in support of the school. The closure proposal goes through a stormy consultation process and is ratified by the Education Committee in March, despite dissent within the Labour Group.

The plan goes to the DfE for ratification on the basis of closure at the end of the summer term. Boys are to be transferred to Homerton House, despite parents' protests. A visit by HMI in March reports that progress on the Action Plan is on target and praises the school's current management.

The school is contacted by the Clove Club, the Hackney Downs old boys' association, with offers of support.

After a change in committee chairmanships in May, Labour councillors raise doubts about the closure. On 8 June the Education Committee refuses to endorse the closure proposal or the Director of Education's report to the DfE. LEA officials proceed as if nothing had changed. Parents prepare to take the case to judicial review.

On 28 June, the full council rejects the closure proposal and the DfE is informed. The judicial review process is put on hold.

The school celebrates and presses ahead with plans for recruitment and organization for the autumn term.

On 4 July the DfE confirms that the Secretary of State's consideration of the closure proposal has been terminated.

On 13 July the Secretary of State announces that she 'is minded' to appoint an Education Association to take over the school.

On 27 July the DfEE announces the formation of the North East London Education Association.

Throughout August school staff work with EA members to transfer control.

In September the school reopens with only 200 boys on roll but the EA retains the current staff. The HMI inspection planned for October is cancelled.

In late September the school is inspected by three independent inspectors employed by the EA, whose reports are not to be made public.

On 31 October the EA report is published. It recommends closure.

On 14 November, closure is confirmed by the Secretary of State. Staff are issued with redundancy notices on minimum statutory terms.

On 15 November, an application is made for legal aid to allow a group of parents and children to seek a judicial review of the closure decision, with the support of the Clove Club. The application is refused and an appeal is lodged the following day.

The same day the school is instructed to begin the transfer of some boys to Homerton House.

On 5 December legal aid is granted.

On 8 December leave is granted to move for a judicial review.

On 11 December the case is heard before Mr Justice Popplewell and rejected. Leave to appeal is granted.

On 15 December term ends for Hackney Downs boys with a final school assembly.

On 18 December the appeal is heard.

On 21 December the appeal is rejected and the school closes officially on 31 December.

1996   In February the three EA inspectors' reports and the draft version of their final report on the school come to light, amongst other documents.

1

The Poorest Borough

Diversity and deprivation

The London Borough of Hackney is the poorest in England and Wales. It was created by the amalgamation of the former boroughs of Hackney, Shoreditch and Stoke Newington in the 1960s when the Greater London Council came into existence. It stretches from the skyscraper fringe of the City of London near Liverpool Street Station in the south, to the relative affluence of Stamford Hill in the north. To the west lie the trendy terraces of gentrified Islington, and to the east and south, beyond the River Lea, the similarly deprived boroughs of Newham and Tower Hamlets. But on almost every measure of deprivation, Hackney comes off worst – and this has been reflected for decades in its educational performance.

The *Social Atlas of London* (1974) showed a pattern of low attainment in primary schools, low staying-on rates at secondary level, and a high proportion of children from immigrant families in Hackney at the time that Hackney Downs School was going comprehensive.

It is no surprise that this should be the educational situation in a borough with high population density, high rates of illegitimate births and mental health referrals, high air pollution, and a high proportion of poor or unfit dwellings. The only hopeful aspect of that 1974 analysis of the state of the London boroughs was that the Greater London Council's system of transfer payments between the richer and poorer boroughs guaranteed Hackney high levels of spending on education, health and welfare services – all regarded as a means of redressing the imbalance between the rich and poor parts of the capital.

That system ended with the abolition of the GLC and, in 1990, of the Inner London Education Authority. The latter change handed control of its own education service to the borough of Hackney for the first time. According to its own statistics, there was little improvement in the social circumstances of the borough during the lifetime of the GLC, and some deterioration. *The London Borough of Hackney – Its People, Facts and Figures*, published by Hackney's Research and Intelligence Unit in 1995, makes gloomy reading.

The population is still enormously mixed. The large Jewish community which Hackney Downs School served spectacularly well before and after the Second World War has almost completely moved on, apart from an ultra-Orthodox enclave in the north of the borough which has its own privately funded schools. One-third of the total population in Hackney is made up of more recently settled ethnic minority communities, the same proportion as in Ealing but less than in Brent, Newham and Tower Hamlets. The ethnic minorities in Hackney are very diverse. The largest group is of African-Caribbean origin, with other sizeable black communities from Africa and elsewhere. There are also substantial Turkish, Indian, Pakistani, Bangladeshi and Chinese communities in Hackney, including significant numbers of Kurdish and other refugees. Substantial numbers of children do not speak English at home.

Both the ethnic minorities and the white population are deprived. Hackney has the worst overcrowding in London amongst its white community in unfurnished accommodation, and the black African and Indian communities in the borough also fare particularly badly, according to *London's Ethnic Minorities* (1994), published by the Commission for Racial Equality. Levels of post-school qualification are very low. And, at 14.1 per cent of the population, Hackney has the worst rate of long-term illness in London. Hackney children are more likely to be suffering from long-term ill health than anywhere else in London at the time.

Economic activity in the borough is low, with the highest rate of unemployment in London. As a consequence, household incomes are also extremely low. The Hackney Housing Survey of 1993 revealed an average income in Hackney households of £11,900 a year, compared to almost £20,000 in the rest of Greater London. Two-thirds of Hackney households had a gross income of less than

£10,000 a year, compared to only 43 per cent in the rest of inner London and 40 per cent in Greater London as a whole.

Hackney is one of only two boroughs in London where more than half the households include dependent children. Of those families, more than 40 per cent are headed by a single parent, and in more than another seven per cent of families the adults are not married.

Almost 50 per cent of Hackney households are in local authority accommodation. Only 27 per cent own their own homes. The greatest concentration of very poor households is in privately rented accommodation. Thirty per cent of the population receive income support. More than 4,000 families are classified as homeless and live in temporary accommodation. Almost two-thirds of households are without a car, and household amenities are poor. Given the levels of deprivation and unemployment, it is not surprising to find that the crime rate is considerably higher than the London average, with 163 reported offences per thousand people compared to 125 in London as a whole, with offences of burglary almost twice the London average in the mid-1990s.

The politics of Hackney

Not surprisingly, Hackney Council has remained solidly Labour-controlled since the Borough's inception until the 1990s. During the early 1980s, like the Labour Party nationally, the party in Hackney veered sharply to the Left. By the end of the decade it was beginning to swing in the opposite direction, although still split and remaining an unusually fractious group. Local politics were further complicated by the existence of powerful groups pursuing ethnic agendas. As Jake Arnold-Foster, deputy editor of the *Local Government Chronicle*, writing in the *New Statesman*, put it in July 1996: 'Hackney Council has a uniquely dreadful reputation. In-fighting amongst the permanent but faction-ridden Labour majority, waste and inefficiency, political-correctness policing, extensive fraud and internal corruption – all these have helped to define the character of the cursed north-east London borough.' Hackney Downs School was to suffer particularly from 'faction-ridden' local politics.

In 1987, 60 per cent of Hackney children qualified for free school meals, one-third of the children belonged to one-parent families, and 70 per cent of school pupils came from ethnic minority families. But from that year onwards the council was forced to come to terms with substantial cuts in expenditure over successive years as the GLC was phased out.

Furthermore, Michael Barber, a Hackney councillor at that time, later a professor at the London Institute of Education, and now head of the Labour government's Standards and Effectiveness Unit, said in his book *Education in the Capital* (1992), that Hackney's bureaucracy was 'insensitive, inefficient and in places corrupt'. It was described in 1986 in the Arden Report, commissioned by the borough itself, as a place in which 'the unthinkable has become a habit'. Attempts at reform by the Labour Party began in 1986, but the task was enormous.

It was to this troubled council that control of education passed in 1990. The decision to abolish the Inner London Education Authority was tacked on to the Conservative government's Education Reform Bill in 1988 as an afterthought. It was fiercely resisted by the Labour-controlled boroughs in Inner London and by a substantial parents' campaign, but to no avail. The Bill passed into law in the summer of 1988 and up to that time it had been regarded as a point of political honour in some boroughs that little or nothing should be done to acknowledge the new dispensation until it was irrevocably in place.

Neighbouring Islington, which had more or less openly welcomed the opportunity to run its own schools, had a chief education officer in place during the summer holidays of 1988. By that stage Hackney had done no more than have a briefing seminar and another political row.

Councillor Michael Barber made no secret of the fact that he was eager to become the borough's first Chair of Education. He was eventually appointed in September, but for six months the borough had no more than five staff working on plans for the take-over of a service with a budget of almost £100 million and responsibility for the education of 20,000 children and young people, and thousands of adults.

By February 1989, however, Hackney had put an education plan out to wide consultation and it was ready to submit to the Secretary of State as required. By the end of the year, after a poor response to its first advertisement, the borough also had a Director of Education.

He was to be Gus John, an African-Caribbean from Grenada, a former Dominican friar who had moved into local government administration. He was well known as an anti-racist campaigner and had been a member of the inquiry into the killing of an Asian pupil at Burnage High School in Manchester.

The combination of Michael Barber and Gus John should have augured well for Hackney schools. Michael Barber spells out in his book *Education in the Capital*, his concern at the discovery that many black and other ethnic minority parents felt that the ILEA had failed their children. In particular, he said, they felt that teachers did not have high enough expectations of them. It was a view he and Gus John shared.

The new education authority

At the beginning of the 1980s, Hackney's secondary schools had been reorganized by the ILEA to leave just ten. Four of these were for girls only and proved to be popular with parents, four were co-educational and, though popular enough, proved to have difficulty in attaining a balanced intake between girls and boys because of the counter-attractions of the girls' schools. Two schools were left to serve boys only: Hackney Downs and Homerton House, neither of which found the task easy.

The ILEA had begun to express concerns about educational standards at Hackney Downs in 1985. As it prepared to hand over to the borough, it had designated no fewer than eight Hackney schools as 'a cause for concern'. Anyone taking on the administration of education in Hackney was faced with serious problems from the beginning.

Michael Barber's core idea was that education should be run as a partnership. The Hackney Plan spelled out that the partnership should 'ensure that all concerned are involved in the definition of educational objectives, the planning and implementation of strategies to achieve them and monitoring of progress towards them'.

Gus John's particular concern was to raise the performance of the ethnic minority children in the borough who were seriously under-achieving: in particular he wanted to raise examination results and to get parents, particularly ethnic minority parents, more involved in their children's schooling. It was his firm belief that the only true liberation for black children would come through high quality education.

Sadly, the high hopes with which the two men set out were soon dashed. Michael Barber had to relinquish his role as Chair of Education when he was appointed to a senior position at the National Union of Teachers. He moved on rapidly to become a professor of education, first at Keele University and then at the London Institute of Education, although he maintained close links in the borough.

Gus John persisted for seven years in his new job, before taking early retirement in 1996 at the age of 51. Ironically some of his fiercest criticism was reserved at the end for some of the councillors who had appointed him with such optimism, and for some of the black teachers at Hackney Downs who, he told the *Independent on Sunday*, had behaved in a way which was professionally unacceptable and undermining to the management of the school.

The battles which raged around Hackney Downs School once it came under the control of Hackney Council have to be seen against this backdrop of desperate poverty and considerable political unrest and controversy over education, race and other issues.

Throughout the early 1990s the council was convulsed over allegations of maladministration and racism which split the Labour Group in two, both sides attracting support more widely within the London and the national Labour Party. It was this split which finally deposed the Hackney Labour leadership in May 1995. By this time the Hackney Downs School closure process had also become bedevilled by allegations and counter-allegations which had more to do with politics than education.

When Gus John and Michael Barber began to push through ambitious plans for Hackney schools, it was inevitable that attention would focus on a school like Hackney Downs, and equally inevitable that there would be dispute about how far its poor performance was the result of the desperate deprivation of its pupils, or was the fault of its managers and teachers, or of the LEA itself.

Hackney as a whole paid a high price for the faction fighting – by no means a simple Left/Right split – within the ruling Labour Party which was eventually referred to the National Executive Committee of the Labour Party for resolution in 1996. Hackney Downs School paid the highest price of all.

The rest of this book concentrates on how a once-proud and successful school was destroyed by the vitriolic politics of Hackney even though a coalition of staff, parents, and many of its eminent former pupils believed it could have overcome its difficulties and lived to triumph another day.

2

The Beginnings

The early years

Hackney Downs Middle Class School for boys – the 'middle class' reflecting the 12- to 15-year-old age span of the pupils and only coincidently their social status – opened its doors in 1876, just six years after the 1870 Education Act made elementary education up to the age of 10 both free and compulsory. To understand why its eventual closure in 1995 caused such outrage among so many people, both in Hackney and in the country as a whole, it is necessary to look at how and why it came to be held in such high regard by so many, right up to the moment the high-powered campaign to save it ended in the High Court.

The new school at Hackney Downs was the proud foundation of the Worshipful Company of Grocers, who hoped to do for North London, in the expanding suburbs which already housed workers to service the City, what their educational philanthropy had already done for other places. In Hackney their intention was to provide a practical rather than a classical grammar school education, and the school was launched with an unusual curriculum for its day. The bias was to be in the direction of commercial subjects and English literature, leaving Latin, then the badge of the gentleman, to be taught as an 'extra' after hours. The fees were to be kept relatively low, and 10 per cent of the places would attract scholarships to be awarded on the results of an entrance examination. The school was built on a triangle of land between two railway lines and facing the Downs, one of the few green lungs in that already heavily built-up part of London.

The first head was an enthusiastic supporter of the Grocers' newfangled approach to education. The pronouncements of Herbert Bowen, who opened the school with a roll of 210 boys and four assistant masters, have an uncannnily modern ring. 'The mere accumulation of facts may come at any time; but the wise and right treatment of a few, should be our constant treatment while the learners mind is young', he wrote in his book *Studies in English* in 1876. 'Some facts there must be of which to treat; but the mere piling together of facts is as the piling together of loose stones without mortar and without a design, as the attempt to build a house without tools, or without a knowledge of their use.'

Bowen placed a high value on his mother tongue, putting English Literature, then a subject scorned by the universities, at the heart of his curriculum, very seldom used corporal punishment and, as enthusiasts will, was soon pressing the Grocers' Company for extensions to the original red-brick Gothic buildings which they had provided to accommodate 500 boys when the school opened.

Those buildings were soon extended, and were remarkable from the start in one respect. The fifteen classrooms, library and domestic offices of the original school included a large semi-circular hall-cum-theatre which would seat 800 people. The theatre was to play a crucial part in the life of the school for over half a century.

Bowen's reign did not last long. The brave new enterprise quickly ran into difficulties. In 1880 the school roll, which had been steadily increasing, unaccountably fell back and the accounts began to show a loss. There were rows – another uncanny precursor of modern concerns – about the lack of religious instruction and school prayers, which the head did not favour. A master was dismissed, without the approval of the governors, for striking a pupil. In 1881 Bowen resigned without his loss apparently being mourned by his pupils, the governors, or the Company, which had lost faith in his idiosyncratic and somewhat austere approach.

The school had found itself in a genuine dilemma. It was, by trying to follow a more modern educational path than was usual in the Victorian public and grammar schools, putting itself at odds with the ambitions of the parents. The fathers of the Hackney Downs boys were predominantly bank officials, civil servants, professional and businessmen. They had ambitions for their sons, and if those ambitions – for scholarships to public schools such as St Pauls and

Merchant Taylors and then to the universities – were to be met, then Hackney Downs had to provide a traditional classical education.

The school bowed to the market. It appointed as its second head Revd Charles Gull, founder and commander of the Dulwich College Rifle Corps, who rode a horse to school and personally carved the joint at school dinners. Latin and corporal punishment took their more usual place in the scheme of things and Hackney Downs slotted itself into the minor public school hierarchy.

Yet Hackney Downs never became entirely indistinguishable from schools elsewhere: perhaps because it had a theatre at the heart of the Victorian building to exert a dramatic influence. During the later years of the nineteenth century the school's productions of Gilbert and Sullivan operettas became renowned throughout London. Or perhaps because the Hackney Downs boys, even under the fierce tutelage of Revd Gull, were never oblivious to the social conditions of East London beyond their high walls. Money was raised for the East London Church Fund, and the debating society tackled subjects such as conscription, Jewish immigration, railway nationalization and women's suffrage.

By 1906 the school buildings had been extended to include an ingenious swimming pool which could be covered in winter to provide a gymnasium, extra classrooms, playing fields, and fives courts and had reached the state of solid Victorian grandeur which some Hackney residents and old boys of the school can still remember.

Almost from the beginning, the school had enormous support from an active old boys' organization. The Clove Club, which took its name from the spices which adorn the Grocers' Company coat of arms, was actively involved in many school activities, taking major responsibility for some sports clubs. With a few temporary periods of quiescence, the Club remained committed to the school to what turned out to be an extremely bitter end.

At this stage of the new century, with publicly funded education expanding rapidly, the Grocers' Company became worried by the ever-increasing costs of running the school, and decided to hand its creation over to the newly established London County Council in October 1906.

By now Hackney was also changing. The middle classes, who had sustained the school in its early days, were moving out. Poorer residents, including large numbers of Jewish immigrant families, mainly from Eastern Europe, were moving in. Although fee-paying continued, within two years of the LCC taking the school over, its more generous scholarship scheme resulted in 38 per cent of the boys being exempted from payment. By 1934 the proportion had reached 49 per cent.

The school flourished under its new management. A Welshman, William Jenkyn Thomas, took over the headship, the sixth form developed art, science and commercial streams, and by 1931 the school roll had reached 675 and further building extensions were completed. By the time Jenkyn Thomas retired in 1935, old boys of Hackney Downs were appearing at the top of their trees in medicine, science, politics, business and academia.

And yet the school still remained somewhat different from other London day schools. By this time it was educating a high proportion of Jewish boys. The new head, Thomas Balk, integrated the two communities more closely by abolishing Saturday morning lessons, which the Jewish boys had been unable to attend, and by including them, after negotiations with the Chief Rabbi and the Archbishop of Canterbury no less, in assemblies which had previously only been held for Christian boys. Hackney Downs' experience of successful multi-cultural education had deep roots.

After the War

The school was severely disrupted by the Second World War. Technically it was evacuated to East Anglia as soon as hostilities began, but gradually boys began to drift back to London and by 1943 part of the school was re-established at Hackney Downs, and effectively it functioned on two sites for the rest of the war. The after-effects of hostilities were dire, in physical terms at least. The top floor of the school was in ruins, the gymnasium roofless, the rear playground was full of debris from bombed-out buildings, and the swimming pool had been used as a source of water for fire-fighting. Staffing difficulties were inevitably acute.

Gradually the school rebuilt itself both physically and academically. Its preparatory department for the under-11s was phased out when the 1944 Education Act abolished fee-paying, and from that time all boys entered the school at age 11 by means of the selective London County Council Entrance Examination.

It was after the war that the school's dramatic tradition was triumphantly revived with a production of *Macbeth* in 1947 and *Romeo and Juliet*, starring a young Harold Pinter, in 1948. By 1947 an educational revolution was already being planned, although it took far longer than anyone anticipated to realize. In that year the LCC set out its proposals to reform secondary education on comprehensive lines in the London School Plan. Changes of government and, more crucially, lack of funds for new buildings postponed those changes for more than a dozen years. Other parts of London 'went comprehensive' while Hackney Downs continued its life undisturbed as a successful three-form-entry grammar school.

On the night of 18 March 1963 disaster struck. Three months earlier the school theatre had been renovated with the help of parents, and the first production on the enlarged stage with its new lighting system was to be Anouilh's *Antigone*. The dress rehearsal was successfully completed on the Monday evening. The following morning much of the school lay in smoking ruins.

By a bitter irony, the fire was evidently caused by a fault on a dimmer switch in the new lighting system in the theatre. From there the flames spread to the upper corridor and the Victorian landmark tower, and threatened the gymnasium and the library. When an assessment was made of the fire and water damage it emerged that most of the heart of the original school building had been lost.

Hackney Downs did not close, even temporarily. Alternative accommodation for the damaged classrooms was found almost immediately. Even the production of *Antigone* went ahead with borrowed costumes in a neighbouring school hall. But in many ways the devastating fire marked the beginning of a new and much more difficult era for the school.

Going comprehensive

By the time major rebuilding began in 1965, to include a kosher kitchen, an assembly hall specially designed for dramatic productions, and an extended library, the Inner London Education Authority (ILEA), which had succeeded the LCC, had plans well advanced to phase out all its grammar schools. In the summer of 1966 it was announced that Hackney Downs would expand to become a six-form-entry comprehensive with a 'balanced intake'.

The Labour government was by this time pressing for a completely comprehensive system, locally the school population was rising, and the new development of the Hackney Downs site offered scope for much-needed extra places. Internally the move was welcomed because there was genuine support for comprehensive education among the parents and the staff of the school. Even the old boys' association, the Clove Club, supported the change, largely because they accepted that the staff felt very positive about it. Hackney Downs took on the new role which was proposed for it, not just willingly but with enthusiasm.

Building work continued until 1970, and in that year the fire-damaged Victorian core of the school was demolished, leaving in effect a purpose-built comprehensive school with some Victorian remnants, including the science block and the swimming pool, on the original site. In September 1969 Hackney Downs received its first comprehensive intake of 180 boys.

According to John Kemp, who took over as head in 1974 and published a memoir of his time there, *The Last Thirty Years* (1991), when he retired, the ILEA was amazed when the Hackney Downs staff agreed to go comprehensive. Some of the teachers were doubtful, he says, and some were scared, but the majority were fired by the idealism of the times and became committed to the idea that the new school could give a wider range of boys access to the advantages previously confined to the few.

After the fire, staff had for a time shared premises with a half-empty and run-down secondary modern school and had observed lively and alert children in a limited and depressing environment. Teachers were convinced, Kemp says in his memoir, that Hackney Downs could offer a great deal to such children.

3

Gathering Clouds

Hackney Downs – the showcase

For a time Hackney Downs flourished as a comprehensive and became the apple of the ILEA's eye. But conditions were then favourable in a way in which they were not 25 years later. To ease its transition, the school was allocated a high proportion of 'grammar' ability boys for its first few years through the ILEA 'banding' system which attempted to give its comprehensives a theoretically balanced intake – 25 per cent high ability, 50 per cent average, and 25 per cent below average. These are crude measurements but they did something to keep ILEA comprehensives roughly 'comprehensive' in intake, for a time at least.

But an increasingly impoverished inner-city borough does not naturally produce children in those neat proportions. The Hackney 'norm' for children of above-average performance was one of the lowest in the country at about 10 per cent. By the 1980s only a handful of the school's intake of 180 boys would have reached the old grammar school entrance standard.

The comprehensive school decided in the beginning that mixed-ability classes would work well, for the benefit of all, if they had a good proportion of able pupils in them, generous resources and excellent teaching. At first, Hackney Downs had all these things, and even as the proportion of able children dropped it felt that, exhausting and demanding as the system was, it was producing results to be proud of.

The school became a media pet. Visitors from overseas were pointed in its direction. Drama and creative writing flourished and a cohort of outstanding women teachers was recruited. Exam passes were startlingly good in many subjects. A serious effort was made to overcome the disadvantages of an all-boys school through attempts to counter any 'macho' tendencies and to introduce boys of many cultures to the idea of equal opportunities for all. Local employers welcomed applications from Hackney Downs boys. The school was vandalism-free and felt safe.

However, by the mid-1980s there were serious worries, some of them sparked by factors entirely outside the school's control, some internally generated. For those looking for an explanation of how a 'sink' school can be created by the 'market' in school places, Hackney Downs offers a perfect case study, and one where the slide began well before the overtly market-oriented changes of the 1988 Education Reform Act which eventually sealed its fate.

At this point Hackney Downs had 825 boys on roll, already down on its high point of over 900. Its pupil–teacher ratio was a generous 12.5:1. But only five boys achieved five A to C grades at O-level in the summer of 1984, although there were at least 21 Band 1 (grammar school ability) boys in the year. Worse, 28 per cent of the year group gained no exam passes at all.

Hackney itself was changing dramatically. The child population dropped rapidly in the 1970s and the ILEA closed or amalgamated six secondary schools in the borough in 1980. As a successful school, Hackney Downs was untouched by the reorganization, but to some extent this was a disadvantage because amalgamated schools were actually at a staffing advantage during a particularly difficult time for London schools because redundant staff were kept on until natural wastage restored the designated pupil–teacher ratio.

It was also becoming clear that the popularity of boys' schools was beginning to wane. The conversion to co-education of a neighbouring girls' school provided 120 extra boys' places on Hackney Downs' doorstep. Up until the mid-1970s Hackney Downs was always over-subscribed. By the mid-1980s the school was getting only 120 applications a year for its 180 places.

It was at this time that Hackney Downs began to find its spare places filled by newcomers to the borough, very often children who spoke no English, latterly a proportion who were refugees traumatized by events in their home countries. This intake was increasingly augmented by a growing number of boys expelled from other schools. The school gradually lost its high-ability intake, limited though that had been. It became, in all but name, a secondary modern school – something which happened, as Sir Peter Newsam, the ILEA's former education officer has pointed out, to many comprehensives in the inner city.

And it became a peculiarly unstable secondary modern school at that. Population change meant that the Jewish population living in parts of Hackney departed – by 1976 there was hardly a Jewish boy left in the school. The racial, cultural and linguistic mix changed rapidly and continuously. During the 1970s and early 80s about half the pupils were of African-Caribbean origin, and John Kemp says that the school made great efforts to meet their needs. In the early 1980s the intake became even more diverse as wave after wave of newcomers arrived. Bangladeshis, Vietnamese, Turks, Kurds and Somalis came to Hackney Downs. By 1990 there were 27 home languages being spoken. None of this was unmanageable on its own: but combined as it was with other difficulties, the school was becoming more and more stretched.

Staffing was an increasing problem. Turnover was high, and when the ILEA began to cut its teaching force in the mid-1980s in response to government financial pressure, it introduced a system of compulsory redeployment which, for the best of motives, took away schools' ability to select their own staff. Inevitably inner-city schools with the highest turnover took more than their fair share of teachers redeployed from other parts of the capital. Not all were necessarily poor teachers, but there would always be a risk that some were disaffected by a compulsory move, especially if they found themselves unwillingly in a school in a highly deprived area and a school with more than its share of problems. It is certainly arguable that schools in inner-city areas are by definition those least able to get by on a diet of unwilling recruits, temporary appointments and a high proportion of 'supply' staff. But that was what Hackney Downs increasingly got.

Changing perceptions

At the same time as the school was trying to cope with this avalanche of social change, national perceptions about schools were also changing, at the Inner London Education Authority as well as elsewhere. In the early 1980s the ILEA decided to undertake a five-yearly review of its schools and chose Hackney Downs as one of six 'good' schools for a trial run inspection. The report was glowing. Two years later the school went through the same process for real. Nothing much had changed, according to John Kemp, except the ILEA's perception of what made a good school. The Conservative government had become more hostile to comprehensive education, rigour had become the buzz word at the Labour-controlled ILEA, and the new inspection report concluded that while Hackney Downs was socially impressive, its academic standards were not good enough.

It is perhaps worth quoting the conclusions of that 1985 report in some detail because it illustrates the genuine tension schools face in inner-city areas, a tension which is not caused by sloppy thinking or ignoble motives, but by a genuine concern for young people who face such enormous difficulties out of school. That concern for their care inside school can come to dominate a school's thinking.

David Hargreaves, then the ILEA's Chief Inspector, now Professor of Education at Cambridge University, wrote in July 1985 in his formal report on Hackney Downs:

> The school has much to recommend it. Its policies have been consistent with the principles of comprehensive education. Mixed ability teaching operates across the 11–16 age-range, group sizes are small, pupils have the opportunity to negotiate some of their learning and there has been considerable curriculum development in many areas of the curriculum. Much of the teaching is distinguished, a variety of appropriate styles being used. The school has played a leading role in implementing the Authority's initiatives. The school now needs to implement its intention to offer a more balanced curriculum in the fourth and fifth years and to make its offer at 16+ as attractive as possible.

The school is to be congratulated upon developing highly positive relationships between pupils and staff and also within the staff. This is testimony to the deep commitment the staff feel towards pupils and is apparent in the mutual respect that was shown. However there are grounds for concern based on measurable indices of performance. The school has had difficulty in recruiting pupils for the coming school year, public examination performance has been disappointing and the staying-on rate is low. Attendance, though improving, is still unsatisfactory, particularly in the fourth and fifth years. It is essential for the school to retain its present humane and liberal atmosphere but there are indications that a more rigorous approach to whole school policies is needed as a prerequisite to further development . . .

This is a school with so many individual and collective strengths that, given its robust consultative procedures, it should be able to accommodate these recommendations without prejudicing what is a most civilised and humane working environment which is a credit to the whole staff.

The report made many detailed proposals for improvement, but it was the last really optimistic report Hackney Downs was to receive. It is a useful point at which to start a description of how, within a decade, the Grocers' Company School, which had flourished for more than 100 years, met its end.

It was shortly before this in 1984 that Jeff Davies, one of the authors of this book, found himself assigned by the ILEA to Hackney Downs School as a probationary teacher. Jeff had gained his honours degree in history at Manchester University as a mature student after a brief spell as a trainee accountant, and took a postgraduate Certificate in Education at the London Institute of Education. He was no stranger to London, having been educated at Highbury Grove School, Islington, when it was a grammar school, and becoming deputy head boy under headmaster Rhodes Boyson the year it became a comprehensive.

While he built his career over the next decade, Jeff Davies felt that he had gained as much experience as if he had worked in at least three different schools. It was out of devotion and loyalty to the pupils and staff he had worked with for so long that Jeff Davies remained at Hackney Downs to the end.

On top of the ILEA's concern about academic standards, the mid-1980s saw Hackney Downs face a whole series of further crises. The first was the loss of the sixth form when the ILEA set up a sixth-form college in Hackney. The head of Hackney Downs admitted that the change made economic and academic sense for A-level students who were being taught all over the borough in tiny groups. Even so, the school felt bereft, the balance between academically highly motivated youngsters and the rest was irrevocably altered, and Hackney Downs became, he thinks, less attractive to new teachers.

Also in the mid-1980s the staff themselves made enemies. Hackney Downs attracted, as many inner-city schools do, a high proportion of politically idealistic teachers. At various times it employed some of the most high-profile Left-wingers in East London who were disliked at the ILEA and at the National Union of Teachers HQ. They were highly unionized and unreservedly supported the national industrial action of the mid-1980s. Whatever the rights and wrongs of the teachers' case, it has perhaps been forgotten how disruptive that battle was in many London schools.

When the pay disputes were settled, Hackney Downs staff found another cause for which they felt they needed to fight. In 1986 they demanded that the ILEA should remove the asbestos which had been built into the 1960s structure of the school. Again the cause was a just one, although not everyone at the ILEA saw it quite like that at the time. Asbestos was not a trivial issue.

For a short time the whole school was closed completely, and for most of the autumn term large parts were closed as the ILEA carried out remedial work step by tedious step. Alternative premises were found and either used or rejected month after month. Temporary timetable after temporary timetable was drawn up, imposed and discarded. The school descended into organizational chaos.

As the headteacher put it in his memoir: 'There were times when we were hanging on by the skin of our teeth. For example, when a gas leak closed the science block (where most classes were being held) and it was found that the replacement pipes needed to run through ducts found to be asbestos-contaminated.'

This episode had a damaging and, as it turned out, irreversible effect on Hackney Downs' roll. With the school crippled by building work, far fewer 11-year-olds than normal started at Hackney Downs in the autumn of 1987. The school's popularity as first choice for local families was never fully restored.

From this point on, Hackney Downs carried a reputation as a hot-bed of Left-wing ideology, a reputation which antagonized politicians of both the major parties. The reputation persisted long after the high-profile trades unionists had moved on. Given the high staff turnover in Inner London schools generally, and Hackney schools in particular, this did not take long. Unfortunately, some names, including some militant Inner London Teachers' Association members, remained on the staff roll for ILEA administrative reasons long after they had ceased teaching there, causing unnecessarily high staff costs which were to haunt the school later.

This period of union action, and the ill-will it generated at County Hall, seems to have coloured the views of some of those involved in the final battle for the school's future in 1994 and 1995, even though by that time the school was staffed by almost entirely different people. To the end, many at Hackney Downs were convinced that they were still being punished for union militancy in the 1980s which had nothing to do with them individually.

Staff divisions

The staff were also shaping up for a self-generated row which was to dog the school until it closed. By this time Hackney Downs employed a significant proportion of women on its staff and a significant proportion of ethnic minority teachers, some of whom were uncompromising about what they regarded as the best means of raising black boys' achievement. The mix was to prove explosive.

There were two focuses of discontent. In July 1989, not long before John Kemp retired, the staff Women's Group organized a day's in-service training at which some grievances were aired. The group clearly felt that in a boys' school women staff faced particular difficulties of harassment, especially if they were not fully supported by their male colleagues. The Women's Group complained about disparaging remarks being made in the staff room –

not just sexist remarks, but 'racist, heterosexist and dis-ablist comments'. They felt that such attitudes from some male staff had an impact upon how the boys also behaved. They also found it unacceptable for staff to use aggression to manage pupils and called for an end to physical and verbal abuse of all kinds. One black male teacher was a particular focus of discontent.

The notes on the Women's Group meetings are strident, making much use of capital letters, but they also indicate how far the school had come since 1985 when it had been congratulated by the ILEA for its liberal and humane values and when relationships between staff and pupils had been notably positive. The Women's Group's complaints sparked a furious reaction from some of their black male colleagues, who felt that they were being targeted. The staff split and the rift continued until 1994.

Black staff at Hackney Downs had already set up a Black Staff Group, and there was also a Black Parents' Group in existence by the autumn of 1989. These two groups eventually linked together to form the Black Staff and Parents' Group (BSPG). Correspondence, initially from both groups and then from the joint organization, followed the same format – closely typed sheets, unsigned and sometimes undated, but on a very distinctive printer and copier.

From the beginning the tone was uncompromising, although at first the aims of the black staff involved seemed unexceptionable. They were well versed in the research which indicated that black students in general and black boys in particular performed poorly at school to a large extent because schools' expectations of them were too low, so that they were at risk of being stereotyped as low achievers. Hackney Downs had never been a school where racial discrimination was tolerated, but it could have been fairly asked, as any school might be asked, whether institutional attitudes were unwittingly depressing the performance of some of its ethnic minority boys.

In fact, a detailed analysis of examination results at that time, using ethnic codes, showed that black and Asian boys did better at Hackney Downs than the national or Hackney averages. If anyone was doing badly in comparison with national norms it was white boys, some of whom, coming from very deprived backgrounds, had been allocated to the school to fill spare places.

At first the Black Staff and Parents' Group pressed the need to keep parents generally informed, to give them a voice within the school, to enable them to monitor their children's achievement and to produce a more welcoming atmosphere in which they would find it easier to ask questions about progress. It only gradually became clear that their interest in these desirable things was on behalf of black parents exclusively and that the audience they addressed and began to involve in their meetings and campaigns was the highly selective one of the local African/Caribbean community.

The first surviving missive to the head from the Black Parents' Group, following the Women's Group meeting, was even more alarming to the headteacher than the Black Staff Group's intervention. It took furious exception to its own interpretation of the women teachers' complaints about sexism. A woman member of staff who was actually present at the meeting says: 'I certainly do not recall a spirit of "blaming". Rather it was a forum to air concerns and canvass staff support and opinion as to how we could improve the situation. Some women did experience appalling abuse.'

The Black Parents' Group's letter denied that sexism had anything to do with the boys' upbringing in single-parent families – a gloss which had *not* been included in the notes of the meeting circulated in school. So-called 'woman hatred', it claimed, was no more than the normal misbehaviour of children and should be tackled by teachers able to gain the respect of their students and motivate them to learn.

> We gain a strong impression from our children that some teachers adopt teaching styles that are more appropriate to the play centre or youth club. Teachers should be able to deal with the misbehaviour of adolescent boys and not cop-out by labelling this behaviour as a psychological defect.

The head's reaction at first was conciliatory. In a letter to the chair of the Black Parents' Group, he accepted that the issues raised by the two staff groups – the Women's Group and the Black Staff Group – were complex, and suggested organizing a meeting for parents, governors and staff to discuss them. He planned to invite the

ILEA equal opportunities adviser, herself a black woman, and eventually came up with a date at the end of the autumn term, 1989, just before his own retirement.

The head denied that women staff were making simplistic connections between black boys' behaviour and their home background, but pointed out that adolescent boys were often in a state of rebellion and that conflict at home might transfer itself into rebellion against teachers or anyone else in authority. This might express itself particularly in an antagonism towards women teachers in a male environment.

> Whatever might go on in one or two rooms, or with one or two people, the truth is that most women on the staff are amongst the hardest working, most professional people in the place, not at all encouraging 'play centre' styles. And some of those professional women do experience sexually-biased insult, anonymous or not . . . It's very risky to suggest that in some way those women bring harassment upon themselves.

The tone of the Black Staff and Parents Groups' joint reply to the head, unsigned, of 13 December 1989, was contemptuous. The problems, the group said, were 'inappropriate classroom strategies' and 'covert racism' which was the product of the school as an institution, not 'psychosexual explanations' for certain types of rebellion. The meeting proposed for the following week was not convenient for the Groups, the letter said, nor did it address the Groups' concerns. 'A whole school in-service day where the Black Group are in an advisory capacity (and integrally involved in the arrangements, considerations and focus) would definitely seem to be taking the matter more seriously.'

This spat might seem trivial in the light of all the other problems which Hackney Downs faced at the end of 1989. But it is significant in that it highlights an ideological rift – setting some, though by no means all, of the ethnic minority staff against the rest – which deepened catastrophically over the next couple of years.

Financial pressures

The final pressure on the school during the late 1980s was financial. By this time Hackney Downs' roll had fallen to 693 and was already predicted to fall further. There was increasing worry about the numbers choosing the school at 11+, and the ILEA was going through a series of budget cuts which were pushing the pupil–teacher ratio up sharply.

At a crisis meeting of governors in April 1987 there was anger at the ILEA's threatened pupil–teacher ratio of 17.9:1 as it affected schools in areas as deprived as Hackney. The governors argued that a school such as Hackney Downs, where half the pupil intake was now bi-lingual, and where many had behavioural and emotional problems, should be treated more favourably than others with fewer problems. A little later, with class sizes already above 25 even in practical subjects, the head was beginning to complain publicly about the number of boys now arriving at the school mid-year. 'The trickle of new pupils, often with little or no English, is tending to push class sizes up as the year goes on. We have to take pot luck with boys coming into Hackney Downs and we seem to get more than our fair share of awkward customers.' This was a problem which dogged the school to the end.

Lack of capital grants also impinged on the school. It took two years to repair and refurbish two science rooms which were burnt out after a break-in in 1985. There were delays in the provision of new computer rooms a little later and the first of many head's reports to governors focusing on little or no progress on building work. Ominously the school's physical history was beginning to catch up with it. The remaining Victorian buildings and the 1960s blocks alike were beginning to show their age. No sooner had work on the science labs and the computer rooms been completed than wet rot was discovered in the historic swimming pool building. It took four months to repair the damage and remove the scaffolding. The deteriorating buildings were to prove a major factor in the school's loss of popularity with local parents, which accelerated the fall in the roll. Educationally and socially aware parents became particularly reluctant to send their sons to a school in such a bad state of repair.

The ILEA inspectors continued to keep a close eye on Hackney Downs right up to the moment of hand-over to Hackney Borough Council. Their final report, in November 1989, was still mainly concerned with recommendations on improvements which were needed to classroom organization, homework policy, examination monitoring and a more differentiated curriculum to challenge more able boys. The school's informality, they commented, could indicate good relationship but risked appearing confused and unbusinesslike. Good pupil–teacher relationships, which had been the highlight of the 1985 report, appeared to be threatened by a developing 'tough' sub-culture as the boys moved up the school. And by now inspectors were openly appalled at the physical state of the school. 'It is lamentable that the school has been allowed to fall into a state of such disrepair when staff and pupils are expected to have a sense of pride in their working environment.'

John Kemp retired at the end of 1989, as the Inner London Education Authority, abolished by the Conservative government, prepared to hand over its responsibilities to Hackney. Good things remained at Hackney Downs when he went, he says in his memoir, but there was a feeling by then that something dramatic had to be done if the school was to survive. The school was handed over as one of eight Hackney schools which the ILEA regarded as 'at risk'.

The staff were aware of the school's deterioration but they were ready to give their support to a new head who, if he attracted the wholehearted support of the new local education authority, seemed to have every chance of pulling the school around. The governors and ILEA officers appointed John Douglas, a young man who, although he had no previous experience of London schools, evidently offered Hackney Downs energy and enthusiasm. The staff began the new school year in 1989 full of optimism about the future.

4

Hackney Takes Over

Issues of quality

The fate of the schools in the poorest of the London boroughs had always been one of the major concerns of those who opposed the break-up of the ILEA. Schools in areas like Hackney were already complaining that the ILEA, forced into budget cuts by an unsympathetic Conservative government, was not meeting the needs of the most deprived areas of the capital. But it was widely held that a larger authority would, in the long term, be able to administer education more effectively than a number of small ones.

As the most deprived, and amongst the most politically turbulent of the Labour-controlled Inner London boroughs, Hackney faced enormous problems in setting itself up as an LEA. What it probably least wanted to hear was that a large proportion of the schools it was inheriting were 'a cause for concern', including Hackney Free and Parochial which turned out to be 1990's 'worst school in Britain' according to the popular Press. The new Education Committee, led by its Chair Michael Barber and its Director of Education, Gus John, were immediately faced with serious issues of quality even before they had set up their systems for running the schools.

But the ILEA's view was quickly confirmed. In 1990 HMI reported on visits they had made to a number of Hackney schools over the previous eighteen months. They concluded not only that Hackney schools had acute problems, particularly over staffing, but that the problems were getting worse. Schools, they suggested, would not overcome these difficulties on their own.

In the secondary sector, they found that falling rolls, the redeployment of teachers and prolonged industrial action had had a damaging effect on staff morale. The introduction of the National Curriculum and the rest of the provisions of the Education Reform Act had coincided with the upheaval of the ILEA's demise. Everyone in the education service in Hackney, they observed, was under constant pressure that made it very difficult to stand back and plan for the long term.

HMI visited eight out of the ten Hackney secondary schools and came to some dismal conclusions. In four, although none was outstanding, the quality of the work came close to the national average which, in a seriously deprived inner-city context, was no mean achievement. In the other four, which inevitably included Hackney Downs and the other all-boys school, Homerton House, they found that between one-half and three-quarters of lessons were less than satisfactory.

In their report on all Hackney schools they said:

> In the poorer schools and in the less satisfactory lessons in the successful schools the pace is slow, the work has little vitality, there is a lack of differentiation, low expectations of what pupils can achieve and excessive noise; lessons are inadequately prepared, teachers have insufficient competence or confidence in the subject matter they are teaching and they do not offer pupils the degree of intervention and support that they need.

Pupil attendance was low, staff absence and turnover were high and in public examinations the Hackney schools inspected lagged well behind the national average. In 1989 around a quarter of pupils nationally were gaining 5 A to C grades at GCSE. In the Hackney schools the proportion ranged from 7 per cent to 13 per cent. Despite having the most deprived and disruptive intake and being a boys' school, at this stage Hackney Downs' results were still holding their own with the other Hackney secondary schools.

Teacher recruitment had become so difficult in parts of London like Hackney that recruitment of overseas teachers was now common. 'Consequently schools are increasingly heavily dependent upon teachers with little or no previous experience of local circumstances or even of the education system in which they are expected to teach.' Some teachers in Hackney, HMI concluded, had given up the struggle. No staff development had been feasible for many years: nor was the situation likely to change unless some way was found to stabilize staffing.

There was strong evidence to support the conclusion that if Hackney's educational problems were not uniquely difficult, their sheer scale required a radically different approach if the education of its pupils was ever to be more than second best, HMI said.

'To improve the quality of education for the pupils in Hackney will require the strenuous and co-operative efforts of all the partners in the education service', they suggested. But nothing was likely to be achieved unless the central problem of teacher recruitment and retention was solved.

Hackney Council, understandably anxious to prove that as a Labour authority now entrusted with the management of education for the first time it could not only cope but triumph over adversity, went into the fray with vigour. An Action Plan in response to the HMI Report was drawn up covering every aspect of the service, from the crisis over teacher recruitment and retention, to under-5 provision, partnership with parents and governor training.

Strategic objectives were set, staffing structures were described, monitoring systems set in place and plans were costed. As a blueprint for an education service it was exemplary. Sadly, as far as Hackney Downs was concerned, it was not worth the paper it was written on because its promises – for instance, the upgrading of science and CDT facilities, action on staff stability, the provision of a 'secure and structured learning environment', and above all, the 'extensive programme of major and minor works to improve school accommodation' – were either never delivered or delivered too late to save the school.

The LEA's immediate objective was a major effort to rescue Hackney Free and Parochial School, which had hit the headlines in early 1990 as a failing school. All credit must go to those who worked hard to remove this very public label. But it has to be said that the input made at Hackney Free and Parochial School by the LEA and the Diocesan Board of Education was never replicated at Hackney Downs where it could have made an equally dramatic difference.

Betty Hales believes that Hackney Free and Parochial School's revival depended on a combination of factors:

1 Early retirements/redundancies, favourably financed at the beginning of the period of improvement, to allow for proper strategic staffing planning and improvement. (At Hackney Downs it took concerted efforts by many senior managers over a period of four years to achieve the same level of staffing restructuring.)

2 A number of 'exclusions' of particularly problematic pupils during the initial period of change. (Many of the boys 'jettisoned' by Hackney Free and Parochial School found their way to Hackney Downs, exacerbating existing pressures. It is worth noting, however, that many of these boys remained at Hackney Downs until they left school to move onto further education or useful employment.)

3 A large investment in new building to make the school more attractive and educationally viable. (Hackney Downs never saw any of the promised similar major building work, which could have made all the difference to recruitment, morale and efficiency.)

4 Proper advisory and consultant support which was targeted and consistent at the strategic time. (Although Hackney Downs received some similar support, it was never as successful as it could have been because it was not part of a planned intervention programme and often became counter-productive.)

5 The identification and appointment of a strong permanent headteacher. (Hackney Downs had four short-term headteachers in the space of two years at a time when the school was particularly vulnerable.)

A new headteacher

With major challenges facing the borough of Hackney as a whole, John Douglas took over as head with a brief to pull Hackney Downs back from the brink. In an interview with the *Hackney Gazette* he expressed his optimism about his new job, aware of the school's 'terrific reputation' and committed to seeing the school through to a new period of growth and success 'greatly helped by the school's good atmosphere, dedicated staff and supportive parents'. There can be few endorsements so rapidly destined to end in disillusion.

John Douglas had two deputies: one a long-standing member of staff, the other having joined the school the previous year. Their particular areas of expertise were pastoral care and management systems respectively. A term later Elizabeth (Betty) Hales joined the school as third deputy head in May 1990.

Betty Hales describes her arrival in her own words:

Returning to Hackney, where I went to primary school, was like 'coming home'. I had never worked for ILEA although all of my teaching had been in North and East London in a variety of establishments, including a private girls grammar school in Walthamstow, where I had established the Physics department in the newly opened Forest Girl's School in 1981. I had also worked in an FE college in a socially deprived area of Edmonton, achieving excellent exam grades with students, many of whom were not dissimilar to those at Hackney Downs. I had played a strategic role in establishing the new co-ed sixth-form college in Leyton in the mid-1980s, originally Leyton Senior High for Boys.

My promotion to Deputy Head was during my tenth year of teaching at the age of 39. It had been an active time of establishing a successful career, whilst my own three children, two of whom have specific learning difficulties, were growing up. All of this puts the eventual closure of HDS into perspective. There was and is no one who can claim to care more about the value of education for the working classes, or to have more relevant or direct experience of putting quality in place, given the right resources and backup.

When I first arrived at HDS I was struck by its uniqueness and the amazing contrasts. It was not a place where you could be complacent or bored. The staff were intense and vibrant. They supported and educated me in the skills needed to survive the large proportion of extremely challenging pupils and eccentricities of many staff, both newly appointed and those who had been in post through many turbulent years.

By normal standards the new management team was a powerful one committed to raising achievement for working-class
pupils and under John Douglas' leadership the new senior
management took on the school's problems with some vigour
and optimism.

The school buildings

John Douglas' problems were exactly the same as those of his predecessor, but instead of improving under the impact of his energetic
new approach they became rapidly worse before he had been given
a reasonable chance to find his feet. In theory the simplest problem
to solve at Hackney Downs was that of the buildings. A survey in
January 1990 provided eight pages of defects, ranging from broken
windows and leaking roofs to serious decay in the physics block and
the gym. The whole of the Victorian swimming pool building was
now in need of major repairs. This was a pool which was used not
only by Hackney Downs pupils but by other schools in the neighbourhood. The science block had cracks in its walls and the attached
greenhouse was beginning to collapse. The playground needed
resurfacing and was becoming dangerous, and the walls of the
school-keeper's house were shifting.

The new head's efforts to make refurbishment of the school a
priority for the council were backed by the LEA's science adviser.
She expressed her concern in writing to the school and to the LEA
after a visit in September that year. She found two labs out of use
because of lack of essential maintenance and damage due to water
penetration. The rest of the science accommodation, although
usable, was not much better.

But John Douglas was butting his head against a brick wall not
of Hackney Council's own making. The council might set strategic
objectives for refurbishment, but it was the government which disposed. Hackney submitted a bid for £10.4 million for capital works
in 1991/2. This was to include improvements to meet the provisions
of the National Curriculum, for disabled access, and for planned
maintenance to 'begin to stem the serious decline in the condition
of buildings'. The allocation for the previous year had been £1 million and there were commitments in existence from the ILEA which

left a shortfall of £1 million. There was effectively no money available for any new commitments. Hackney Downs' buildings continued to deteriorate inexorably until the school closed.

After more than a year in the job, in March 1991, the headteacher was still writing to the Director of Education about the 'general and deteriorating condition of my school's buildings and structural environment'. The school staff, including caretakers and cleaners, he reported, had worked wonders to help create a welcoming and pleasant environment which impressed parents. But all this had been achieved

> within what is essentially and undeniably an utterly demoralising situation where roofs continue to leak: the gymnasium roof still leaks from storm damage of February 1990; our playground surfaces are deteriorating dangerously; our science block is in a disgraceful condition, only matched by the dreadful state of the swimming pool's shower and changing rooms.

He complained bitterly that apart from urgent repairs no work had been done on the school since his appointment and that incredible amounts of time had been wasted pressing for action and chasing up promises of action, on preparing for meetings which did not take place and discussions with officers. Hackney Downs, he said, needed positive action and investment now.

The head's two-page letter received a four-line acknowledgement from Gus John who said that he was awaiting information from the Head of Client Services to enable him to reply more fully. But as staff watched as other local secondary schools' building problems received attention, the conviction grew that the school was simply being left to decay.

In June, John Douglas was eventually sent a full list of the school's defects by the Deputy Director of Education, and in mid-July confirmation that substantial work on the school roofs would be carried out during the autumn term of 1991. Beyond that there would have to be further consultations.

That same summer the school-keeper requested a replacement for the 50-year-old and now rotting greenhouse attached to the science department. It is interesting to note that four years later, in

March 1995, Betty Hales, by now acting head, was informed by the same Deputy Director that repair of the structure was the school's responsibility and that dangerous glazing should be removed or protected by a solid hoarding as it posed a danger to pupils in the playground! In 1992 conditions deteriorated after yet another fire. By the end of that year HMI were complaining that parts of the school were 'squalid'.

Difficult pupils

John Douglas had other, equally serious, problems. He soon found that the pupil intake was becoming ever more problematic. The autumn term of 1990 was not unusual. After term began, a further twenty boys were directed to the school, going into all year groups. Two of them remained for only a brief period. Nine of the permanent newcomers came directly from overseas, two from the USA displaying extremely disturbed behaviour, three from Bangladesh and one each from the West Indies, Ireland, Cyprus and Turkey. Five were non-English speaking. Of the other nine, four had transferred from other Hackney schools, having been 'advised' to leave, four came from schools elsewhere in London, and one from Buckinghamshire after a family breakdown.

In Betty's words again:

When I first arrived at Hackney Downs I could not quite believe what I had come to. So many pupils far more challenging than I had ever encountered before across all cultural and racial groups. Those who would not sit in a seat, let alone do any work, but simply wandered around the room chatting to their friends, who sneered if you tried to get them to take notice. Little refugee children who were so needy, some so potentially bright. The little Kurdish boys who threw themselves to the ground the day that the police helicopter came low over the playground. (The last time they had seen a helicopter it turned out that a man in a uniform leaned out of the side and fired a machine gun at the people below.) Those same children when autumn came cramming their pockets full of berries 'in case they ever got hungry and needed something to eat.'Two new Somali boys who took handfuls of food that had been discarded to the pig bin and crammed them into their pockets for the same reason.

All newcomers had to be assessed and arrangements made for special language help or other support to enable them to cope in a normal classroom situation. The following year Betty Hales carried out an analysis of the school's 'casual' intake over a full school year. Between September 1991 and July 1992 the school admitted 62 boys at intermittent intervals. Of these 24 were causing concern over their behaviour at their previous schools, eight had been truanting, eight had been 'unhappy' at another school, seven had been permanently excluded, including one who had been at a residential special school, and one 15-year-old Turkish boy arrived speaking no English at all.

This was at a time when the Educational Psychology Service in Hackney, upon which work with the most disturbed children depended, had been disrupted following the transfer of control from the ILEA to Hackney. Normal service was not resumed until July 1990 but there were continuing difficulties over unfilled vacancies and a curtailed service to the school throughout the following year.

It is perhaps not always obvious to outsiders how much time 'difficult' children absorb in a school situation. The regular liaison meetings between school staff, the school's educational psychologist (when one was in post) who visited on average about once every two weeks, and the educational social worker responsible for attendance issues, reveal the complications this constant influx of new children often brought with them. Staff shortages meant that the Education Welfare Officer, responsible for chasing up absentees, was only in school for one morning a week.

In an area of multiple deprivation, even making and maintaining contact with parents can be difficult. Very often liaison is also needed with the local social services department, although in 1990 it was not clear whose responsibility this was, the school's or the EWO's. The school also suffered from its proximity to the Pembury Estate which became notorious at that time as one of the first sites of domestic crack cocaine production in London. Dealing with drug-related issues, in liaison with the local community police offi-cers, became a constant feature of school life at this time.

In the EA report which eventually led to the school's closure it is stated that incidents involving drugs were not routinely reported to the police. This was never true and Hackney Downs senior and pastoral staff enjoyed a close relationship with the local youth and community police team who regularly complimented them on the sensitive and thorough way in which all incidents of law-breaking were handled.

All this soaks up the time of senior school staff who are as a result diverted from more overtly 'educational' concerns. Those senior staff found it particularly unhelpful later to be accused of 'crisis management' and of taking on the role of heads of year, knowing as they did that the crises were real and the heads of year were well-nigh overwhelmed.

In the classroom, teachers were faced daily with children whose problems were simply not amenable to any solutions which the school could offer and whose behaviour was bizarre, unpredictable and sometimes violent. For example: 'Two brothers in Years 7 and 8. Both have very poor attendance and the older boy is disruptive in class. The school had not been notified that the family is involved in an investigation over sexual abuse of children or that the mother has attempted suicide.' The possibility of home tuition for the boys is discussed in a liaison meeting but it appears that the family may in any case be on the point of moving to another part of London. All the officials involved appear to be swimming around in a sort of liaison soup, with the school still technically responsible for edu-cating the boys in a coherent way.

Planning improvements

In the spring of 1991 the school made a bid to the Prince's Trust for funding to run a twilight hours Homework and Activities Pro-ject and to modernize the library and reading room. This was an exciting project which could have achieved a great deal for boys in a highly deprived area. The head was optimistic that the bid would be successful when the Trust committed some funds for the read-ing room improvement. Work began on this basis.

In the summer of 1991 a senior teacher represented the head at a Trust meeting in Scotland ostensibly to finalize the details of the bid. But following this meeting the Trust withdrew its support and asked for money already allocated to be returned. The reasons for this devastating setback were never fully explained to the deputy heads or staff, but many felt later that this loss of sponsorship further strained the relationship between the school and its head and the LEA. The school was left to pick up the bill for the work already started.

When the head of humanities left, he was replaced by Jeff Davies, who combined this responsibility with that of head of upper school and careers. This heavy combination of jobs was symptomatic of the strains imposed by preparations for Local Management of Schools which threatened to reduce the school's budget severely.

Jeff Davies immediately took the upper school in hand, rationalizing the examination entry system, integrating assessment and achievement with the pastoral work being done at Key Stage 4, and generally working to improve the rigour of teaching and pastoral work. The parents of all boys whose behaviour was giving cause for concern were written to on 1 October 1992 and asked to make urgent appointments to discuss their sons' problems. Partnership with parents and the improvement of academic achievement were always top priorities, but were sometimes overwhelmed by circumstances within the school and the neighbourhood.

The sheer scale of the behaviour problem had by now become huge. In the autumn of 1991, John Douglas' second year as head, the regular liaison meeting with the school's support personnel was told that fourteen of the term's intake were causing urgent concern and might need referral to the educational psychologist, extra support in class, or already had statements of special educational need or were members of families involved with social services for various reasons, including child abuse. Concerns about ten other older boys were also referred to the meeting. Time did not improve matters for Hackney Downs. A year later no fewer than 37 boys were officially referred to the single educational psychologist responsible for the school. Both the school and the educational psychology service were on the brink of being overwhelmed by the needs of Hackney Downs boys.

In one extreme case, a father actually broke his son's wrist in front of a teacher when told about his son's misdemeanours. This case led to a full child abuse investigation and it was brought to light that the father also severely beat the mother and the younger children in the family. It is a measure of the social deprivation and need in the area that social services decided to leave those children in the family home.

All cases were treated seriously and referred to social services so that both the child and parent could access appropriate help. But child protection issues are very time-consuming and detract from other, no less important and directly relevant work. It is too simplistic to say that teachers should concentrate only on education. School is often the front and only line of defence for otherwise defenceless children.

The headteacher and senior staff were actively trying to contain poor behaviour in classrooms throughout this time. At the beginning of 1991 the policy of simply sending disruptive pupils out of class was clearly not improving the school's behaviour problems because they tended to roam around the building. It was also absorbing unacceptable amounts of senior management time in monitoring what was going on.

A referral room was set up on a temporary basis to receive pupils sent out of their normal classes, and a procedure established to make discipline more consistent, to make sure that boys sent out of class were suitably monitored and occupied, and that incidents were reported to senior staff and to parents. The room was well used, with anything between seventeen and 30 boys being sent there each week. The most common misdemeanours were disruption of lessons and extreme rudeness to staff. Without exception, the boys concerned came from extremely deprived circumstances and had histories of very difficult behaviour at previous schools. Many families found their sons impossible to control outside school as well as inside.

The referral room did not solve the problem of unruly behaviour, but it made some improvement to the atmosphere of the school. Inexperienced staff, of whom there were many, felt more supported by the system and used referral as a way of demonstrating to parents the seriousness of their son's problems. Referral also helped by establishing proper channels of communication between heads of year and tutors, and made the responsibilities of heads of department and classroom teachers for behaviour more explicit. In-service training was provided to clarify staff roles and responsibilities.

Regular meetings of deputy heads and heads of year were also established at this time with the aim of providing boys with some consistency of approach and offering mutual support to middle managers who sometimes felt that they were using sticking plaster on gaping wounds. It soon became noticeable that one department was not using the referral room, so consistency right across the school was difficult to establish.

Attendance and punctuality

The school also made strenuous efforts to improve problems of poor attendance and punctuality, identified by the LEA's attendance survey in 1990. In January 1991 the headteacher wrote to parents to explain the procedures for notifying the school of a boy's absence, and for the imposition of a detention for lateness twice in one week. This also required a greater sense of organization amongst the staff, some of whose register-keeping had been criticized by inspectors. The effect was not dramatic, but attendance had begun to creep up from an average around 70 per cent in 1990 to peaks over 80 per cent by mid-1991.

This was not a problem unique to Hackney Downs. The senior adviser, launching an attendance survey the previous year, had come across some intractable problems. Where pupils were referred for specialist help at off-site units, for instance, it was sometimes impossible for the 'home' school to know whether they were attending or not. There was also a proportion of 'transient' children in the borough living in temporary accommodation who came and went unpredictably. Schools were unsure at what point they could legitimately remove a child's name. A similar problem arose when children were allocated to a school for the start of Year 7 but never turned up. One school noted twenty such cases and neither school nor the authority had been able to trace them.

These children haunted the attendance figures like ghosts,

pulling down the averages and leaving numbers of children unaccounted for although ostensibly in the education system. Other Hackney schools were reported to have no educational social worker support, so the follow-up of persistent non-attenders was actually impossible for a time. The ability to follow up children attending Hackney schools but living in another borough also proved extremely difficult, at least for a time after the demise of the ILEA.

LEA inspection

The new LEA's initial response to Hackney Downs' problems was to send in its own inspectors and advisers to 'monitor' more or less everything. In the spring of 1990 there was an LEA review, at three weeks' notice, about which the headteacher complained that he had not been consulted. Science provision was also reviewed by the science adviser who was critical of the state of the buildings and of less than consistent teaching and learning. An attendance survey took place in January 1991.

That month Gus John wrote sympathetically to John Douglas, congratulating him on the progress he had made so far, and offering further 'support' in the guise of a 'substantial visit' by advisers to explore a number of issues such as management and organization, curriculum offer and delivery, school policies and practices, and the professional development of staff. The school was given ten days' notice of this visit which took place on 29, 30 and 31 January 1991, one year after John Douglas had taken up his post.

The headteacher's note to staff about the visit was a model of temperance. It was, he told staff, a visit for development purposes and not to be taken as 'ominous'. 'In many ways it makes complete sense and we need to look at what positive outcomes can result from it.' But by this time there was growing evidence that some staff were becoming disillusioned by the constant external pressure on the school and the amount of time and energy being absorbed by these constant 'visits'.

Even so the senior management team did not give up. Betty Hales, two terms into her new post, carried out a significant amount of work on discipline and classroom management/curriculum delivery in the spring and summer of the year. But that January visit was to prove crucial in the relationship between the school, its governors and the LEA, as much because of how its findings were presented as what they actually revealed.

On 10 April 1991 the school governors met at the request of the LEA's chief inspector so that the report resulting from the school review could be presented. The completion of the report had taken fifteen weeks which, by the standards of Ofsted which must report back to governors within five weeks, is a long gestation period. No inspectors had contacted the school with either information or advice during this period. However, neither the school nor the governors complained about the delay until the governors became uneasy when they were told during the Easter holidays that the report was not available for them to see before their meeting.

On 10 April the head and the chair of governors, Helen Baxter, were informed that the report was still not ready but that the chief inspector would present the recommendations that evening. On arrival at the meeting the governors were outraged to discover that the report and its recommendations had been withdrawn without explanation.

A frosty exchange of letters between the chair of governors and the Director of Education failed to clarify just what was going on except to indicate that the Director was considering making a report on the school to the Education Committee and that if the governors thought they were being ill-treated by the LEA they should be aware of 'folk much less well disposed to the school than the Directorate and Hackney Council are' who might ruin any real prospects the school had of turning itself around. There were those who considered this to be a hint that closure was already being considered.

When the Review report eventually arrived on 12 May 1991, the inspectors commented on the school's appearance of 'neglect and disrepair' which must have been galling to those who had suffered and complained about this state of affairs for years. They were encouraged by the absence of litter and graffiti and by the pupils' generally good behaviour, gratifying comments for the deputy heads and pastoral staff who had been working hard on these issues in extremely difficult circumstances.

But in general the tone of the report was unfriendly and highly

critical. It noted 'dangerous fissures' in the staff – presumably a reference to the continuing activities of the Black Staff and Parents'
Group – and found a lack of clarity about roles and an absence of
whole-school policies. At least it felt the school was fortunate in its
appointment of headteacher and deputies and congratulated John
Douglas on his grasp of the need for structures and those he had
already put in place. The school, however, the advisers warned, was
so unstructured that it was near the point of no return. They concluded ominously: 'There are no options for the senior management
team to discuss whether or not the recommendations contained in
this report are acceptable for they have the force of law.'

The inspectors made 28 recommendations in all, covering management, attendance, homework, curriculum, staff meetings, a
curriculum analysis, examination entries, discipline, learning
difficulties and links with primary schools. There were no recommendations about what should be done by the school or the LEA
about the deteriorating physical condition of the school or about
the demoralizing problem of mid-term entrants. A follow-up review
was scheduled for the following October.

The school's reaction to this was undoubtedly prickly. They had
concerns about the accuracy of some aspects of the report and the
fact that some of what they regarded as inaccuracies were used as
a basis for critical generalizations. Shortcomings, they felt, had been
regarded as generalizable, while examples of good practice had not,
and they perceived a gap between what the inspectors had said while
they were on site and what emerged later in writing.

Staff were upset to find little or no comment in the report on the
good social atmosphere and on better pupil behaviour, nor any academic comparison with the performance of other Hackney schools,
even though the examination results were holding up well in difficult circumstances, or on the lack of parity of intake.

John Douglas was quite open with his staff about the incident of
the delayed report and Gus John's decision to send in two advisers
to help implement the recommendations on organization and curriculum which had been published. But there is a note of
desperation beginning to appear in his communications. He concluded his note to staff: 'I have outlined what I want to see reviewed
or developed by departments by the start of the new academic year

. . . All of this is entirely within our contractual responsibilities and obligations as teachers, managers and headteacher. There is anyway no choice in the matter.'

The two advisers were expected to stay at the school for two terms. In fact they worked at the school for the rest of the summer term, a total of six weeks, and did not come back in September. No explanation was offered for the withdrawal of their support, strengthening growing staff suspicions that the LEA was already thinking about closing the school.

The staff also noted that, in contrast to the treatment of Hackney Free and Parochial, no injection of funding for buildings, resources or staff restructuring was offered to Hackney Downs, nor was it suggested that the school should exclude any of its difficult pupils, as Hackney Free and Parochial had done. From this point on, the relationship between the Hackney Downs staff and governors, and the LEA, became increasingly soured by suspicion.

Ironically the intake that year rose, perhaps an indication that parents were becoming a bit more confident that change and improvement were under way. The school roll in September 1991 stood at 430, still desperately low, but the intake of 126 Year 7 boys made that the largest year group by some 40 boys and pushed class sizes in that year up to an average of 25. Parents may also have been impressed by GCSE results which showed just under 16 per cent of pupils gaining the magic five A to C grades, and 40 per cent of passes overall at grade C or above. (The Hackney average for five A to Cs was 17.9 per cent that year.)

The published statistics gave the impression that a quarter of the school's pupils still left without any exam passes at all, the worst result in Hackney. But this reflected the huge number of 'ghost pupils' – boys who had never attended at all, who were being taught off site, or simply could no longer be traced – on the roll. Every boy who was actually attending Hackney Downs sat at least one GCSE that year, with the non-English-speaking pupils taking, at least, art.

In the autumn term there was a 'follow-up' review, this time by six LEA inspectors. This time the inspectors commented on the fact that they had received a more positive reception from school staff and that the school had begun to take their previous recommendations seriously, although there was still evidence of practice lagging behind policy and procedures. Of their previous recommendations they found some progress being made on the majority. They produced 24 more recommendations, with target dates, to consolidate previous progress and continue work on attendance and punctuality, discipline, curriculum and management and organization.

The governors too were taking an active interest in the review processes, setting up an action plan working party to monitor progress and report back to the full governing body regularly.

By this time John Douglas was clearly becoming anxious about the school's 'precipice-like' existence and about the effect the constant reviews were having on staff. In November 1991 long-term staff sickness and a complete absence of available supply staff reduced the school, he told the LEA, to 'survival management'. Staffing had not been assisted by an LEA 'freeze' on appointments that summer because of a budget crisis. The freeze was not lifted until October. Local management was not yet in force in the former ILEA area.

At the end of 1991 John Douglas wrote seeking an urgent meeting with the Director and senior staff to discuss the future of the school. He clearly welcomed the help he was now receiving, but felt that this was not enough to help him cope with the escalating problems he faced.

Increasing problems

By January 1992 anxiety had turned into a sense of serious crisis. The report back to governors on the October review of the school had, the head told the Director of Education, been extremely negative and any sense of progress had been lost. He was incensed that the impression had been given to the meeting that the school had been given sufficient support. The short-term appointments of LEA advisers he evidently regarded as inadequate. He complained about 'inflammatory and sweeping' statements about attendance, exam results, exclusions, amongst other matters, and indications that the LEA now regarded the school's future as being in serious doubt through no fault but its own.

There was little in the second review which was not inherent in the first, in the headteacher's view, and progress on the first set of recommendations put the school in a good position to make progress on the second. He was very afraid that if the meeting accurately reflected his feeling that the LEA had abandoned Hackney Downs, then staff would give up and many would leave.

By this time many staff were deeply disillusioned by what they saw as constant criticism from the LEA, without any attempt being made to offer the level of support the school needed to turn itself around. Many were becoming seriously worn down and levels of sickness were increasing.

John Douglas was apparently reassured of the LEA's continuing support in a telephone conversation, and work on implementing the action plan continued. Within weeks HMI were back at the school on a one-day visit which raised again specific problems of teaching and learning and discipline. HMI made it clear that they were keeping the school's progress under review and that progress was now a matter of urgency. The governors were also putting pressure on the staff, seeking departmental reports on progress in relation to the review. These were presented to the governors in March.

Hackney Borough Council's now constant budget difficulties were also impacting hard on the school. In July 1991 the LEA froze the recruitment of teachers from outside the Borough. Hackney Downs staffing was cut by two teachers just before the end of term at a time when there were two outstanding vacancies. John Douglas complained to the LEA about this decision, coming as it did on top of the net loss of nine teachers over the previous eighteen months since he came to the school, and an imminent reduction of his deputies from three to two. He complained that he was being left with insufficient staff to cope with special needs pupils and pupils needing to learn English as a second language.

During the early part of 1992 the relationship between the head and some of staff was further soured by an industrial dispute between the National Union of Teachers and the LEA over the issue of cover for absent staff and the redeployment of staff prior to the introduction of Local Management of Schools. This was another bitter row provoked by the breakdown of negotiations on a borough-wide cover agreement. After the breakdown, the NUT imposed a ban on all cover after the first day. The LEA responded by attempting to dock the pay of teachers refusing to fulfil their obligation to cover for three days. Hackney Downs was particularly vulnerable on the redundancy issue and the school NUT branch resisted the identification of Teachers Above Authorised Numbers (TAANS). The dispute rumbled on throughout 1992, leading to increasing unpleasantness between staff.

Finance was also becoming an increasing problem for the Borough of Hackney in general and for Hackney Downs in particular. Local Management of Schools was due to be introduced in 1992. It was obvious to the LEA, to John Douglas and his senior management team and to the governors, that Hackney Downs was not viable under any conceivable financial formula based, as it had to be, on pupil numbers. Even though under John Douglas' headship the school was attracting more pupils each September, its roll remained below 450.

The implementation of LMS for the 1992/93 financial year caused management and governors severe problems. It seemed likely that the imposition of the formula would lead to significant staff losses, but as the financial year approached, governors remained unclear about costings and the LEA's figures. The replacement of teachers became increasingly uncertain and posts were being advertised as one-term-only contracts, so adding to the general instability of the institution.

In the summer of 1993, as part of the LMS staff reductions, three long-serving and very experienced members of the school staff with head of department responsibilities took early retirement. This was a serious blow to the school, especially as their posts could not be advertised externally. The technology department was taken over by a highly respected black teacher, with the assistance of a recently qualified assistant teacher. Unfortunately he was taken ill, took early retirement in 1994 and died soon after the school closed. The post of head of PE was combined with that of head of year.

The replacement of the head of science was even more contentious. There were two internal candidates, the number two in the department, who was male and white, and a young black female biology teacher. At the interview, the science adviser from the LEA made it quite clear that she favoured the more experienced candidate but the interview panel split on racial lines, the two white members supporting the adviser's view and two black parent governors voting for the black candidate despite the advice of the LEA representative. The casting vote was eventually made in favour of the more senior applicant by a black teacher governor.

Some members of staff were clearly unhappy with the outcome of the interview for the head of science post. Others were both surprised and displeased when the biology teacher was appointed to a vacant head of year post very late in the term. Divisions within the staff were now reaching crisis point and the health of senior staff was beginning to suffer.

Pressure on Hackney Downs was relentless. Following a briefing by HMI, four LEA inspectors visited the school again in the autumn of 1992. They found few examples of good lessons and many poor ones. They raised concerns about declining GCSE examination performance and concluded that the school was at risk.

But the rescue of Hackney Downs was rapidly becoming an issue out of either the head's or the senior management team's control. The efforts that John Douglas was making were being undermined from within by a small minority of the staff, and from without by changes imposed by government to introduce LMS, the National Curriculum and league tables.

5

A Divided Staff

The Black Staff and Parents' Group, which had been a thorn in John Kemp's side before he retired, proved even more difficult for his successors to deal with. With the school under constant pressure to 'improve', the 'fissure' which the inspectors had identified within the staff was rapidly becoming a chasm. This was not an issue of racism within either the whole school or the staff. Race relations at Hackney Downs had always been, and continued to be, good. The problem lay in an extreme and to some extent separatist view of education espoused by some, but by no means all, black staff at the school. The Caribbean didactic style of teaching, enforced by physical discipline, was much admired by some, even though corporal punishment was outlawed in British schools. And there were undoubtedly some black parents, who used physical punishment on their children themselves, who agreed with this philosophy. Many parents, when told about their sons' misdemeanours, often said to Betty Hales 'You should beat him.' At the same time, other black parents supported the school's more mainstream approach.

Almost as soon as he arrived, John Douglas, like his predecessor, began to receive communications from the Black Staff and Parents' Group (BSPG), typed but generally unsigned. Their first letter to him returned to the theme of the 'faulty foundation on which some educational practice was based at Hackney Downs', in other words the row with the Women's Group which had simmered on for over a year. The BSPG argued that the academic achievement of black pupils was the responsibility of the school, that social and family factors were not an issue for teachers, and that the school should appoint an equal opportunities co-ordinator, whose prospective duties the group spelled out, as a matter of urgency.

A handwritten note reached John Douglas four days later, also unsigned, to inform him that the Group believed there was a need for an incident book to record racist incidents in the school, to be kept and monitored by the black staff.

The head's written reply was the soul of reasonableness. He agreed that the appointment of a co-ordinator might be helpful, but pointed out that the post-holder would certainly expect a responsibility allowance and the school's budget for such allowances was overspent. When he had time to complete an urgently needed review of posts and allowances, he would give the matter serious consideration.

On the issue of the 'incident book', by now apparently in existence, he was less conciliatory. Such a book might serve a useful purpose, but it should be a whole-school document held by the senior management. 'I have already had it said to me by a pupil that the nature of its present existence has caused some confusion amongst pupils who have been told of its existence; this can only cause pupils to believe that Hackney Downs is a divided school with a divided staff.'

Undeterred, the BSPG returned to the attack within a couple of weeks, emphasizing the depth of the ideological rift between some of its members and the school's management. The letter begins assertively:

In Hackney Downs School there is an assumption that pupils must first be taught how to behave before they can achieve. At a recent staff meeting it was suggested that the school should devise a set of rules on behaviour and if these rules were not adhered to certain sanctions would be put into action . . . The proliferation of school rules is nothing more than an attempt to deal with the effects rather than the causes of the problem. It must look at classroom practice.

The letter went on to offer the Group's view on how classroom behaviour might be improved and to reiterate the need for the still existing incident book to counter the effects of racism in the school. 'The Black parents strongly believe that this book must continue to be maintained and administered by Black staff.'

Some black parents might have been happy with this situation, but the rest of the school undoubtedly was not. By the end of the following term, July 1990, white staff were becoming unsettled by the whole business. The BSPG was eager to pursue grievances felt by some black staff and students, and was holding regular meetings for black parents only. Invitations to these meetings were given out by black staff, directly to black students, with instructions to pass them directly to black (not white in mixed-race households) parents and not to allow white teachers to see them. Fortunately many black parents were unhappy with these procedures and complained to the senior management, so the school quickly became aware of what was happening.

The headteacher wrote to the Group to complain that pupils themselves were expressing confusion over what letters were being handed to which pupils and why, and what meetings were occurring for which parents and why. There had also been occasions, he complained, when pupils had spoken of going to see a black teacher or had mentioned the incident book in ways which had either been deliberately intended to challenge a teacher's authority or had had this same effect. 'I am also concerned that within this general atmosphere of staff uncertainty and confusion, we have seen an increasing number of occasions when certain pupils have spoken loudly of racism in circumstances which I do not believe involved any racism whatsoever.'

In spite of the evident strains now being imposed on the school by the activities of the BSPG, the headteacher still tried to conciliate. He encouraged the election and co-option of black parents to the governing body, suggested that the Group should be more formally integrated into school structures and that he should be invited to their meetings to improve liaison and understanding. His overtures were fairly peremptorily dismissed.

The working of the school's maths department at this time is central to an understanding of how difficult this issue became. The head and deputy head of maths were both black and involved in the BSPG. It had been their custom for some time to enter promising students for maths GCSE early. But the means to achieving this end was to offer small groups of mainly black students extra tuition. Some of the same boys also attended supplementary Saturday or after-school classes organized by the black community. This established practice was now causing concern to other departments because boys were being asked to go to extra maths tuition when they should have been at other lessons.

The results of this practice looked good for the boys' maths, on paper at least. Some of the boys entered early gained a GCSE grade C. Some were subsequently started on an A-level course the following academic year. What worried Betty Hales, now responsible for exam performance, when she analysed the results more closely, was that the same boys were not going on to gain a GCSE grade A or B in Year 11, which is what their ability indicated should have been within their reach. Betty Hales caused waves when she suggested that the rationale behind early entry should be the subject of whole-school discussion and agreement. Her factual analysis was not welcomed by some staff and she began to experience hostility from some black pupils and parents, and the number of unfounded allegations of racism against her and other white staff began to rise.

Racism was, and remains, a hot political issue in Hackney. The Borough Council at that time employed large numbers of ethnic minority staff. Passionately-held beliefs and a tendency to police political correctness fiercely made these difficult issues even harder to tackle than they might have been in a more homogeneous community. As in the wider community of Hackney, so in Hackney Downs School. The issues raised by the Black Staff and Parents' Group proved incredibly difficult to resolve.

Gus John was kept informed by the school about the problems the BSPG was causing. His response too, at first, was cautious. He was sympathetic to the idea of an equal opportunities' co-ordinator and to some of the Group's other concerns, which coincided with concerns in the LEA's own action plan. But he was seriously worried from the beginning about the Incident Book and about the indications the Group's communications gave of fairly fundamental misunderstandings of how the school – or any school – should function.

The BSPG, he wrote to John Douglas, were failing to understand that they could recommend policies but had no authority to decide matters which were within the remit of management, or that they were accountable to other staff.

By what process and by what authority, for example, is it suggested that reports by students about certain members of staff
should be communicated to those staff, and who would make
decisions about the veracity of such reports or about sanctions
deemed to be appropriate? Those colleagues are effectively
appropriating to themselves functions which you (the headteacher) have not delegated and cannot delegate outside of
your senior management structure if you are to be seen to be
protecting the rights of all students and all staff.

The Director recommended continued dialogue with the Group
about race issues but he advised John Douglas in July 1990 to take
immediate steps to discontinue the Incident Book recording alleged
racist incidents and to make it clear to staff and students that it was
unofficial and did not have his endorsement. Gus John admitted to
the headteacher in a letter that he feared a Burnage-style polariza-
tion between staff, students and parents – a reference to the tragedy
at Burnage High School in Manchester in which he had been
involved as a member of the inquiry team after a boy had died. The
Manchester issues, he suggested, might be usefully used in in-service training at Hackney Downs. In the meantime, he said, the head
had his permission 'to inform those members of staff that you are
intervening robustly with the full authority and support of the
Director of Education'.

However robust John Douglas was encouraged to be, it did not
work. In November 1990 the Black Group announced that, having
seen the published agenda for an in-service training day, they would
treat the issues more effectively 'if they met as a group to address
this agenda from a common Black perspective'. They would meet
during the morning of the training day for this purpose. When John
Douglas insisted, verbally and in writing, that 'mixed' groups would
be more productive, some black staff defied him and met as a separate group.

He then wrote individually to members of the Group, telling
them that he would be discussing the situation further with the
Director. Their action, he said, represented a 'strange and rather
worrying attitude to your professional colleagues and to the need
for the whole school staff to work through issues together'. It also,

he told them, breached their terms and conditions of employment and diverted attention away from the real tasks which faced the school.

The Group was unrepentant. In a written response, they said that in their view, since the head's arrangements for the training day were 'unreasonable', they could not accept his statement that their action was in breach of contract. 'The work was conceived, planned and set purely from within an Anglo-centric context. As a result of this, the Black staff did not have a voice.' However, they had found the introduction and talk from the Director of Education 'useful'.

The equal opportunities co-ordinator

Soon after this, the BSPG presented John Douglas with a detailed description, with diagrams, describing how they saw the still-to-be-appointed equal opportunities co-ordinator functioning. A crucial part of his/her duties would be home/school liaison. The diagrams give the impression that senior staff were to act only through the co-ordinator, who would also have oversight over a whole range of other management functions such as the assessment of teaching and learning styles, the 'observation' of the wishes and choices of parents and the community prior to curricular modification, and ensuring that assessment and record-keeping were appropriate and in accord with the National Curriculum. It is a document which apparently leaves little role in its scheme of things for the headteacher or other senior staff who were actually appointed to run the school.

The feeling grew towards the end of 1990 that the BSPG, albeit with a few powerful leaders and others who went along with them for a quiet life, was effectively running in opposition to the rest of the school. Things did not improve in the following year. Disciplinary issues were increasingly polarized around issues of race, and some staff began to feel intimidated.

Discipline

The head and governors were working to impose an agreed disciplinary procedure. In March 1991 the headteacher proposed introducing a Complaints Book, to be held by the head, to record pupil complaints and the details of how they had been dealt with. This more open system, recommended by the governors, was in response to the Incident Book still held by some of the black teachers. There is evidence that John Douglas felt so beleaguered by this stage that he was seeking advice from colleagues elsewhere about how to tackle Hackney Downs' difficulties.

But the difficulties with his divided staff got no easier. There were a series of disputes over disciplinary issues involving black staff and students and a minority of black parents who were apparently willing to take issues to the LEA in their pursuit of allegedly 'racist' teachers. They began openly calling for the sacking of individual members of staff. The files show the endless paperwork and meetings involved in taking evidence from staff and boys and trying to reconcile conflicting accounts and interpretations of incidents.

In October that year John Douglas wrote to the Director of Education about a dreadful fortnight during which a series of accusations of racism had involved him directly as well as more junior staff.

> In the two weeks before half term I was confronted with:
> 1   A pupil complaint concerning racist abuse of a black pupil by a white member of staff.
> 2   A complaint by a black teacher/class tutor concerning the way a white teacher (the same as in 1 above) had refused to accept a note given by her to two pupils who required early lunches.
> 3   Two follow-up complaints by the parents of these two pupils.
> 4   A Black Staff Group complaint regarding the way I had interrupted a report-back by a senior member of staff (who happened to be black) at our recent INSET day.

In fact the Group accused Douglas of 'abusing his position as headteacher'. His behaviour, they wrote in their letter of complaint, 'reveals the depths to which you are prepared to sink to quieten the voice of black teachers who have a legitimate right to address the staff at such meetings'.

The head acted to defuse each of the issues, but was left, as so often happens with such incidents, with a sour legacy of ill-feeling and nothing fully resolved. There was an irreconcilable conflict of evidence over the use of 'racist abuse' by a member of staff. The misunderstanding between a black and a white teacher over school meals for two (black) pupils with medical conditions had led not only to another accusation of racism but to the arrival of aggressive letters from parents who had given the same racist interpretation to the incident.

John Douglas was clearly most angered by the attack on his own authority and he summoned what he intended to be the first of a number of meetings involving himself and all the black teachers in the school. The Group responded by reiterating their accusation of racism, and inviting him to attend a meeting under the auspices of the Group. 'We would wish to discuss your attitude to these groups and to the implications of your responses to various issues raised by these groups since your appointment as headteacher.'

On 8 November the appointment of an equal opportunities co-ordinator was finally made, although not without further ill-feeling. The interviewing panel consisted of the chair of governors, a co-opted governor who had previously been an elected parent governor, the school's development adviser and the headteacher. A parent governor had also been appointed to the panel but telephoned to say that she could not be present, having been delayed elsewhere. The second in charge of the maths department, a black woman, was a candidate, but after interview the post was given to a white male teacher who had chosen to work part-time in order to undertake his share of child-care responsibilities and who had carried relevant head of department responsibilities previously. The appointment was for one year. The appointment of a white man clearly did not please the BSPG. The disappointed candidate instituted a formal grievance procedure with the local authority on the grounds that the interview panel had been incorrectly constituted after the sudden withdrawal of the parent governor. The complaint was investigated and dismissed by the LEA.

It seems clear that the BSPG expected that a black staff member would be appointed to this post, which they had pressed for and which they saw as taking precedence over heads of year, and curriculum and pastoral deputy heads. The governors were clearly not minded to go along with this shift in the school's line-management and power structure.

By now thoroughly exasperated, particularly by a report about a BSPG meeting at the end of November about which, as usual, he had not been informed, John Douglas issued a four-page memo to all staff on 4 December 1991.

In a meeting called via the normally official means of school communication to parents (namely pupil post), appearing to therefore be part of the school's formal organisation and service to parents, things were said about the school, its management and myself which clearly caused parents considerable concern and anxiety. Amongst information given at the meeting there was also misinformation. Staff with special responsibilities within the school were present, lending further 'official' credence to the meeting.

In co-operation with the Director of Education, John Douglas laid down ground rules for the future conduct of the black groups. They were not to use school organizations or facilities. Meetings of all groups of staff were to give him an agenda and a report back on their discussions. Meetings with parents were to be organized only with his authority. All meetings were to meet basic standards of professional behaviour.

He wrote to all parents explaining what was happening and inviting them to a meeting to discuss concerns. The official Parents' Association was also to be given a high priority.

He reiterated the school's commitment to overcoming underachievement, particularly amongst ethnic minority boys, and its opposition to all forms of racism and race discrimination. But he emphasized that these issues needed to be addressed by the whole school on behalf of all its pupils, not by small groups.

Let me make it absolutely clear that I am not seeking to deny black parents or any parents the right to meet independently and to work to their own agenda, nor their right to require the school to be accountable. But the school cannot hope to be pro-active with parents or be accountable if parents have a perception of a divided school, with one section of staff inviting them to meetings and displaying high levels of alienation from other staff and from the senior management of the school.

The Black Staff and Parents' Group responded within days with their own memo, justifying their existence. John Douglas might have attempted to end the conflict within his staff, but the other side evidently had absolutely no intention of ceasing hostilities.

6

Crisis

HMI visits

Throughout the whole of John Douglas' period as head, HMI were also showing a keen interest in the progress of the school. By October 1992, when two inspectors arrived for their second visit that year, HMI had been in the school six times in four years. The visit on 22 October, at a week's notice, was ostensibly to look at the work of Year 7 as part of a random survey to look at how children were settling into their first year in secondary school. John Douglas did not appear to his colleagues to regard it as particularly significant, although when they arrived, HMI looked at classes in other years as well as Year 7.

When they reported back it became clear that they were extremely unhappy at the state of the school. They criticized discipline and classrooms barely under control; attendance which had slightly improved but was still unsatisfactory; poor punctuality; unsatisfactory or very poor teaching and learning; low GCSE entries and poor results, and a physical environment which was grim, dirty and, in some areas, 'squalid'. They concluded that the school had deteriorated since the previous visit in February and was now a cause for serious concern.

This HMI visit was to prove crucial. John Douglas found himself immediately involved in a row with the LEA for allegedly not informing them of HMI's plans to visit. He had assumed that HMI would inform the LEA automatically of their intention to visit one of their schools. A phone call logged at the school from the LEA on 17 October (the day after HMI's letter announcing their visit was sent), asking for documentation on progress since the last HMI visit, gave the impression in retrospect that someone at the LEA knew before the school did that HMI were coming again.

But quite apart from that technicality, it now seemed clear that the LEA was increasingly blaming the head and senior staff for what they identified as the lack of progress being made to improve the school, and the head was evidently becoming resentful at having to carry the can for what he saw as a disaster not of his making.

The latest HMI visit he had found particularly galling: he had, he said, been offered little chance to respond, question or challenge, there had been no discussion of the school's particular problems with its intake and staff or of its efforts to improve, and HMI had not visited any lessons by the school's most successful staff. The LEA responded immediately by sending in four advisers on yet another inspection visit. Senior staff by now felt very conscious that they were receiving an inordinate amount of inspection but little in the way of advice and support.

On 11 November 1992 Gus John attended a governors' meeting at Hackney Downs to express his concern at the latest turn of events. HMI, he told governors, were expecting a response from him in reaction to their latest critical report. The threat of a full HMI inspection hung over the meeting. Gus John was particularly critical of the school staff's apparent lack of intention or capacity to change in the light of everything that had happened to highlight their shortcomings.

External pressures, he also warned the meeting, were ever increasing. The government was putting through legislation which would enable it to take over failing schools and turn them into grant-maintained schools – or close them down. Hackney Downs was so small that it would fare very badly under Local Management of Schools. And he was about to launch a review of secondary education because of the worrying number of surplus places in the borough.

There were, Gus John told the governors, three options he could put to the Education Committee: close the school outright; turn it into a mixed school, although that would be difficult as it would exacerbate the surplus-place problem; or possibly discuss a merger with Kingsland, the oversubscribed nearby mixed school, to form a popular school on a split site.

A stormy discussion followed during which it became clear that governors did not share the Director's view that the school had received 'more than its fair share of advisory time' during the last couple of difficult years. Nor was there universal acceptance of his view that the staff were largely to blame for the current state of the school. They were 'working their butts off', as one governor put it, and had been asked to do far too much in too short a time. Senior staff might have received help, but classroom teachers had not. Other governors complained that no notice had been taken of issues that the Black Staff and Parents' Group had tried to raise. Some governors saw Gus John's three alternatives for the future as simply school closure by one means or another.

John Douglas tried to separate out the issue of falling rolls: numbers, he said, were rising. On the issue of school improvement, he pleaded for more time to allow measures which were already under way to bring results.

At the end of the meeting Gus John left with the governors' reluctant approval to proceed with discussions between himself and the headteachers on a phased amalgamation with Kingsland School. He would report back to them on that issue, and on the HMI and LEA advisers' reports within a few weeks.

The staff reaction to this turn of events was angry and bewildered. An open NUT meeting, attended by many non-union as well as union members, published a document in defence of what they saw as unwarranted criticism of their performance at the governors' meeting – the minutes of which had not been published. They hit out at the local authority which they said had intervened with its reviews but had not provided the means for the staff to implement review recommendations. At the same time staff had been cut, including the vital support staff who dealt with special needs pupils, staff turnover had gone up (one tutor group had eight maths teachers in a term), replacements had been less experienced and temporary or from an agency, and there had been a lack of consultation and of clear whole-school policies.

For several weeks as the term drew to a close Betty Hales found herself running the school without senior management support. Ken Russell, deputy head, was on extended sick leave and John Douglas spent considerable time at meetings at the education department. She relied heavily on the support of the pastoral team to keep the school afloat and on NUT members who relaxed their action over cover during this crisis. When members of staff received anonymous notes objecting to the levels of co-operation Mrs Hales was achieving, she took the issue to an NUT meeting where a resolution was passed reminding all NUT members of the rules on professional conduct.

Betty Hales had always regarded her continuing membership of the NUT as a strength in her dealings with Hackney Downs staff, but she was increasingly aware that some members of the LEA did not share this view. She believed that the school's notoriety, gained in the industrial action of the 1980s, lingered on.

A new headteacher

After four difficult weeks, one day before the school broke up for the Christmas holidays on 17 December, the governors were told that John Douglas was to move to a new job, responsible for 'special projects' within the LEA and also seconded to take an MBA, and the Hackney Downs headship was to pass immediately to Peter Hepburn, who would be seconded from his current job as deputy head at the other Hackney boys' school, Homerton House. He would be supported by Daphne Gould who was to come to Hackney as a consultant following her retirement from a successful headship in neighbouring Tower Hamlets and a period serving on the National Curriculum Council. It has to be asked what the LEA thought it could gain by making another short-term appointment to the headship of Hackney Downs School at this stage, given all that was known by 1993 about the importance of committed leadership to school success.

However, it is clear from the governors' minutes that the Director of Education was seriously concerned that the government might step in and take control of Hackney Downs if some drastic action were not taken. He had already met HMI to discuss their most recent findings and would be meeting them again in the New Year to discuss the LEA's response, he told the governors.

Governors complained that the appointment of a new head was their responsibility. They were stunned at the turn of events, and sad and disappointed at the way John Douglas' headship had ended, they said.

Governors also complained that the additional support Peter Hepburn was being offered now would have been helpful much earlier. Gus John agreed that consultants might have been useful, but because of budget constraints he had preferred to rely until now on his own advisory service.

The governors had severe reservations about how the new regime would work at such short notice and about how staff, parents and pupils would react. The Director warned them that if governors could not work with the senior management, the LEA had the right to rescind its responsibilities and take over the running of the school itself.

The governors insisted on meeting Peter Hepburn and Daphne Gould before making a decision on the LEA's proposals. In the end they voted to accept the appointment of the new headteacher. John Douglas's three years at Hackney Downs were entirely unexpectedly over.

The two deputy heads – Ken Russell, who had just returned from sick leave, and Betty Hales – felt very slighted by the way the new dispensation had been agreed and announced. They had been told of John Douglas' departure just before the governors' meeting at which it was confirmed. After discussing their reactions, they agreed that it would be in the interests of the school to work constructively with the new acting head and the consultant.

They met Peter Hepburn and Daphne Gould during the Christmas holidays to brief them on the school, the staff, pupils and governors in the hope that all four of them could work together to prepare for an expected Ofsted inspection. Betty Hales and Daphne Gould immediately warmed to each other, finding that they shared a passionate commitment to high achievement and quality education for working-class children.

For her part, Daphne Gould later stated that it took her only a very short time to confirm for herself that the information and impressions she had been given of the school in those early meetings were accurate and well-informed. She took on board Betty Hales' judgements about the quality of the school's staff and the extent of the social and educational needs of the pupils, which were extreme even for Hackney.

The responsibilities the new senior management team faced were by now pretty awesome. None of the problems identified during the later years of John Kemp's headship nor during the years John Douglas had been in charge had been resolved. There had been *some* improvements, but some problems had deteriorated. The staff and to some extent the governors were still deeply divided and increasingly demoralized. Fears that the school could not survive in its present form were exacerbated by the effects of LMS and the threatened review of secondary education in Hackney.

Meanwhile, the local authority itself was running into serious difficulties. On 5 February 1993 a letter went to all council staff from the chief executive concerning allegations of corruption and fraud in the housing department. Seventeen people had been dismissed for fraud. Such allegations did not concern the schools directly, but they were unsettling for all Hackney Borough employees, especially in the light of rumours that malpractice was not confined to the housing department.

Running Hackney Downs would have been a daunting task even for a very experienced head, but for the second time Hackney Downs was placed in the hands of a head in his first appointment, and in this case only a seconded appointment. Some of the staff found his approach brusque, others appreciated what they regarded as 'up-front' management. His approach to the disaffected black teachers, it soon became clear, was to 'include them in', although Daphne Gould expressed reservations about this. It was not, as it turned out, to prove any more successful than previous attempts to resolve the deep divisions in the school's staff.

However short-term their commitment, Peter Hepburn and Daphne Gould took on their new roles with energy. By now it was known that the school would be inspected by Ofsted, probably within a year or eighteen months, and Peter Hepburn's first priority was to prepare for that. He was a manager with a 'systems' approach, whose main means of communication with staff was through memos, forms and meetings.

A new broom

Almost as soon as the January term started, the new head was tackling the issue of pupils who might come to school but 'bunked off' the lessons they disliked. The head's own patrols of the corridors had picked up numerous miscreants, and he consulted heads of year to work out a more effective way of checking that boys attended the lessons they were supposed to attend. Over the next couple of months he attempted to tighten up the disciplinary system already in place and make it more consistent. Most responsibility for good order rested with the heads of department, with a wider support system for pupils out of control. Peter Hepburn agreed with the view that sanctions and rewards were not the only answer: that suitable work, planned to engage the attention of all pupils, was also crucial.

But as time went by, the other senior staff became concerned that the number of exclusions was rising rapidly: the number of temporary exclusions went up by 50 per cent during the year, and nineteen boys were permanently excluded compared to eleven the previous year and only seven during the following two years when Betty Hales was in charge.

There is a genuine question about exclusion rates: many 'improving schools' improve by removing their most unruly pupils. This may ease the load on staff, at least temporarily. But it leaves unresolved the questions which Hackney Downs had to some extent committed itself to answering: how do you educate in the mainstream pupils with extreme learning, emotional and behavioural difficulties? Is exclusion a solution or does it just shift the problem somewhere else?

The new head also produced an action plan on liaison with primary schools and the local community, and he and the senior management team began work on the school development plan, which would be required for the Ofsted inspection. This set specific targets, for instance to improve attendance and punctuality by 5 per cent, to improve the atmosphere and appearance of the school, and to improve classroom management and teaching.

His plans are interesting not least for the light they throw on the state of the school as it existed when he took over. For instance, his plans to improve the school atmosphere include not only a code of conduct for the pupils but also 'a staff code of professional ethics'. The school's appearance was to be improved by removing graffiti and removing broken and unused furniture from teaching areas, as well as improving display and presentation in the foyer, corridors and classrooms.

As far as classroom performance was concerned, Peter Hepburn asked for the production of comprehensive and differentiated schemes of work by the autumn of 1993, better planning and monitoring, and more incentive for pupils and wider recognition of their achievement.

Yet the fact was that, in spite of the Christmas appointments and the avalanche of paper policies Peter Hepburn introduced, the school was still suffering from the disruptive behaviour of many 'casual' entrants with multitudinous personal problems. In spite of representations from the school, the LEA at this time offered no possibility of the school's avoiding admitting any applicant while it had spare places in the relevant year group – which of course it almost always had.

Peter Hepburn's plans to defuse the situation regarding some black members of staff were no more successful than his predecessors'. Attempts by other staff to curb serious classroom disruption by a minority of black students were invariably met by abusive, and uncannily similar, complaints from parents. Staff at all levels, and the head himself, were accused of racism in letters sent to the school and to Gus John directly. The majority of parents from the ethnic minorities at the school remained consistently supportive throughout the difficulties which the school experienced. But there is no doubt that many staff were worn down by the determined disruption of a small minority.

The LEA still proclaimed its good intentions towards Hackney Downs, but seldom, it appeared, had the capacity to fulfil them. At the very beginning of his headship, the schools services manager promised Peter Hepburn better information on mid-term entrants, most of whom, she accepted, were either new to the country, with little or no English, or coming to Hackney Downs from other schools and with a record of behavioural difficulties or exclusion.

'In such cases we will try to involve the educational welfare service at an early stage. Unfortunately I cannot give you a firm timescale to complete this work, as the head of admissions is on maternity leave and a review of the education welfare service is also under way.' The council's obsession with reviews was not confined to Hackney Downs School.

Almost exactly a year later, as Peter Hepburn was about to end his stint at the school, Gus John commented in an internal memo (which was copied to the school), that though the school had a legal obligation to admit applicants, he realized that this meant that the school had to spend an enormous amount of senior management time on 'the many disaffected and disruptive students' who arrived on its doorstep.

This memo is significant in that it acknowledges the efforts made during 1993 to calm the school, introduce behaviour management techniques and give 'excessive' amounts of time to those students and families who would co-operate. It conceded that the support services had not always been as responsive as the school might have wished, not because individual officers were indifferent, but because they too were snowed under by the conflicting demands on their time.

> Given the fact that the school is needing to do a good deal of work to prepare for Ofsted and is still very vulnerable, unless we are setting it up to fail, we have to look seriously and urgently at how it is resourced to manage all those damaged students who end up there. It is not an unreasonable expectation on the part of the school, but one we must resolve at senior level. The issue comes up over and over again each time the carousel goes around and off-loads more kids at Hackney Downs.

It would be difficult to find a clearer statement of Hackney Downs' fundamental problem, or clearer confirmation that it was not, in fact, getting sufficient support from the LEA to deal with it.

The nature of the problem

In September 1993, the deputy head Ken Russell completed an audit of the form lists of the school which listed six problem areas:

- attendance/punctuality/truancy;
- behavioural difficulties;
- emotional difficulties;
- non-statemented special educational needs;
- language deficit;
- statements of SEN.

Of a school population of 467 boys, he found that 101 were exhibiting behavioural problems, 99 had, by the school's definition, special learning needs, 90 had language problems, and 41 were persistently truanting from school or lessons. Of course these totals include boys with multiple problems: those who truanted constantly and misbehaved violently when they did come to school. But only fifteen boys had official statements of special educational need which entitled them to extra help. Absenteeism was a particular problem in Year 11, as it is in many secondary schools. Language needs were fairly evenly spread among the year groups, because whatever efforts the school made to teach boys without English effectively, more non-English speakers constantly arrived to join all the year groups. Special educational needs boys were also fairly evenly spread among the year groups, but behaviour was a particular problem in Year 9, with 38 boys out of 110 causing difficulties. It is interesting to note that this was the same difficult year group that HMI had seen when they were Year 7 and had concluded that standards of behaviour and achievement at the school had deteriorated.

Looking at the audit figures another way, there was not a class in the school which did not have 50 per cent of its boys exhibiting one or more of the six difficulties the school had defined. There was remarkable consistency across the year groups and the school as a whole. In September 1993, 264 of Hackney Downs' 467 boys had a problem, some had more than one, and a significant number were a danger to themselves and others.

Much of Daphne Gould's time was taken up dealing with

individual cases of disruptive pupils and a small number of less than satisfactory teachers, some of whom she successfully eased out of the school. But the level of disruption was an ongoing problem and the level of suspensions was high. Setting off the fire alarms was a constant pastime among the more difficult children, for which they were generally temporarily excluded if caught. Dangerous activities included playing on the railway embankments just beyond the school grounds, and climbing onto the roofs. Permanent exclusion usually happened only after a number of warnings for serious misbehaviour.

Daphne Gould also worked vigorously to improve depressing aspects of the school which were outside its immediate control. She took furious exception, for instance, to the standard of school meals for the 440 boys, 340 of whom were entitled to a free meal and for many of whom it was their main, or indeed their only, meal of the day. In a teaching career of 39 years, she said, the standard of meals at Hackney Downs was the worst she had ever seen.

Throughout the year of Peter Hepburn's headship, difficulties with the Black Staff and Parents' Group continued. In the March the head agreed to allow the Group to meet on school premises again, in spite of the Director of Education's wish that the Group should disband and the reservations of some governors. The decision was not welcomed by some other staff, some of whom complained about the Group's unprofessional behaviour.

However, the longest and most disruptive dispute between the school and the BSPG was over the resignation of the second in the maths department. She informed the headteacher in writing at the end of May that she would be leaving the school to take up a new job in September. The LEA and chair of governors were informed but before the LEA had acknowledged her resignation, effective at the end of August, which it did on 1 July, she was having second thoughts about her new job which she apparently discussed with the head. The day after the formal acknowledgement of her resignation from the LEA, she wrote to the head confirming that she wished to withdraw her resignation.

This request threw both the school and the LEA into some confusion, as no one initially seemed to have any idea whether or how a resignation could be withdrawn in this way. At the school level, the head told his colleagues that as her resignation had already been formally accepted by the LEA, the whole matter would have to be referred to governors. At their July meeting the governors confirmed the recommendation of the head and chair of governors not to allow the resignation to be withdrawn. They were advised that to allow her to withdraw her resignation might lead them to be held liable for her breaking her new contract of employment.

There was also a financial rationale behind the decision. Staff rationalization for LMS was still being pressed forward, and a maths vacancy had already been advertised at a lower salary than was currently being paid for a deputy head of department. All staff who had left that year had either not been replaced at all or had been replaced at a lower point on the salary scales. Other staff were having their duties redefined to save money.

The row over the governors' decision rumbled on throughout the autumn term, Peter Hepburn's last, and was to prove the catalyst for an even greater row after he had left. That story will be resumed in the next chapter.

Hard work but little reward

There is no doubt that Peter Hepburn, Daphne Gould and the deputy heads worked extremely hard during 1993 to restore Hackney Downs' reputation. LEA advisers came to the school to look at the maths, English and music departments, and gave favourable reports on them. There was a significant improvement in GCSE results in the summer of 1993, vindicating policies introduced by John Douglas and the new examinations policy introduced by Jeff Davies. But the state of the buildings still caused serious concern, as did the disproportionate number of boys with learning, behavioural and emotional difficulties.

Staffing continued to cause concern, with key members of staff sick and vacancies which the school could not fill. But Betty Hales' approach to the issue of cover for absent colleagues, using the supply budget to buy in some very effective Australian teachers, had largely taken the sting out of the issue. Her contention that staff needed time out of the classroom for legitimate professional purposes, and her careful monitoring of the supply teachers who came in, improved morale and the atmosphere in the staff room, and ensured co-operation when it was needed in a genuine emergency.

Even so it was not proving easy to provide the stability which the pupils needed. Monitoring of pupils' work and improved recording systems were still only at an early stage.

At the governors' meeting in November 1992 at which he made his final report, Peter Hepburn announced that he had been appointed to a headship in Hertfordshire and would be leaving at the end of term.

It had already been agreed between the two deputy heads, Daphne Gould and the LEA in September, that Ken Russell, the deputy head with 27 years' service at Hackney Downs, would become acting head when Peter Hepburn left. Betty Hales would be his deputy and Daphne Gould would continue her two-year advisory appointment at the school. For the second time the school governors, now chaired by Councillor Pat Corrigan, had little direct involvement in the appointment of their headteacher.

As Peter Hepburn left it was announced that Ofsted's inspection would take place in May. The key staff, including the deputies and the pastoral team, who had continued to offer each other considerable support throughout this time, were left feeling that a year in the life of Hackney Downs had been wasted, not through the fault of Peter Hepburn, but because his temporary appointment had simply not provided the stability which the school had needed during a crucial year. But the senior staff were optimistic that they could work with Ken Russell, who was as committed as they were to improving the school, and that they could face Ofsted with some confidence that the school could pull back from the brink.

7

Going Co-ed?

Soon after Peter Hepburn and Daphne Gould moved to Hackney Downs in January 1993, and as Gus John had predicted at the November 1992 governors' meeting, the London Borough of Hackney decided to review its secondary school provision to make sure it was 'sufficient and suitable' to meet local needs up to the end of the century. It was known that the Department for Education had been pressing the borough for some time to reduce its proportion of surplus school places and that it believed that the borough could dispense with a secondary school. But the Director of Education's priorities by the beginning of 1993 were quite different. His concern was to make sure that there were enough places to meet future demand, which was rising.

Hackney's secondary schools had been reduced to ten in number by the ILEA reorganization in the 1980s, and were by 1992 running with a considerable proportion of empty places – 1,035 out of 8,250. However, the empty places were not evenly spread across the ten schools. Some schools were significantly more popular than others, with most vacancies concentrated in the all-boys' schools, Hackney Downs and Homerton House, and most of the girls' and mixed schools were either full to capacity, or full in Year 7 and therefore beginning to build up their numbers towards capacity. Because there were four girls' schools available and only two boys', there was also a serious gender imbalance in the intake of the mixed schools, with too few girls on roll.

However, the child population was already rising and by 1993 the empty places appeared to be filling up fast, in spite of the long-standing tendency for a high proportion of the borough's children to opt for secondary schools outside Hackney. The Director based this review on the premise that pupil numbers would continue to rise steadily to the end of the decade and that by 1997 Hackney would need all the secondary school places currently available. The figures, based on primary school rolls, were quite clear on this point. Projected secondary school total rolls were as follows:

1993	7,463
1994	7,633
1995	7,833
1996	7,979
1997	8,181
1998	8,528
1999	8,842
2000	9,040

By the year 2000, the Director was suggesting in February 1993, the borough would actually be about 1,000 secondary places short. In addition it was also known that one of the girls' schools was seeking to decrease its intake by one form (30 pupils), which would make 1996 a more likely year for secondary school accommodation to become virtually full.

The long consultation process on the future of the secondary schools was launched at Education Committee in February 1993, a month after Peter Hepburn took over as acting head of Hackney Downs. There are no grounds for suggesting that this was not a necessary exercise for the borough as a whole, but every reason to believe that for a school like Hackney Downs, already in crisis, it added a new dimension of instability which could do nothing but harm to its fragile reconstruction. Many in Hackney, including the majority of the school's staff, began to believe that this destabilization was deliberate.

Given that the DfE was highly unlikely to give permission for a new mixed school to be built to meet the unmet demand for co-education in parts of the borough, the initial proposals were based on the feasibility of reorganizing the existing ten schools. This could be done by amalgamating two existing schools into a new co-ed institution, although by the Director's calculations this would have to be on a split site because no existing buildings could be taken out of use. Alternatively, a mixed school could be created by converting one of the boys' schools, Hackney Downs or Homerton House.

In May the recommendation was made that Hackney Downs should go co-educational, admitting its first mixed intake in September 1995. All the other nine schools would retain their existing character. It was assumed that Homerton House would increase its intake and effectively fill up with boys whose families continued to prefer a boys-only school, and Hackney Downs would cater for the additional girls in the growing secondary population. The change of character at Hackney Downs would need DfE approval and it was hoped that this might be obtained by the Christmas of 1993, leaving eighteen months for the necessary conversion to be made.

Looked at in purely logistical terms, the scheme made sense. There were clearly too few families wanting boys-only education in the borough to support the two boys' schools as they were presently being run. If the demand was diverted to a single boys' school, that school, in theory, would fill to capacity. But this left a huge question mark over how Hackney Downs was to attract enough girls to boost its intake enough to make it viable under the LMS formula, when the other mixed schools in the borough were already having difficulty recruiting enough girls to ensure a gender balance. It also demonstrates the usefulness of a strategic body which is responsible for planning education across borough boundaries. From the beginning staff and governors at Hackney Downs asked where their girls were to come from and never felt that the LEA was able to answer the question satisfactorily.

However, the school was really faced with Hobson's choice. With 450 pupils it would not be viable under LMS. Improving the quality of the school and building up its intake as its reputation improved would take years, not months. In the medium term the alternative to taking the chance of going co-educational would quite possibly be closure on financial grounds. Educational officials admitted to the governors that the scheme was a high-risk one. With hindsight it is possible to see that it was never really a runner at all.

Cutting the intake

But there were more immediate preoccupations. In his report to Hackney Downs' governors on 20 May, Gus John broached the question of the transitional arrangements which would have to be made before the school could accept its first co-educational intake. His view was that even though the school was only half full, it would help in completing the necessary building refurbishment and alterations if the number of pupils on the site were to be reduced even further. He suggested that in the school year 1994/5 the Year 10 boys at Hackney Downs should transfer to Homerton House and complete their last two years of secondary education there.

This shift of pupils to the neighbouring – and in the eyes of many pupils – rival boys' school, would allow for two years of building work. This would provide new toilets, changing and shower facilities for girls, and allow for upgrading the dilapidated science department, adaptation of the CDT areas, renewal of the roof and windows, structural repairs to the science block, and internal and external redecoration. The following year there would be further improvements and renewal of the school boilers and windows in the swimming pool building.

At the same time Hackney Downs would need to liaise closely with Homerton House over teaching and curriculum, transport and learning support. The LEA did not envisage any changes in staffing during this period but suggested that all appointments and promotions should be on a temporary or acting basis for the duration, although they had to admit during the consultation that this was up to the governors. In reality, the governors were always reluctant to go against LEA advice, and found it particularly difficult now that their chair was also the chair of the Education Committee.

Crucially, while the roll of Hackney Downs School was deliberately, albeit temporarily, reduced in size, additional funding for small-school protection would be provided. 'To ensure that the curriculum could continue to be provided, extra resources would be added to the school's budget to ensure that an establishment of 23 teachers in addition to the head would be maintained.' Most governors and the SMT interpreted that as a promise that while the school's roll was artificially depressed, the high unit costs which would inevitably result would be met because they were a result of deliberate and considered LEA policy. It did not cross their minds that those unit costs would eventually be held against them or that promises made and accepted in good faith might be withdrawn.

Meetings were held for Hackney Downs staff and for parents during May and June. The staff meeting was well attended. Four parents turned up for one of the parents' meetings, though another was slightly better attended. Staff concern centred on the transitional arrangements with Homerton House and the insecurity inherent in the proposals for teachers. Not everyone was convinced that the school roll had to be reduced even further to make the transition to a mixed school possible. Parents were concerned about the effect on pupils of an enforced move to another school while the building work went on, about the LEA's financial guarantees for the transitional period, and about the school's future if it failed, in the end, to recruit enough pupils as a mixed school. But the overall feeling at both meetings was that the co-educational option was probably the best available to ensure any sort of future for Hackney Downs.

At this point the governors of Homerton House threw a spanner into the works by objecting to the proposal to transfer Hackney Downs' Year 10 pupils to their site. As an alternative, the LEA suggested that freezing the Hackney Downs' Year 7 intake in September 1994 and 1995 would be preferable. This would reduce the school to four and then to three year groups, and it would only return to five year groups after another two years, but the LEA's promises of financial cushioning for this period seemed firm. In 1995 girls would be admitted for the first time and in 1996, in spite of its still depleted numbers, Hackney Downs would return to LMS funding and effectively be responsible for its own salvation. In response to a specific question to LEA representatives at a staff meeting to discuss the proposal, staff believed that there would be financial cushioning for the six years that the missing year groups would affect the total numbers on roll.

At a special meeting on 28 June the Hackney Downs governors discussed the proposal to go co-educational and heard it recommended warmly by the acting head, Peter Hepburn, who was soon to announce his departure for a headship elsewhere. The governors accepted the proposal unanimously and the LEA began to draw up firm proposals to submit to the DfE for approval.

In July the Education Committee approved the proposals for Hackney Downs, although detailed work on the capital and revenue funding had yet to be prepared. The closure of either Hackney Downs or Homerton House, both low recruiters, was specifically rejected in the Director of Education's report, on the grounds that the borough would need their places in future.

The final proposal was that Hackney Downs' Year 7 intake should be frozen for only a single year – September 1994 – to facilitate the building works. The two-year 'breathing space' had been rejected as too expensive. It was also suggested that shared teaching arrangements between Hackney Downs and Homerton House might also be useful during this period. There was no suggestion that the 'lost' intake would eventually 'return' to Hackney Downs. The implication was that the school would have to run with one year short of its total roll for a full five years, though there was no discussion of the detailed financial implications of this. The 'frozen' Year 7 was to be included in the statutory proposal to go to the DfE.

The LEA's timetable was tight. If the DfE did not give the go-ahead to the plan by January 1994 it would be difficult to avoid recruiting boys as normal in September that year. That would set the whole scheme back by twelve months. Although Hackney Downs' future might depend on going co-ed, and that by now was what most people involved believed, the road was going to be a long and complicated one. Whatever other merits the plan had, an immediate enhancement to the stability of the school was not one of them.

Doubts emerge

However sound the plan seemed to the Education Committee that July, serious doubts soon began to emerge. One of Daphne Gould's responsibilities was to produce what was essentially a feasibility report for the governors on the transition to co-education. It was presented to governors as a confidential report that summer and did not make encouraging reading. Mrs Gould did not pull her punches.

The premises, she said, were grossly neglected. Two rooms had suffered fire damage which had never been repaired. Unrepaired broken windows had caused further deterioration by letting the weather in. The school, she said, needed a completely new science department if it were ever to meet the needs of the National Curriculum. The Victorian science block might then be converted to other use, but could not satisfactorily now be used for its original purpose. The swimming pool needed new changing rooms for girls, which would also make it more accessible to the community. The main building needed structural repairs and refurbishment. The Sports Council had been approached with a plan to bring the sports facilities up to a standard suitable for the school and the community. In 1993 the pupils could be offered only a modified PE curriculum.

On other matters, such as discipline and attendance and the curriculum, she reported some progress, but a great deal still had to be done. The school suffered from a high level of noise produced by pupils and some teachers. The boys' school culture included shouting, verbal abuse, and high levels of aggression and violence. Some boys were still spending time out of lessons, wandering around the school and creating disruption.

Most depressing perhaps was her analysis of the support the LEA had been able to offer during 1993. The school was still feeling overwhelmed by the proportion of special needs pupils and difficult youngsters being admitted to fill 'casual' vacancies. The process of assessing the amount and kind of support such boys should receive was slow and time-consuming. This placed considerable pressure on resources and teaching staff.

Hackney Council was addressing the enormous task but should realize that identifying need was only part of the problem. Appropriate support was just as essential and would take time and additional resources. There might be greater need, she thought, for central provision to be developed with vision and innovative skill. There were also implications for social services which should be working more closely with the education service and responding more quickly to the needs of distressed families.

Even when help was offered, problems could not always be resolved. Two Hackney Downs boys were offered places in a special unit. Both were so aggressive that it was not felt that the offer of a third place could be confirmed because a similar boy would make the group unteachable. Yet Hackney Downs teachers were expected to teach them as part of mainstream classes. In the end neither boy took up the place because their families refused to give permission: they both stayed at Hackney Downs until the end.

Other LEA initiatives had also failed to produce the results expected, Daphne Gould reported. A steering committee to monitor the progress of the various support services did not produce the action expected. Liaison with the support services was slow and time-wasting. Boys who needed urgent action taken on their behalf should be dealt with in days and weeks, not months and years. 'Daily contact focuses the mind', she said with the voice of experience. The LEA needed to consider the risk that casual admissions of inordinate numbers of pupils with considerable learning and behavioural difficulties would jeopardize, if not destroy, the education of the majority of pupils at Hackney Downs. A new LEA referral process would need to establish clear guidelines if it were not to realize its potential for chaos.

Daphne Gould concluded sombrely:

The management of HDS has an enormous problem which faces it daily. It is one of priority. The senior staff are permanently reacting and therefore can never be proactive. The demands of the pupils are constant and time-consuming. They seek attention and get it. To fail them is to create even greater difficulty which will need to be managed later. However, this results in all future planning and the task of real management taking place after school. Quality time for planning is not easy to identify in HDS and yet this must now be a priority for a successful future.

8

The 'Race War'

Another new headteacher

The last few weeks of Peter Hepburn's headship had been very stressful for everyone at the school. The parent of a pupil whose behaviour had become extremely dangerous and who had been excluded, was pursuing an allegation of racism against the acting head. The child was emotionally disturbed and receiving treatment from a child psychologist at a local hospital. Hackney Downs had been attempting to have a statement of special educational needs finalized for the boy ever since he had joined the school. In spite of the boy's evident problems, his mother believed they were caused by racism at Hackney Downs. At the same time Helen Thomas, the extremely competent head of English, was experiencing serious difficulties with some black pupils in her classes. The feeling among some white staff was that they were being made the target of unfounded allegations and that their classes were deliberately being made even more difficult than they would normally be.

The view of the school's new head of special needs is significant. He had joined the school that summer after running an off-site unit for persistent truants in another part of Hackney. He succeeded a long-serving and highly respected teacher who had been the victim of a tragic hit-and-run road accident earlier in the year which left him with brain damage. The post of head of special needs was a difficult one at Hackney Downs, not only because of the numbers of boys with SEN but also because of the opposition of some of the black staff to efforts to modify children's behaviour in any way. The new head of department's predecessor had met opposition from the BSPG and he was aware that he was moving into a problematic area.

He was assisted in the department by another new special needs teacher, and together they undertook an audit of needs within the school and began to work on strategies to deal with the extreme problems of some of the pupils. As a newcomer to the school, able to look at its problems with a fresh perspective, the new HoD said that he had never encountered more problematic children in such high concentration anywhere else. He confirmed what Daphne Gould, who was working almost exclusively with the boys with problems and their families now, had also found: that the sheer concentration of individual difficulties at the school was almost overwhelming.

The school had also been in a state of uncertainty about the headship and other senior appointments since Peter Hepburn had announced that he was to move on at the end of the year. Betty Hales had met with Gus John during the summer and discussed the difficulties over the Black Staff and Parents' Group with him. In the September, at a second meeting with Gus John and his deputy, it was agreed that Ken Russell would take over as acting head, with Betty Hales as his deputy. She did not wish to compete with Ken for the headship in the best interests of the school. They were surprised that no arrangements were finalized about salaries or formal appointments, and nothing was put in writing.

For the rest of the term it was felt that preparations for the Ofsted inspection began to slip. Increasingly there was an air of tension and anxiety about the school, although many staff continued to work loyally to keep the show on the road.

At the end of a turbulent year in 1993, with the future of the school as a potential co-educational institution still under consideration at the DfE, the acting head, Peter Hepburn, left and was replaced by Ken Russell. The new acting head took over at the beginning of January.

At this stage, Gus John appeared to be significantly more optimistic about the school's future. He presented a report to the final meeting of governors in 1993 which congratulated the staff on the improvements achieved the previous year, on the improved exam results and on the fact that the intake had risen for the third year running. He had suggested, and the governors approved, that Daphne Gould should remain at the school until the end of 1994 and take charge of the planning for co-educational status.

The mood was a reasonably cheerful one at the level of the LEA and governors. As Gus John put it to governors:

> While the school is nowhere near coming out of the woods, I am confident that the management and staff, even with Peter Hepburn gone, have the capacity to continue to build upon their significant achievements since January 1993. The significant improvements in the ethos of the school, in behaviour and discipline, in attendance and in examination results have already resulted in a morale boost among the staff.

But however well 1993 was perceived to have gone, Ken Russell and Betty Hales took over a school in a severe state of uncertainty, with an Ofsted inspection due in five months' time. The school still reverberated with the after-effects of the Black Staff and Parents' Group row over the departure of the second in the maths department.

The term got off to a disastrous start. Relations between the school and the LEA had been made more difficult by an appeal decision to over-rule the exclusions of three very difficult boys, who arrived back at school at the beginning of the January term. Exclusions were still running at a high level. There had been 25 exclusions of between one and eleven days during the previous term, some involving the same boy more than once. There had been six indefinite exclusions, which were intended to allow time for consideration of future educational provision for the boys concerned. It was three of these which were over-ruled by a panel of governors and an education officer. At the same time, setting off the fire alarm became a form of pupil sport which disrupted lessons two or three times a day.

Worse, on the very day that Ken Russell was writing to parents warning them that he would exclude fire alarm offenders in future, street fighting broke out outside Hackney Free and Parochial School in Dalston between boys from Hackney Downs and Homerton House on one side and pupils at the Hackney Free and Parochial School on the other. One serious incident, involving an 'invasion' of the rival school, fighting and chases involving boys brandishing bricks, hit the local and national newspaper headlines

and put enormous pressure on Hackney Downs senior staff to identify and punish the culprits. A massive amount of time was spent
trying to establish which boys had been where they should not have
been and when. When the investigations were complete it was clear
that very few Hackney Downs boys had been involved and the incident had been exaggerated by the media; but later, when the school
became national news again, the headlines from this incident were
referred to again and again.

Staff relations were also proving very difficult. Some black staff
remained unco-operative and appeared to be engaged in activities
unconnected with, and even antagonistic to, the school's agenda.
At this time unauthorized letters were going to some pupils' homes
on Hackney Downs headed paper; a pupil discovered off-site without permission appeared to be running errands for a staff member;
and the head, Ken Russell, subsequently revealed that his family
had received threatening phone calls. These were similar in nature
to several that were received later in the school office from callers
who asked for Betty Hales by name. Questions were also being
raised about payments which seemed to have strayed outside the
school's accounting system.

General unease was exacerbated by an entirely unrelated row
going on both locally and nationally about the decision of a Hackney
primary school headteacher not to let her pupils attend a performance of the ballet Romeo and Juliet. The national Press seized on
the case with their customary enthusiasm for anything they perceived
to involve 'political correctness' and 'loony Lefties'. It was a long,
messy and heated row, impinging on the Hackney Downs governors'
meeting in January, and a row which did nothing to improve relations between LEA officers and Hackney teachers generally.

Ken Russell only presented one headteacher's report to governors, at that January meeting. He was working, he told them,
without a salary scale or a contract of employment. He then outlined his concerns over staffing and finance. The school was to
undergo a financial audit at the end of term, and he complained
that he had been given only two weeks' notice of a full-day visit by
HMI to consider the school's suitability to go co-educational.
Senior management time was once again being soaked up in preparations for an inspection, he said.

He also outlined his worries about pupil behaviour, pointing out that if discipline was to improve significantly this would only be over a period of time and if sufficient resources could be targeted at assessment and liaison with parents. Enabling heads of year and form tutors to undertake preventative work on behaviour would be one of his priorities.

Within weeks of his first governors' meeting, at the beginning of February, Ken Russell went on sick leave and never returned to Hackney Downs.

At this very difficult time, Daphne Gould was consulting architects about necessary building work to accommodate girls, and HMI arrived in school to discuss the feasibility of co-education. The inspectors' feedback was equivocal, although they emphasized that the co-education decision would be not theirs but the Secretary of State's. They said that they had observed excellent behaviour among pupils and also some which was totally unacceptable. They had seen lessons of high quality and others which were unsatisfactory, homework regularly marked and other books apparently marked rarely if at all.

HMI encouraged the school to launch a classroom monitoring scheme, which was already being planned, and complimented senior managers on the quality of their existing planning. On the whole the senior management team felt reasonably encouraged that the improvements they had brought about had been recognized. But they were not altogether surprised to pick up hints that the school might not be regarded as a suitable environment for girls. It was a worry many of them shared.

Crisis over the maths department

But if January had proved an extremely difficult month, February turned out to be a disaster. When at the beginning of the month Ken Russell reported sick, Betty Hales found herself temporarily in charge of the school, initially for one month, without salary upgrading. It turned out to be the month that the activities of the Black Staff and Parents' Group became a crisis.

Betty Hales and Daphne Gould had met Gus John and the Deputy Director at Gus John's house, within two weeks of Ken

Russell's taking sick leave because it was already becoming apparent that he was unlikely ever to return to the school. Ms Hales had made it clear that she was only willing to take on the acting headship on condition that the LEA took action over certain problems outside the school's immediate control.

In Betty Hales' own words:

> I never for one moment considered taking the easy option of refusing the appointment as acting head or of taking long-term sick leave myself (as I was advised to consider by more than one Hackney officer and, as it seemed to me later, many would have preferred). I had worked for four years with the frustration of being deputy to a succession of heads who, I felt, should have been tackling some very serious issues more firmly. Some problems just don't go away if you avoid them. If the LEA had wanted a weak and malleable figure-head they made a mistake and got the wrong person. I have never run away from a problem in my life – but nor have I instigated or encouraged one to develop for my own ends.

Betty presented a short-term action plan, dated 25 February 1994, which covered three main points:

1   Changes to the fire alarm system which was going off three times a day. It was agreed that the LEA would alter the alarms so that they could not be so easily activated.
2   Help to re-establish staff morale before the Ofsted inspection, in particular by lifting the embargo on permanent appointments. At the time all appointments were being made on a temporary or acting basis.
3   The LEA to accept that the student population presented overwhelming difficulties which could only be resolved by an acknowledgement of the extent of the problem and an input of extra resources. Betty Hales favoured establishing an on-site unit staffed at special school levels to address learning, language and behavioural problems.

This action plan, which was a condition of her accepting the acting headship, seemed to be received with sympathy, but no assurances were given on points 2 and 3, and Daphne Gould advised Betty Hales not to push any further. Betty states that it took about eight months for her to conclude that firm management at Hackney Downs, which seemed to be producing worthwhile results, was not necessarily what was wanted by the LEA.

It was at this time that the discontent among some black parents and staff erupted. A governors' meeting had been scheduled for February because of the imminence of the Ofsted inspection. This became the focus of agitation among black parents because it was also to consider a letter from the head of maths. Dated 7 February, and harking back to the events of the previous summer term, this letter sought the re-instatement of his deputy as the price of his continuing at Hackney Downs himself.

Immediately before the governors' meeting the school began to receive a shoal of pro-forma letters, delivered by black boys, signed by black parents, addressed to the governing body and indicating that they had been circulated to the Hackney Council for Racial Equality and the Hackney Black Staff and Parents' Group. The letters expressed the parents' concern at the problems in the maths department and formally requested the right to be present 'in line with the normal procedural conventions' as observers at the governors' meeting. Fifteen of these letters, which give no indication as to who circulated them for signature in the first place, are still in existence. Senior staff have since spoken to a number of black parents who say that they believed the letters were official communications from the school and constituted an invitation to the meeting.

On Thursday 24 February the governors arrived at the school with no idea that a group of angry parents would be present expecting to attend the meeting, and in particular the discussion of the head of maths' letter to them. The letter was introduced as a special agenda item and it was agreed to take it at the beginning of the meeting, before dealing with the Ofsted inspection, which was the main business.

The meeting immediately resolved that discussion of the letter would be treated as confidential – normal procedure for governors dealing with any item concerning named members of staff – and that therefore no observers would be accepted. It was also agreed that the acting head and the LEA adviser should remain to take part in the discussion.

At this point the chair of governors, Councillor Pat Corrigan, adjourned briefly so that he could meet the parent representatives in another room. He returned to the meeting looking severely shaken, commenting only that an incident had taken place which he would not discuss but about which he would seek advice from personnel staff the following day.

The meeting resumed its discussion of the head of maths' letter. It concluded that it would not reverse its decision on the resignation of his deputy 'which was based on principles of equal opportunities and professional responsibility'. It reasserted its commitment to the agreed procedures for appointments and selection. It resolved that it could not be held to ransom by threat of resignation and would respond in those terms. And it agreed finally that it would notify the parents of its decision and clarify the position to them.

A motion to reinstate the deputy head of maths was immediately proposed by a parent governor but found no seconder. The acting head repeated a previous request that for health and safety reasons all visitors, including governors, should sign the visitors' book in the school office on arrival. The discussion had taken up so much time that the Ofsted discussion was postponed to a further meeting in March.

The head of maths' resignation letter was dated that same evening. It was on the acting head's desk the following morning and faxed to the Director of Education's office soon afterwards. Betty Hales and two senior officers from the LEA informed him that morning that a complaint of gross misconduct had been made against him, and that he was suspended from duty until the matter had been resolved. By the end of the day she had written to him confirming his suspension.

It turned out that the head of maths had already been appointed to a post at another school before his late-night resignation, which was formally accepted by the LEA a week later. Neither the LEA nor the rest of the senior management team had been given any indication that the maths department was to lose its head just weeks before Ofsted arrived. The complaints upon which the head of maths was suspended were never taken to a formal disciplinary hearing for adjudication.

Campaign against the school

The day after the governors' meeting, the school erupted. A group of boys reacted angrily to the head of maths' absence, which was commonly being called 'unfair dismissal'. At 12.10 on 1 March, just three days after the suspension/resignation, and just as Year 11 was leaving maths and Year 10 were moving from English to maths, about 60 upper-school boys refused to go to lessons and went to stand outside the school. They claimed that they were holding a demonstration to get the head of maths reinstated. It is not clear how so many pupils became familiar with an inaccurate version of what had happened at the governors' meeting and subsequently.

Senior staff acted quickly. All staff were notified of the incident and asked to keep the younger children in their rooms. Only one black teacher disregarded this advice and was found taking her group to the front of the building because 'they had wanted to know what was going on'. Senior staff stood outside the school to observe the demonstration in the hope of checking any incipient violence. At that stage Daphne Gould decided that in the interests of safety some pupils should be sent home early.

Press interest had by now been aroused by the protesters, and the local and national papers were taking an interest. Pictures of boys brandishing placards outside the school gates were published and versions of the week's events began to appear in print. The idea that a 'race war' was 'bringing the school to its knees' made good headlines, although neither the school nor the community was divided simply along racial lines.

A war of words raged around the heads of parents and boys as the existing Black Staff and Parents' Group, and a new organization calling itself Hackney Downs School Parents Against Low Educational Standards Action Group, bombarded the community with angry leaflets, many addressed to parents at home. It has never been explained how the Group obtained home addresses for the school's pupils.

The Action Group wrote to Gus John on 17 March demanding that inspectors replace senior managers at the school and that urgent measures should be taken to appoint a permanent head and more permanent high-calibre teachers. They wanted their demands met by the end of the month or parents would take action 'of a more public nature'.

The Action Group turned out to be a less than representative body, even of black parents. Many black parents complained to the school later that they had been led to believe that the Action Group's meetings had been organized by the school and they went to them on that assumption. They were also angry to find that their signatures on an attendance sheet were later attached to a petition as if they had signed that too.

Even more strident were leaflets widely circulated in the community offering a lurid version of the affair and its 'trumped-up charges' and calling openly for parents to remove their children from the school. There were meetings on 16 March and again on 30 March at the United Reformed Church, and another leaflet telling parents in detail how they could transfer their sons to other schools either in Hackney or in neighbouring boroughs. By the end of term 60 boys had left the school, many of higher ability, a devastating reduction in the school roll at a time when every empty place counted financially.

Throughout the fierce controversy many families, including black families, were contacting Betty Hales and deputy head Jeff Davies to express their support for Hackney Downs. As one parent put it:

That letter sent by the black teachers and parents group didn't and couldn't of affected the way in which I see Hackney Downs School, and I like the teachers, except one. That teacher is racist himself. I have realized this two years ago and I keeped this name in mind . . . I am happy with Hackney Downs and I will remember it as a good school, I would like to thank all the teachers who have been very helpful to my son. I am specially writing to you Mr Davies as my son says you have been very kind and a good teacher. I want to say a lot of things but I can't write good English. Please forgive my mistakes. I wish you a successful life and also happiness but in the future only God knows what will be.

Pat Corrigan responded to attacks in the leaflets by explaining in a letter to parents how the Black Staff and Parents' Group had been attempting to influence policy in the school for a period of three years. He spelt out details of the Incident Book held in 1990/91 by the black staff and the definition of a 'racist incident' not only as verbal or physical abuse but as 'black boys failing to achieve high academic results in subjects taught by white teachers'.

The headteacher was being asked to approve a practice whereby black pupils would report white teachers, without their knowledge, to a black teacher, who would enter these reports in the book. The Black Staff and Parents' Group would then determine what action to demand that the school take against those named by the pupils.

Time and again, he said, the school and the LEA had made it clear that the Group was perfectly entitled to focus on the quality of teaching and the achievement of the pupils, but there should be a whole-school approach to these matters, in which black teachers should play their part with their white colleagues.

Quoted in the local newspaper, he said: 'The future of every child in Hackney Downs School is too important to be sacrificed to the personal agenda of ruthless people who pose as the defenders of educational standards.'

Mr Corrigan also responded to the concern of some parents that leaflets, which he dismissed as 'mischievous and vindictive', were being distributed directly to parents' homes. The school, he said, was investigating how their pupil address lists came into unauthorized hands.

The aftermath

Betty Hales was determined to reunite the staff, pupils and parents. She wrote to all parents in mid-March, partly to introduce herself as the new acting headteacher, an appointment now confirmed by the governors, and partly to encourage parents to work as partners with the school to ensure a high standard of education for their sons.

A week later she wrote to the parents of 64 boys, mainly in Years

10 and 11, informing them that there were aspects of their behaviour and attitude which were totally unacceptable.

> The staff at Hackney Downs school are hard-working, well-qualified professionals and should not have to work in conditions in which they are insulted or abused by students, or in which the efforts they make to provide good quality education for all our students are flouted by a minority who are not prepared to abide by our rules.

She asked parents to sign a return slip guaranteeing their son's future behaviour.

Press interest in the school continued unabated right through March, using up precious management time at a moment when senior staff should have been concentrating on preparations for the inspection. Pressure from the protesters became so unremitting and malicious in March that the school and the LEA considered taking legal action to quell it, and began to build up evidence which would enable them to take out injunctions against named persons. Some senior members of staff received abusive anonymous letters at this time.

While this war was being waged in the community and the Press, life in the school went on, constantly throwing up new problems. But despite all the difficulties, real progress was now being made. Betty Hales took a series of assemblies designed to unite and motivate the school community. At the end of a serious session about the relationship between parents and pupils there was spontaneous applause from the school, and she began to feel that there was real hope for Hackney Downs. The school was being kept open at weekends, and many staff used the time to come in to prepare for the inspection and to allow students to complete GCSE coursework.

It took until April for the governors to arrange interviews for two acting deputy head posts. They promoted Jeff Davies, head of humanities and upper school, and Helen Thomas, head of English. While waiting for these appointments to be confirmed, they took over the roles on a temporary basis, handing over some of their other responsibilities to their second in departments.

The school now found itself in serious staffing difficulties. They were without a permanent head of maths and English. The head of modern languages and the head of Year 10 were already on long-term sick leave and seemed unlikely to return. Both were teachers who had been at the school for many years. The head of learning support, as already stated, was away after a serious car accident which had resulted in permanent disability.

At the start of the summer term the head of technology took long-term sick leave with a serious blood disorder which eventually caused his death just weeks after the school closed. This left the technology department in the care of a newly qualified teacher, assisted by a newly qualified supply teacher. These two young men took on the challenge of National Curriculum technology and worked late, night after night, to make sure that pupils were adequately prepared for their GCSEs. The LEA's technology adviser provided valuable support at this time, as did the humanities adviser and a new link inspector. Such support was rare enough for staff to comment on it at the time.

Temporary and supply appointments filled the gaps in staffing just before the Ofsted inspection and the school began to feel a little cautious optimism about the future. Parents too began to rally round the school and outsiders began to comment on the improved behaviour of boys on the street and in the community. Some parents expressed their gratitude to staff when they came in to discuss disciplinary problems and a handful agreed to come into school to help support boys in class.

At this stage two-thirds of the staff were holding acting appointments, including the whole senior management team, the heads of Years 9 and 10, and the heads of English, maths and technology. Astonishingly there were signs that morale was improving and a feeling that at last the school was on the way up again.

One of Betty Hales' priorities at this time was to work out a staffing structure which took account of the strengths of the staff she still had. But numbers were so low that this involved many staff carrying heavy dual responsibilities across the management and pastoral roles. Even so she was able to convince the Hackney Teachers' Association (the local branch of the NUT) of her good faith and enlist their support in some of her proposals for the inspection period and for the long-term improvement of the school.

The HTA were able to facilitate consultations with another Hackney school which had just gone through the inspection process. Getting onto good terms with the NUT, notorious for its militancy, was not something Hackney education officials or head-teachers generally attempted, and there is good reason to suppose that Betty Hales did not earn many brownie points at Hackney education offices for her efforts. She regarded building good relations with staff and their unions as an essential part of her job.

Another concern was to get to grips with the learning needs of the boys. Betty Hales had already developed a fairly sophisticated method of relating pupils' verbal reasoning scores on intake to their GCSE performance to give an indication of how much 'value' the school was adding over five years. Year 7 entrants were being routinely screened and assessment was being extended to other year groups to help identify areas of need.

That March, the learning support department assessed the reading ages of Year 10 boys, those who would be taking their GCSEs in the summer of 1995. A significant proportion were still in the early stages of learning English; a few had statements of special need; many more, it was felt, had emotional and behavioural difficulties which justified a statement. This view was shared by Daphne Gould, the locum educational psychologist assigned to the school and, it turned out, the Ofsted inspectors. Of the 78 14-year-olds tested, only ten had a reading age equal to or above their chronological age. Fifteen had reading ages below age 10. The majority were more than two years behind their chronological age. This was the cohort of boys which was held up to scorn eighteen months later because only 11 per cent of them gained five good GCSE passes. In fact 11 per cent was a major achievement, and even more important was the fact that the A to G grades that year were among the most improved in London. Hackney Downs was getting even its lowest achievers some qualifications.

One way or another the school struggled to the end of the Easter term, hoping for a respite over the holiday. But there was one more bomb-shell to come. On 21 March the Department for Education wrote to Hackney's Director of Education rejecting the proposal to turn Hackney Downs into a co-educational school. After careful consideration, the DfE official explained, the Department had not been convinced that the school was in a position to cope with the change of circumstances which would result from the introduction of girls.

They went on: 'There is no certainty that the school could provide an adequate environment for girls, or that it could recruit a sufficient number of girls for a balanced intake.' The senior team was devastated, since the school was already such a different place from the one which HMI had visited just a few months earlier and now had the potential in their view to become so much better. Suddenly Hackney Downs' future was thrown into jeopardy all over again.

9

The Ofsted Inspection

Preparation

The summer term began with Betty Hales and Daphne Gould working seven days a week to prepare for the inspection. In spite of the disruption which still continued, especially amongst a group of Year 11 boys, the school's documentation went off to Ofsted on time. The Headteacher's Form for the inspection gives an interesting snapshot of the school at a period of great stress.

The roll in January 1994, before the exodus of some black pupils, stood at 436, slightly down on the previous year and significantly down on 1992 when there had been 454 boys in school. Two factors had led to this decline: the high number of exclusions during Peter Hepburn's headship, and the fact that Daphne Gould had at last persuaded the LEA to stop mid-term admissions until a proper support system had been introduced to deal with the acute difficulties most of these boys brought with them. Ironically, with hindsight, this decision can be seen to have been against the school's best interests. Although Year 7 admissions had been going up, the falling roll opened the way for allegations that the school was becoming more 'unpopular' when closure eventually became an issue.

In her personal statement to Ofsted, Betty Hales gave the inspectors a brief outline of what she saw as the school's major problems: a staff structure depleted at the middle management level; long-term pressure leading to long-term sickness among staff; instability created by there having been three acting heads within four terms; and the unrest both inside and outside the school caused by the head of maths' suspension/resignation. The education of the pupils, she said, had been severely threatened during the year through no fault of the school.

Describing the school's pupils, Betty Hales commented on the worsening language and ability imbalance among the pupils and the severe difficulties caused by the intake of boys who had been excluded from other schools, now amounting to 5 per cent of the total roll. Extra pressure was placed on the school by pupils with limited English arriving from abroad, some of them severely traumatized. Levels of aggression were increased, she suggested, by boys mentally and/or physically damaged by their environment.

The school was eligible for 'Section 11' support (the Home Office grant for special language teaching) for more than 80 per cent of its pupils. Sixty per cent of them were eligible for free school meals. Pupils had arrived at Hackney Downs from 50 primary schools and spoke 33 languages at home.

Attendance rates had improved to just over 82 per cent that year, with half the absences unauthorized. Among older boys there was still a problem of long-term truancy: 'it is suspected that a number of boys in Year 11 have not only "dropped out" of school but also out of society. A number of these boys are known to the police, who have been involved with some of them on numerous occasions', Betty Hales reported to Ofsted.

The examination results had improved again the previous summer, with 22 per cent of boys achieving five 'good grades', and 89 per cent gaining at least one pass, compared with 9 per cent and 75 per cent in 1992. Just over half the Year 11 leavers had continued in education after leaving Hackney Downs the previous summer term. On the value-added measures for London schools pioneered by Professor Desmond Nuttall in 1989, Hackney Downs had come near the top of the Hackney 'league table'. Even when the A to C score dipped to 11 per cent during the last two turbulent years that the school was open, the A to G results, which are the more relevant for a school recruiting mainly Band 3 boys, remained high, a fact which was noted later by HMI.

While all this information was being assembled for Ofsted, the normal life of the school lurched on, improving in some ways, but still subject to unexpected crises which distracted staff from their core tasks of teaching and management. With two senior maths staff now gone, the school asked a consultant, a senior GCSE examiner for London University, for urgent help in assessing the present state of the department and assisting the remaining staff to prepare students for their GCSEs. The consultant worked with the head of PE, who had volunteered to take over as acting head of maths.

The consultant's report was not encouraging. With only five working weeks before the submission of course-work, he found that Year 11 pupils had not yet completed any assignments. He recommended that the pupils transfer immediately to a similar syllabus which did not demand course-work at all. With his help, the department implemented a revision programme for the boys coming up to the examination and a scheme to help Year 10 pupils, with a year still to go to GCSE, to make a start on their projects in good time.

The consultant was very critical of the department's 'weak and insecure' policy document which did not appear to have been approved by governors or senior management. And he particularly objected to the policy of entering boys from lower years for GCSE, which he said was an inappropriate policy for all but the most exceptional students who might be expected to gain an A or an A* grade. Far from being an 'excellent' department, as the recently departed head of maths had claimed during the recent troubles, the consultant concluded that the Hackney Downs maths department had serious long-term weaknesses.

Objections

At this stage the long-term direction of the school was still in doubt because the LEA had decided to seek an urgent meeting with DfE officials to see if they could reverse the decision on becoming co-educational. In the middle of April it was left to the Hackney Teachers' Association to put into words what many people at the school were now thinking: that the uncertainty and disruption of the last few months, culminating in the rejection of the co-educational plan and the uproar over the head of maths' departure, had left the school in such a vulnerable state that the Ofsted inspection should be postponed.

In a letter to the governors, circulated to the LEA, the headteacher and national NUT officials, the Association raised two issues of major concern: first, that the uncertainty over the school's future status had made it impossible for the school to produce a valid development plan as required by Ofsted; second, that instability had been exacerbated by the LEA decision, the legality of which the union now questioned, not to admit Year 7 boys in autumn 1994, and by the failure to advertise and appoint permanent staff to fill the many vacancies at the school, including the headteacher's post.

> Many posts are presently filled by teachers who are 'acting up', teaching a subject that is not their specialism, teachers who are agency staff (not in all cases recognised as qualified teachers by the DfE) or are trained insufficiently, in one way or another, for their present roles.
>
> This has stemmed directly from the uncertainty about the school's future and is the educational equivalent of planning blight. It is not the fault of the individual teachers involved in such blight nor of the acting management team, who have mended and improved an interim staffing structure with ingenuity and professionalism. Quite simply, they have been put at risk by the indecisiveness and lack of forward planning of the LEA.

The Assocation asked the governors to seek a postponement of the Ofsted inspection until the autumn term to allow the school time to revise its development plan in the light of its likely continuation as a boys', not a mixed, school and to allow time to fill its vacant posts with the confidence that it could recruit from a good field of candidates once the uncertainty about the school's future had been removed.

'We would welcome an inspection on this basis, given our record of public examination results and other successful performance indicators, which have been achieved under recent difficult circumstances', the Association's recommendation concluded.

The governors discussed this approach from the NUT at their meeting on 18 April, and turned the request down. The union continued to voice its unease. At a meeting with Councillor Pat Corrigan, the chair of governors, they made much the same points, but also urged that there should now be a vigorous campaign to recruit Year 7 boys for September, that permanent teaching and management jobs at the school should now be urgently advertised and filled, and that the LEA should consider extra financial help for Hackney Downs to help it to recover from the planning blight induced by the failed reorganization proposal. They welcomed an assurance from Mr Corrigan that the LEA was committed to the continuation of Hackney Downs as a thriving boys' school if it turned out that the DfE confirmed their refusal to let it become co-educational.

Within weeks, however, there were the first ominous hints that the LEA might be having second thoughts about its whole strategy on secondary school provision. A meeting of secondary heads in May highlighted the whole borough's worries about pupil behaviour, disruption and exclusions, and the difficulties Hackney was having in meeting the needs of its most disruptive pupils in a climate of cuts.

Almost as an aside, Gus John indicated that he was puzzled by the failure of the two boys' schools to recruit enough pupils at a time when the demographic trends were pointing to a shortage of boys' places in the borough. The assumption was that boys were being sent in increasing numbers out of Hackney rather than to the two under-subscribed boys' schools. No one imagined that the events of the previous term at Hackney Downs, or the disruption involving pupils from both schools, were unconnected with this trend. But whatever the cause, Gus John suggested, the future of one of these schools could be at risk.

This was the first of a number of occasions when Betty Hales was to hear of comments about the school within the LEA which had not been made known or discussed with her or the governors first. She quickly came to believe that she was not being given the backing or support by the LEA which would help her, as a newly appointed acting headteacher, to fulfil her responsibilities. She shared these concerns with Daphne Gould, who said that she would raise them with Gus John. Betty Hales found Daphne a great support throughout this difficult time, a fact which may not have been fully appreciated by the staff who remained to some extent unaware of all the difficulties the school faced.

The inspection

The Ofsted inspectors spent a week in the school in May, some of them returning the following week to look at the work of Year 10 pupils who had been on work experience during the official inspection week. Fourteen inspectors observed 140 lessons, about 19 per cent of the total. They also attended assemblies, tutor groups and extra-curricular activities. All full-time and most part-time teachers were seen in action at least once, and written and practical work was scrutinized. There were also extensive formal and informal discussions with teaching and non-teaching staff, governors and pupils and with the school's education welfare officer. It is some indication of the level of parental participation in educational issues that the inspectors' meeting for parents attracted only nine parents and only fourteen bothered to return a questionnaire which sought their views on the school.

Betty Hales' immediate reaction to the inspection was one of relief. She found the team a highly professional and supportive one which seemed to understand the school's problems with its difficult intake of boys, its buildings and its staffing deficiencies. The immediate feedback seemed supportive rather than threatening, although the inspectors made the point that designating the school as in need of special measures might be in the school's interests as it would spur the LEA into providing more support. The senior team were not entirely convinced by the logic of that argument.

The inspection over, the school returned to its new routines. GCSE exams got under way and end-of-year exams were also introduced for the first time in early June for the other year groups. An activities week, as a break from the normal curriculum, was planned for the end of the summer term. Slowly the staff saw behaviour in school beginning to improve.

In spite of the senior staff's best efforts, some disruptive activities and incidents continued in school and out. At the end of May, Betty Hales wrote to parents asking them to contact her if they received letters allegedly from the school which worried them. She had received complaints from families who had been invited to meetings on school headed paper but with an illegible signature which turned out to have no connection with the school. Other families had received letters which apparently indicated that arrangements had been made to transfer their son to another school.

The Ofsted report

On 9 June Betty Hales began the day by attending the funeral of the school's former head of art, who had resigned just a year before because of ill-health. She went on to attend the governors' meeting convened to hear the informal feedback from the Ofsted inspectors.

The dry, official language of the inspectors' report, which was eventually published in August, gave some comfort to the school's friends and rather more to its enemies. In its introduction, it laid bare the difficult environment within which the school functioned. Although ostensibly a comprehensive school, the report noted the fact that very few boys were of high ability. In Year 7, the intake year, 64 out of 90 pupils (more than two-thirds) had reading ages at least one year below their chronological age, and 45 – half of the intake – had reading ages three years below average. Turnover of pupils was high – 15 per cent in the Year 7 group – and every year group had a high proportion of boys admitted after being excluded from other schools. The majority of these boys did not have English as their mother tongue and some were known to be involved in crime.

Nearly 68 per cent of the staff held acting or temporary posts at the time of the inspection, more than half had been at the school for less than two years and more than half of those were on temporary contracts. The school budget was being drained by high levels of long-term staff illness and uncertainties in planning as a result of circumstances beyond the school's control.

In the light of what happened later it is perhaps wise to spell out the logistics of the school, as reported by Ofsted, in May 1994, at the last point at which Hackney Downs had pupils in every year group. The school roll at that time was 431. There were 31.7 full-time equivalent teachers, giving a pupil–teacher ratio of 13.6:1 and an average class size of 18.5. The total expenditure per pupil had been £2,900 in 1992/3 and was estimated to be £3,300 in 1993/4 after the roll had been unexpectedly depressed by the departure of 60 pupils of families disaffected by the Black Staff and Parents' Group contention.

This was generous provision, although not outrageously so for a very small school with a very high proportion of children with language and behavioural difficulties. It is now a commonplace to say that schools which are effectively secondary modern schools should not be judged as if they were comprehensive. It is arguable that by this stage Hackney Downs was in some ways closer to being a special school than a secondary modern, so great were the special needs of many of its pupils.

The school had not provided any information to Ofsted about the Key Stage 3 assessments of 13-year-olds which should have taken place the previous summer. (In fact most Inner London schools had refused to implement these tests.) But they were able to report a significant improvement in GCSE results. The proportion of students gaining five or more A to C grades had gone up from 9 per cent to 21 per cent and those gaining five A to G grades from 45 per cent to 59 per cent. Eleven per cent of boys gained no GCSE passes in 1993 compared to 25 per cent the previous year. In addition fifteen boys gained City and Guilds Technology qualifications.

While hardly outstanding, these results did show some progress was being made and that the school was within sight of the LEA average, especially for pupils with five A to C passes. (Hackney Downs 21 per cent, Hackney as a whole 25 per cent.) Fifty-two per cent of the school's leavers in 1993 had remained in education, 28 per cent had found jobs and 20 per cent were unemployed.

It must have been unusually difficult for the Ofsted inspectors to make judgements on Hackney Downs at that time. Betty Hales had only been in post for four months, the future of the school as a boys' school had been in question until a few weeks before Ofsted arrived, and the reverberations of more than a year of unprecedented disruption by the Black Staff and Parents' Group were still upsetting the institution, boys, staff and governors alike. A significant proportion of the staff, through the NUT, had asked for the inspection to be postponed.

Judgements, however, had to be made. The inspectors, to no one's real surprise, decided that the school was not giving its pupils a satisfactory standard of education and required 'special measures' as laid down by the 1993 Education Act for failing schools.

It offered four main reasons for this decision:

1   There was underachievement among the majority of pupils in two-thirds of the subjects of the National Curriculum, in religious education and other curriculum provision. Levels of attainment overall were unsatisfactory (compared to national norms).
2   There was regular disruptive behaviour, poor attendance and high levels of truancy and a risk of physical harassment between groups of boys.
3   There was a high proportion of unsatisfactory teaching. Expectations were low; there were high levels of staff absence with the result that many teaching posts had to be filled on an acting basis.
4   There was a limited range of teaching strategies and class control techniques which, combined with staffing turbulence and poor parental support for the school, had a deleterious effect on learning.

Some of the inspectors' more detailed comments seem to contradict their austere conclusions, and they identified, even at this stage, encouraging signs that the school might be pulled round. They found a small proportion, 7 per cent, of lessons where standards were good. And they commented that in spite of the fact that all classes were difficult to teach because of 'an undertow of poor and bizarre behaviour' which set the pattern for others, the school's examination results represented a creditable performance by the pupils and teachers. The pastoral system, they said, endeavoured to give support to boys who needed it, but was overstretched, and although there was no indication of racial tension there was evidence of bullying, which the staff were dealing with.

More hopefully they found staff morale buoyant in spite of all the school's difficulties and, more significantly, given what is known about the effect of the headteacher on school quality, found in Betty Hales a head who had been, in the few months since her appointment, very effective, who had improved staff morale and had begun to tackle the serious staffing problems and set up new management systems in a number of areas.

The inspectors were scathing about the state of the school buildings. They found two blocks boarded up, one because of subsidence and the other because of fire damage and vandalism. The fabric of the whole school, from 1960s blocks to the original Victorian science labs and swimming pool, showed signs of poor maintenance and general neglect, with leaking roofs, rotting window frames and peeling decorations. The school itself had tried to keep the main block in a reasonable state from its own resources, but in general, the inspectors concluded, the buildings did nothing to enhance the boys' education.

Vandalism, litter and graffiti were problems against which the staff were waging a constant war. The science block contained a number of health and safety hazards related to the gas and electricity supplies and there was a recurrent problem of rain leaking onto pupils' work in technology and art.

Ofsted proposed ten key issues for action for the senior management, governors and LEA:

1 the improvement of pupil behaviour;
2 stabilization of the school's staffing, to be followed by a raising of teachers' expectations of pupils;
3 measures to ensure value-for-money through improved financial management;
4 broadening of governors' oversight of the curriculum and finance;
5 closer analysis of the damaging impact on the school of mid-term admissions of boys with behavioural problems;
6 a rolling programme of repair and refurbishment of the buildings;
7 greater support for bilingual children;
8 a review of the special needs statementing process to cover more pupils;
9 urgent action on health and safety matters;
10 a review of aims for collective worship in order to meet statutory requirements.

Increasing pressure

While the school was digesting this, there were other issues causing constant pressure. The borough was in dispute with the DfE over funding for the appraisal scheme which it was expected to implement that year. Schools were thrown back onto their own resources, which meant that teacher appraisal in Hackney did not get off the ground in 1994. There was also a dispute between the teacher unions and the Inner London LEAs over an Inner London supplement of £822 a year to compensate teachers for the high cost of living in London. In Hackney this was being taken away from staff when they were given promotion, since it had been made discretionary for new staff.

This affected Hackney Downs staff more seriously than most, given the need to ask staff more or less routinely to take on extra responsibilities on an acting basis. Those who had taken on promotion and considerable extra responsibilities in good faith were finding themselves only a few pounds better off as a result. At the time of the inspection two-thirds of the staff were affected by the loss of the £822, including both deputy heads, two heads of year and the acting heads of English and maths.

Betty Hales, who was sympathetic to the teachers' case, raised the issue with the governors at their meeting on 23 June. They discussed the issue as it affected some Hackney Downs staff and urged the LEA to restore the allowance so that teachers could gain from their promotion in the way that they anticipated.

At the same governors' meeting, Betty Hales also presented a paper explaining why she believed the LEA should be urged to allow the admission of Year 7 pupils the following September, as some parents were already requesting admission to the school now that the co-educational proposal had been dropped. The NUT supported this proposal and had raised the issue with Ofsted.

This governors' meeting was not clerked in the normal way and notes taken were never presented in the form of minutes. Fortunately, several governors kept a record of the proceedings and the votes taken. The governors voted seven to two in favour of both these proposals. Only the chair and one other LEA governor voted against, and there was one abstention.

Betty Hales had attempted but not succeeded in having a pre-meeting with the chair before the formal meeting and was unaware of LEA opposition to both her proposals on the allowance and on Year 7 admissions. She is now convinced that this meeting, at which the LEA view was voted down, affected attitudes towards the school in the next few months. Even at the time she realized that winning two crucial votes without the support of her chair of governors was not necessarily a triumph.

Staffing

After the Ofsted inspectors' visit, but before the findings had been confirmed by HMI, efforts continued to stabilize the school's staff. A new slimmed-down staffing structure was produced to meet the looming financial crisis brought about by the drop in the school roll. When one of the temporary deputy heads resigned to go overseas, it was decided to run the school with a single deputy until the roll increased again. This would obviously put much extra work onto the head and remaining deputy, but they were prepared to take this on in the best interests of the school.

The head of maths post was advertised and interviews held, but the successful candidate chose to reject the offer, apparently in the light of the school's difficulties. The governors decided to ask the acting head to continue running the department and made two main-scale maths appointments to fill the vacancies. Because of the low roll, no other posts could be advertised externally because, although there were subject vacancies, the school was fully staffed in terms of actual teachers.

Three head of year appointments were made internally, one going to the head of music and the others to two of a number of very able Australian-trained teachers now at the school, both recent appointments. Technically the Australians were still 'unqualified teachers' because neither the LEA nor previous heads had registered them for the Overseas Qualified Teachers' Scheme which ensures that overseas teachers' qualifications meet British criteria. At this point Betty Hales made sure that five of her staff were registered and all successfully and quickly qualified. A head of English was also appointed at this time. The science and technology departments remained causes for concern; but given the appalling working conditions and the impossibility of appointing new staff, there was little that could be done to improve these subject areas. They were included in the development plan as areas of urgent concern in the medium term while in the short term they relied on newly qualified and/or overseas teachers.

A very experienced and competent teacher had volunteered to take over the modern language department – not her subject – when it proved impossible to attract applicants from outside. The acute shortage of good modern language teachers was affecting all Inner-London schools at this time.

10

Special Measures

The headship

Betty Hales and the governors were astonished to learn from Daphne Gould in June that the headship of the school was to be advertised by the LEA with a closing date two weeks before the end of term. Betty Hales had been led to believe that the post would not be advertised before the autumn and there had been no discussion with her or the governors prior to the decision to advertise. Quite apart from the extra pressure the decision put upon the acting head, who had to turn her mind to an application, the lack of consultation set alarm bells ringing. At the beginning of that July HMI visited, as required, to confirm Ofsted's conclusion that the school required special measures. The staff found the inspectors supportive and understanding about the school's difficulties and the senior management's efforts to improve the situation. A little later Betty Hales was cheered by an encouraging letter from the school's single Conservative Party governor, who thanked her and her staff for the immense amount of work they had put into the school during a very difficult year. 'I am certainly aware of the immense pressures on teachers even in normal times. What you and your staff have had to put up with has been, quite frankly, amazing and I have nothing but admiration for the way in which you have all managed to come through it.'

As far as the pupils were concerned the end of that summer term went well. Hackney Downs was the only secondary school to accept an invitation to take part in the Hackney Show, and the school's musicians, led by the head of music, got a rave reception. The first Activities Week at the end of term, on which many staff had put in so much overtime, was a great success. Betty Hales succeeded in getting the school some good publicity to offset the appalling Press coverage which it had suffered earlier in the year. The term ended with an up-beat staff party and a good deal of optimism about the future, even though it was now known that 'special measures' had been confirmed by HMI.

Relations with the LEA, however, were becoming more difficult and erratic, and decisions were being made about the school with very little consultation or, in some cases, no consultation at all. Betty Hales was astonished to receive a fax on 18 July asking as a matter of urgency for her copy and pictures for the coming year's secondary transfer brochure by the 21st, only three days ahead. Whether by accident or design she is not sure, but she had never received an earlier request for the information.

But this was a minor inconvenience compared to the news that Daphne's Gould's consultancy contract was to be terminated at the end of term without explanation. This left Betty Hales facing the task of writing her Action Plan without Daphne's support and without the respite of a summer holiday. The 40-day period allowed for the task starts immediately for 'failing' schools and does not take school holidays into account. And first there was the personal anxiety of her application for the substantive headship to be resolved.

Interviews for the headship

At the second attempt, a governors' panel met at the end of July. There had been twelve applications for the post but the meeting concluded that only two, including Betty Hales', met the criteria for the job. The meeting was then informed that it was LEA policy that headship interviews would only be held if there were three suitable interviewees. It was therefore decided that the short-listing could not go ahead at that time and the post would be re-advertised.

Two governors came away from the meeting with the firm impression that some candidates had been excluded from consideration on flimsy grounds. Betty Hales was later told by an LEA official that the governors could have insisted on going ahead with interviews for two candidates. But by that time the future of the school was in jeopardy and she decided that a complaint about her treatment would be counter-productive for the school; but the psychological distress remains incalculable.

The assumption among most governors was that Betty Hales, in view of the favourable feedback from Ofsted on her performance, would stand an excellent chance of gaining the job. Her application had been backed by an enthusiastic testimonial from Daphne Gould to Pat Corrigan. She complimented the work she had done as deputy head on the curriculum, her budgetary and staff control, her work on performance indicators and 'value-added' measurement of the school's progress, which had led to improved pupil achievement and to raising teachers' awareness of individual and departmental performance.

Since she had taken over as acting head, Daphne Gould said, Betty Hales had shown that she had three essential qualities for the job: enormous capacity for hard work and resilience; vision, supported by clarity of thought which enabled her to plan ahead successfully; and the determination not to shrink from the unpalatable or difficult situation.

In Hackney Downs School the staff were not a cohesive unit, neither were they performing effectively. Elizabeth Hales has used a number of strategies to recognise quality, to reward hard work and loyalty and to challenge unprofessional performance . . . Elizabeth Hales possesses the qualities of leadership; her informed decisions are based upon what is right for the pupils and the quality of their education. However she is well aware that she must carry her staff with her, but not by compromising her own position. I believe that she has the qualities necessary to continue the improving trend in the performance of HDS.

It was clear from this letter of reference that Daphne Gould, who had worked closely with Betty Hales for five terms, believed that the school had at last found the headteacher who could turn it round.

Publication of the Ofsted report

Even the long-awaited arrival of the Ofsted report was dogged by the incompetence Betty Hales was coming to expect from official-dom. The motor cycle despatch rider commissioned to deliver it during August arrived after the school had closed for the day and chose to cram the package into a disused post-box at the school gate instead of finding someone to take delivery. He had to open the confidential package and dismember it in order to achieve this feat. The school discovered a wet and soggy parcel a few days later, left where any passer-by (or reporter) could have taken possession of it overnight.

The designation of the school as needing special measures in that report required both the school itself and the LEA to draw up action plans for improvement. What is remarkable about Hackney Downs' 'key points for action' is the number that required action by the LEA rather than the head and staff. The damaging effects of mid-term admissions of difficult pupils, the refusal to appoint either a permanent head and many permanent teachers (the entire senior management team, including the heads of all the major departments, were on 'acting' appointments), action on the state of the buildings and on some health and safety matters, and a review of the statementing process for pupils with special needs, all required LEA commitment at least, and funding at best.

The governors were also seen by Ofsted as having played less than their full part in the running of the school up until then and were instructed, in effect, to get their act together. To some extent this was a fair comment as the governors, like the staff, had been deeply divided throughout the activities of the Black Staff and Parents' Group, and had included members so disruptive that at times it was difficult to conduct business in the normal way.

However, by the time of the publication of the Ofsted report the composition of the governing body had changed sufficiently to offer some hope that it could play a genuine and constructive role in the school's regeneration. What was much less clear was whether Hackney as an LEA had come to terms by 1994 with the more independent role demanded of boards of governors and head-teachers by the 1980s legislation on school government.

It has already been noted that the chair of the Hackney Downs governors was at this time also the chair of the Education Committee, an unusual situation and one which could be seen as putting the chair in an impossible situation when disagreements arose between the school and the LEA. Communications from Gus John to governors also had a directive tone which had by then become uncommon in other authorities which had fully accepted the greater autonomy of governing bodies and the accountability of headteachers to their governors rather than to LEA officers.

The governors had already begun to move in a more positive direction before the inspection by setting up curriculum and finance sub-committees. The inspectors urged the governors to provide more help and support and to co-ordinate the budget with the development plan: a process, they said, 'well understood by the acting head teacher and senior management team'. In effect, the inspectors were urging the school to take more responsibility for its own management and its future development.

Support for the school

In many ways the LEA, leaving aside the unexplained loss of Daphne Gould, appeared supportive of the school following the publication of the inspection report in early August and its attendant publicity. A joint letter to parents and carers from Betty Hales and the chair of governors, Councillor Pat Corrigan, made much of the positive points in the report: good morale, efficient financial record-keeping, and the role of the senior management team in creating a sense of purpose, and an ethos within which the staff felt that the school's problems could be solved.

The letter emphasized the 'creditable performance' in examinations and the fact that GCSE English and English Literature results were above the national average; that there was no evidence of racial tension or serious bullying and that any bullying which did emerge was swiftly dealt with; that welfare and guidance systems were sound and work experience well organized and helpful.

The letter outlined how the school had already started to respond to the inspection report and promised consultations with parents on the Action Plan and its implementation.

Gus John also went to the trouble of writing to parents and carers commenting that although the report indicated that there was much to be done, with support from pupils' homes this could be achieved. In view of what happened within two months, it is perhaps worth quoting from this letter:

Hackney Downs has a proud history. Like all schools, it has periods of success but also times when success is not so readily achieved. The school enjoys a number of recent achievements, including improvements in examination results, some of which are well above the Inner London average. However, the inspection shows that there is still a lot to be done. With hard work and your support this can be achieved.

In partnership with the governors, staff, pupils and yourselves we will be initiating an action plan to respond to the concerns raised by the inspectors. I am determined to turn Hackney Downs into a first-class boys' school of which we can all be proud. I will ensure that my officers do all they can to support the staff and governors in providing a high-quality education for your children.

Towards the end of August, Councillor Pat Corrigan was still writing to his fellow-councillors explaining what had happened and pointing out that while the report was critical in some respects it also highlighted the fact that the school had made and continued to make significant improvements. It was, he told his colleagues, a basis for future planning and future improvements. He spoke of his confidence that the 'failing school' status would be removed, and expressed his confidence that Betty Hales and the staff could achieve that outcome.

Discussion also continued with the LEA about the possibility of Hackney's obtaining Single Regeneration Budget money from the government which could be used to improve the school's library. In the event the Single Regeneration Budget bid was successful, but only Homerton House School benefited from the money despite its appearing in the LEA's Action Plan as support for Hackney Downs.

The Action Plan

The inexplicable, and unexplained, loss of Daphne Gould could have damaged the Action Plan, especially as she had been told not to enter the school again after the termination of her contract. It was made potentially even more damaging by the fact that the school had also been allocated a new 'link' inspector by the LEA who visited once on 1 August and made no more contact until the following term when the plan was practically finished.

Betty Hales had built up a good working relationship with the previous link inspector, an IT and science specialist, who found himself unable to comment on the fact that his link with Hackney Downs had been broken at such a crucial moment. He continued to offer Betty Hales as much support as he could over the following months, but in terms of inspection support from the LEA, the school felt seriously neglected at this time. Only two inspectors visited in September when the Action Plan was being finalized, and both told Betty Hales that their visits were 'unofficial'.

The letter from the DfE confirming Hackney Downs' new status as a school needing special measures also emphasized the need for close liaison between the school and the LEA during the 40 working days to 10 October which the school had to complete its Action Plan. As the LEA was expected to submit its plan and commentary on the school's plan just ten days later, liaison would have seemed to be essential.

Fortunately for the school staff, who were undisturbed by the liaison with the LEA over the Action Plan for almost the whole of August, Daphne Gould remained not only willing but anxious to do what she could for the school, and Betty Hales and the (acting) deputy head, Jeff Davies, consulted her at her home as they spent much of the summer holidays and September drafting the school's response.

The Action Plan and the accompanying Implementation Plan, which were to go to the DfE, were impressive documents. Taking as their starting point the key points for action identified by Ofsted, Hales and Davies identified fourteen targets for the school. These were:

1 To improve behaviour in lessons and around the school.
2 To ensure that all departments produce individual departmental development plans, in line with the school strategic plan.
3 To encourage pupils to take responsibility for, and ownership of, their behaviour and learning.
4 To foster and facilitate the involvement of parents in the life of the school.
5 To further develop and enrich the support infrastructure for pupils and the school.
6 To reorganize the structures within the school which support and encourage good behaviour and positive achievement.
7 To enhance levels of literacy and language for all pupils.
8 To develop a strategy to improve attendance.
9 To enhance teacher methodology and practice.
10 To stabilize the current staffing situation in order to produce a structure capable of delivering a quality education and with the potential to engender future developments.
11 To undertake a total audit of all resources, including personnel. The purpose of this will be to ensure the effectiveness and efficient use of finances and will inform future planning.
12 To widen and enhance the curriculum offered to pupils.
13 To establish the aims of the school for collective worship in accordance with statutory requirements.
14 To review the use of the buildings in terms of Health and Safety requirements and effective and efficient curriculum delivery.

Target 7 was identified as a priority 'key issue' by the school itself. Literacy needs and the subsequent lack of confidence and ability to access the curriculum, they felt, was very closely linked to behavioural problems, especially for pupils who might be easily led into disruptive behaviour by others. This seems like sound commonsense. To expect good behaviour from pupils who cannot understand or participate in their lessons assumes a level of tolerance and self-control unlikely to be found among angels. Angels boys from inner-city Hackney were not.

Each of these targets was then broken down into discrete tasks, criteria were set for the successful implementation of each task, the personnel responsible were identified, a date set for action, review and completed implementation, and the whole plan costed. A grid was also produced to cross-refer each target and identify those for which LEA involvement would be needed. There was absolutely no indication at this stage how far the LEA was prepared to be involved, or how much financial support they would be able to find to put the school back on the road. But staff were optimistic as the new school year began with a staff training day which set up working parties to take the implementation of the plan forward.

11

The Boys of Hackney Downs

Uniquely difficult?

By the time this book is published the boys of Hackney Downs school will be almost adults, the teachers who remember them are scattered, and the campaign which was fought to keep their school open risks being lost in the folk memory of an East London where the population shifts with relentless rapidity. But still people ask what these boys, about whom so much was written and for whom so much political energy was expended, were really like. The school's staff still maintain that they were unique in the difficulties they presented to the education service and the deprivation of the background from which many of them came. Yet those same staff remember them with affection.

It is impossible to put figures on the level of educational difficulty presented by the Hackney Downs boys compared to other schools in the borough or elsewhere, even though the school's bald statistics, such as the last special needs audit in 1994, support the view that the school had sunk to the bottom of the Hackney pecking order with all that that implies. But there are all sorts of reasons why teachers, parents, LEA officers and local and national politicians do not wish to hear what schools like Hackney Downs are saying. Complaints from the staff are often taken as special pleading to excuse their own failings. Schools similarly placed are not anxious to have the fact broadcast. Other schools under the same LEA may not wish to see money channelled into an institution which, by their standards, is so obviously 'failing'. Those who believe that 'schools can make a difference', as they undoubtedly can, are not willing to believe that there may be some schools where making a difference is almost beyond human capacity. Those who resist 'throwing money at problems' blame teachers for failing to cope with every child who arrives at the school gate. Valid reasons why some children are unlikely to succeed academically are dismissed as 'excuses' for teacher failure.

But those children are still children, deserving of a civilized society's consideration, and in all the political argument over failing schools we need to remember that some children in areas like Hackney carry burdens which those in more favoured areas can scarcely begin to imagine. This chapter brings together some of the individual boys who made Hackney Downs what it was during the last few years of its life. The names of the boys have been changed.

With 60 per cent of the roll identified by the school and the LEA as having special educational needs, many of them in need of specialist help, it did not surprise anyone at the school that HMI saw examples of extremely poor behaviour when they visited Hackney Downs.

Two examples of a 'culture clash' of expectations indicate the scale of the problem. An HMI commented on how noisy the dining hall for Year 7 and 8 boys was and how poor their table manners were. Those who knew the boys were aware that a significant proportion of the children present were Kurdish or Somali refugees who had literally not known where their next meal was coming from up to a few months or weeks previously. Some had experienced near starvation. That some still ate with their fingers (not unusual in their own culture), or took food from their neighbours' plates, was not surprising. For their part the dinner staff were pleased that mealtimes were not unruly and that the newcomers were making progress towards behaviour regarded as more appropriate in a European setting.

Another inspector spent a period with a group of ten highly disturbed Year 8 boys for whom specially designed science practical work had been organized because they could not cope with a mainstream class. These were children who found it difficult to sit still or concentrate for long, some of whom spoke little English, and could barely write. They could have been a danger to themselves or others in a normal laboratory situation. The inspector examined their exercise books for signs of 'progression' and was evidently upset by some minor horse-play and foul language as the class moved out of the lab and a group of Year 11 boys came in.

Complex family lives

The complexities of family life made dealing with some Hackney Downs boys extraordinarily complicated and time consuming: expectations on both sides often failed to find any common ground. One mother, a single parent, told Betty Hales that her 13-year-old, six-foot-tall son was getting so big now that she had to wait for him to fall asleep before she could 'beat him' because she could not reach when he was standing up.

Dealing with crises often took up staff time and energy far beyond normal working hours. One afternoon in 1992, Michael had tried to climb over the locked back gate and had injured his leg badly on a railing spike. Michael was beside himself with worry – not over his injured leg but over his 'domestic' responsibilities. Betty Hales and a colleague tried to contact a duty social worker for help but eventually found themselves driving through the evening rush-hour traffic to pick up various siblings for whom Michael was responsible. The journey took them to Hoxton (about four miles and two bus routes from school) to collect a toddler and pram from a child-minder and then back to meet up with two more young children who were collected from school by a neighbour and then waited at her house until Michael got back with the baby to give them all their tea. Michael knew the way but not the names and addresses of the carers.

The neighbour kindly agreed to care for the three younger children while the teachers took Michael, at long last, to hospital to have his leg seen to. The incident was not over however, since the mother could not be traced immediately. It transpired that she was not the mini-cab receptionist which Michael believed she was, and although the mini-cab office knew where she could be located, they refused to tell the teachers. They did however pass on a message to her and she eventually arrived at Homerton Hospital at ten o'clock that evening where Michael and the duty social worker (who had also eventually been located) were still awaiting his treatment.

Then there was Jason, a 12-year-old, who was found to be in possession of a piece of cannabis resin. After some careful questioning it transpired that Jason had told his friends that he had stolen the dope from his father's supply because he had not been given his pocket money. Jason hoped to sell his goods to make good this deficiency. When Jason's mother was called to school she vocally denied all knowledge of cannabis in the home. However, when told that the police were coming to interview her and Jason at home later that day, she could not get home quickly enough and dragged Jason along the road at a flying pace. The staff assumed she had some tidying up to do.

The school was reluctant to give up on any boy, but was sometimes forced to exclude. David, who had been admitted in 1992 after trouble at other schools, was eventually excluded from Hackney Downs after complaints about bullying and extortion. The headteacher wrote to his mother in despair:

> David rarely attends school. When on site his track record is one of disruption and violence towards others. I wrote to you earlier pointing out that David had been involved in incidents during the week which included throwing stones at a teacher, going into an art room and throwing pots of paint at other boys and out of the window, and taking a pair of sunglasses from another pupil. These incidents are not untypical of his behaviour since we accepted him into school . . . We can no longer give this amount of time and effort to David. We have given him countless chances to start again and each opportunity has been cynically abused.

Parents would often chastise their children physically in front of teachers. The school heard numerous accounts of boys being physically abused at home which seemed to the staff to account to a great extent for the high levels of aggression in the school. There was one boy who was part of the heavy drugs scene. He had his own 'minder' and the message was clear: no one was to interfere with him. Many boys had older brothers who were known to the police and fathers who were part of the local drug ring, adding to the external menace which surrounded the school at times.

Parents did not always wait to be invited into school. On one occasion, Betty Hales and some other teachers were alerted to a problem when they heard very loud shouting in the main corridor. On rushing to the incident they found a new pupil at one end and his mother at the other. She had come into school because he had forgotten something. They were holding a 'conversation' by shouting at each other and they were not holding back on the use of colourful language. Not unsurprisingly that same boy continued to cause problems throughout his school career, and on one occasion, when the Education Welfare Officer needed to visit his home, his mother opened the door completely naked, explaining that she had been interrupted in the bath.

Teachers under stress

Some families introduced Hackney Downs' staff to experiences which do not come the way of many teachers. Paul transferred to Hackney Downs just prior to the Ofsted inspection. He was 15 and had been attending a boarding school for pupils with emotional and behavioural difficulties. His mother was dead and his father had previously been registered as a heroin addict and had only recently regained custody of his son. The school had been informed that Mr B was no longer a drug user. Paul proved to be a difficult pupil to integrate since he was extremely reluctant to accept authority from adults. He was awaiting psycho-therapeutic help. After several letters home and a temporary exclusion, from which Paul did not return, Paul's father attended a meeting with his son at the school with Daphne Gould to discuss the boy's problems.

Betty Hales was in the room next door and heard shouting. Upon investigation she invited Mr B to her office to allow Daphne Gould to talk to Paul alone. Mr B explained to Betty that he 'couldn't stand being talked down to by a middle-class do-gooder'. Betty chatted with Mr B and made him tea and he seemed to become calmer, but after about ten minutes his manner abruptly changed. He suddenly stood up and shouted out 'A toilet, a toilet, I must have a toilet' and he banged his hands on the desk to reinforce this message. Betty quickly ushered him to the en-suite facilities where he remained for some time. He then emerged noticeably calmer and more relaxed.

Betty had used the interval to invite a passing member of staff into her room for protection. She had never before seen a junkie in need of a fix except on television but guessed that this was the only explanation of what she had just witnessed.

Even the Army found Hackney Downs' boys somewhat difficult to handle when a group of 14-year-olds spent 24 hours on an activities exercise, including bivouacking, abseiling, orienteering and an assault course, all of which were thoroughly enjoyed. Daphne Gould wrote in pained tones afterwards that the Hackney Downs contingent had been sworn at by soldiers. There was, she claimed, excessive use of four-letter words and one of the soldiers frequently put his face up to the pupils' faces and used profanity to gain obedience through intimidation. A woman teacher was also insulted.

Violence involving teaching staff was not unknown. Derek, who had arrived from another school in the middle of a term, was as usual unable to co-operate with his teachers in a classroom. He was brought to the deputy head's room where he was set work. Unable to settle, his behaviour was so distracting that Betty Hales abandoned her management tasks and attempted to chat with him as a strategy to calm him down.

Things were going fine and they were almost becoming friends when Betty innocently asked 'And what do you think your mum would say about that?' Derek became completely out of control, smashing up anything he could lay his hands on, standing on the table and throwing china around the room. Another member of staff passing by was called in to help, at which point Derek threatened to jump from the window. He was eventually calmed down but continued to cause disruption around the school on a regular basis until about two months later when he stopped attending without explanation and the family could not be traced.

Nearly a year later a possible explanation for his irrational behaviour became clear with a phone call out of the blue from the Yorkshire police which informed the school that a tape-recorder recovered from a car boot sale had been identified from its serial number as property which had been stolen from Hackney Downs School two years earlier. The person who had been found in possession of the stolen property was Derek's uncle, his mother's brother. This offered a clue to why the boy had exhibited such a bizarre reaction when his mother had been mentioned in an innocent conversation.

Sadly, women staff were particularly at risk from pupil violence, one reason why many staff doubted that a move to co-education would be easy or even possible with some of the most disturbed boys still at the school. Robert had been a major cause of concern since starting at the school three years earlier. He was regularly in and out of foster care and moved house often. His attendance was extremely erratic and despite regular referrals for SEN assessment and help he had never managed to be present at the same time as a carer when an education psychologist appointment had been made.

He spent most of his time when he was at school simply wandering about, either out of class or inside the classroom. His all-round intellectual ability seemed very low. He was very easily led but not actively malicious. He could neither read nor write. To quote from a teacher's report of one incident:

> Miss P was shouting, asking for assistance with a boy that she was holding onto on the Humanities staircase . . . She was trying to restrain the boy and at the same time remove his hood which was pulled down over his face. I helped her to remove the hood and discovered that it was Robert. Miss P was very distressed and it quickly became clear that Robert had grabbed or touched her in a sexually inappropriate way. There were a number of other boys around watching the incident but no one else seemed to be actively involved.

Robert apparently was giggling and didn't seem to understand the seriousness of the allegation. Unfortunately this made the female teacher even more distraught. She was demanding his instant permanent exclusion and it took a lot of tact and diplomacy to calm the situation down.

Many Hackney Downs boys had to contend with family circumstances which made it almost impossible for them to concentrate in lessons or conform to the school's demands for minimal standards of good behaviour.

A boy who had recently arrived in Britain and had been introduced into an established family was made to eat all his meals on the floor while the rest of the family sat at the table. Many boys were excluded from the family holidays, for reasons which it was impossible for the school to fathom. They were left at home to fend for themselves: this included one family who visited Disneyland without their son.

One boy of just 12 was left to look after a young family while mother joined a religious retreat for two weeks. Another boy in Year 9 was left on his own for eight weeks while his mother was on holiday. Father had not lived at home for years.

Discipline at times was made more difficult by accusations of racism and by disputes with parents over exclusions, and by parents unwilling or unable to co-operate with the school when their sons misbehaved. A not untypical incident was recorded by Betty Hales after an interview with Mrs X whose son had been one of two involved in a seriously disruptive incident. It shows how reluctant some parents were to co-operate in gaining the additional help the school believed their sons needed.

Betty Hales recalls that Mrs X accused her of trying to get her sons excluded. She blamed the other boy for initiating the conflict. She threatened to take legal advice if the school talked about the stages of special educational needs referral or educational psychologists. She refused to sign the contract of behaviour.

Yet in spite of continuous crises of this sort, the school did build up good relationships with the majority of its pupils, and gained the loyalty of many severely deprived families who were deeply upset when the school closed. It succeeded, even in its most disrupted final period, in ensuring that the majority of them left school with some qualifications. Looking back on their period at Hackney Downs from the relative tranquillity of teaching posts in other schools, many former Hackney Downs staff ask how other teachers – or inspectors and Education Association members – would have coped in the circumstances they faced day after day.

12

Turning the School Around

The new school year

The 1994 summer holidays had seen the publication of the GCSE results, which proved not as catastrophic as the turbulent two terms just past might have indicated. Somehow, in spite of the turmoil, some boys had achieved something that summer. But Betty Hales was very aware that in percentage terms the school would suffer from the fact that the 67 boys in the year group in January had been effectively reduced to 57 by the time the exams were taken. Of those 67, only four had been assessed as being in Band 1, the old ILEA measure of 'grammar school' ability, but those who had left due to the Black Group's disruptive activities had been among the more motivated and probably gave a welcome boost to the results of the schools they moved on to.

Using the DfE definition of the roll, i.e. all those in the year group in January, 11.9 per cent of the boys gained five A to C grades, and 83.6 per cent one or more A to G grades. Using the more realistic definition of the cohort of boys who were still in school and took the exams, the percentages were 13.7 and 98.2 respectively: in other words, almost all the boys still in the school after the tumult of the spring term gained a GCSE qualification. Using the performance scores adopted by all the Hackney schools, relating grades to ability bands, Hackney Downs performed almost as well in 1994 as it did in 1993, in spite of the enormous disruption the candidates had lived through. Betty Hales was not unhappy, particularly as she felt that the school had now established a healthy staffing situation and structure, apart from the departments identified as having fairly intractable difficulties which needed major investment to resolve.

Betty Hales and others had spent a substantial part of the summer holidays drawing up the first draft of the school's Action Plan as required by Ofsted, and the LEA was working through a similar process, though without consulting Hackney Downs' acting head to any great extent or the governors – who were technically responsible for the school's Action Plan – at all. Governors did not see a draft of the LEA plan until just before it was due at the DfE.

In the meantime several important decisions had been made between the inspection and the eventual publication of the Ofsted report – a period of almost four months – which were to be crucial to the school's long-term future.

The decision by the LEA not to admit Year 7 boys from primary schools in September 1994 had originally been made on the grounds that a year would be needed to alter and refurbish the school ready for an intake of girls in 1995. The plan was turned down in March. In May, Gus John suggested that the loss of Year 7 should stand 'in order to consolidate the recovery which has already begun at the school'.

Betty Hales and the governors were extremely unhappy with this decision. They were only too aware of the financial implications under local management of schools of trying to run with one year group short, not simply for one year, but for the five years it would take the loss of 1994's Year 7 to work through to GCSE. It seemed to them perverse to deliberately make an already barely viable small school even smaller.

At their June meeting – for which minutes were never produced – the governors agreed to make representations to the LEA again and ask them to give serious consideration to admitting Year 7 applicants even at this late stage. Gus John later said that he was never informed about this debate and decision of governors.

Neither governors nor senior staff were clear at this stage about the school's legal position on admissions in the light of open enrolment legislation which permits parents to state a preference for the school they want. They were aware that there was now no over-riding logistical reason for turning 11-year-olds away to allow building work to proceed, and suspected the LEA was on shaky legal ground. Daphne Gould was certainly convinced that the LEA risked acting illegally by turning boys away for September.

As the summer progressed the issue became more urgent. A number of families who already had boys at Hackney Downs asked about admissions for their 11-year-olds. It became clear that other families who had moved into the area and had been told by the local authority to seek places at schools other than Hackney Downs were not happy. Amongst these was a refugee family who had moved into a home just a hundred yards from the school and whose two sons spoke no English and had never attended school before. They were particularly anxious about sending the boys to schools a distance away and about the risk that they might have to be split up.

By the end of the summer term the senior management team had prepared a timetable for September, but were at a loss to know how they should deal with the Year 7 issue. Like everyone else they were expecting that the governors would receive an LEA response to their request in June for a reconsideration of the ban on admissions. It was one of the issues which Betty Hales raised with the school's new link inspector at their meeting at the beginning of August. By this time eight families had made definite requests for admission and a joint Year 7/8 class was timetabled as a precaution.

When she returned to school to process the exam results on 24 August, Betty Hales wrote to Gus John reminding him that the issue still remained unresolved. It was at this point she realized that she had seen no minutes for the governors' meeting in June when the issue had been debated. In her letter to the Director she reminded him of the governors' vote to request a reconsideration. The staff and governors of the school, she said, were of the opinion that taking in a Year 7 which could grow would, on balance, be in the best interests of the school both at present and in the future. Because the school was already receiving specific requests for places and inquiries, she was anxious to discuss the matter with the Director.

I believe there would be more applications if parents were given the information by Hackney admissions section that they may apply to Hackney Downs for Year 7 for September 1994. I understand that some Year 7 boys, recently moved into Hackney, have already been told that there are no places available and have been referred out of the borough. It may also be that some parents with appeals outstanding would prefer to come to Hackney Downs.

Betty Hales wrote this letter because she was unable to contact any senior officer by phone because they were all on holiday. She was increasingly convinced – rightly as it turned out – that the admissions issue would prove crucial to the future of the school. In the end she managed to contact a middle-ranking officer, who in turn made contact with a deputy director, who said that he hoped to have an answer for Hackney Downs by the beginning of term, now a week away. Her first contact suggested that in the meantime Betty should write a formal proposal for officers making out her case.

On 30 August Betty Hales was astonished to receive a copy of a letter addressed to the borough's education department from the DfE, obviously in response to a query as to whether it was in fact legal for Hackney Downs to turn away Year 7 applicants. It was quite clear from this correspondence that Hackney LEA had approached the DfE as early as 1 July for clarification of the legal position. The DfE made it clear in their letter of 19 August that it was not legal to keep Year 7 boys out. 'If applications are received which express a preference for a place in Year 7 at the school this September, the authority must admit those pupils at least up to the standard number.'

By this time Betty Hales had submitted her proposals for admitting Year 7 boys, and she assumed that she had been sent a copy of the DfE letter by the LEA to clarify the legal situation and in effect give her the go-ahead.

Pressure from some parents was growing. One mother wrote a letter which sums up the difficulties faced by many families who sent their sons to Hackney Downs:

> As you know my son Paul already attends H.Downs and has made such wonderful progress that we would like Keith to be afforded the same opportunities. Keith has been accepted for Homerton House but we feel that travelling for him would be very difficult. Keith has never been allowed out on his own and we genuinely fear for his safety. Both my husband and I are working so it would be impossible for us to take him to school ourselves . . . Keith has shown a lot of apprehension at having to go to Homerton House and is very disappointed he will not be with his brother.

The admissions crisis

Betty Hales and her staff knew that the original decision not to admit was crucial to the school's future. Effectively, if Hackney Downs lost a full intake of pupils, it meant that the school roll would begin a precipitous fall and unit costs would inevitably rise. When this did eventually came to pass, the school's low numbers and high costs were used as reasons to justify its closure. In other words, Betty Hales' worst fears that summer were fully justified by events.

The immediate result of her concern was that as the autumn term began, the issue became even more complicated and highly emotive. Betty Hales, now made aware, as she thought, by the LEA that in the view of the DfE the school would be acting illegally if it turned applicants away, had informed parents in a newsletter that the school was expecting to admit a small number of Year 7 boys and that arrangements were being made to teach them in a joint Years 7 and 8 class which would be receiving special attention. Not an ideal solution but, given the special needs of many of the pupils, not as strange as it perhaps sounds to people in schools with a more balanced intake.

She added: 'If you have a son of that year group whom you would like to be admitted to Year 7 so that he can be at the same school as his older brother, please contact us as soon as possible. You may also know of other parents who would like their sons to join us.'

Quite unaware of its possible impact, she distributed a copy of the newsletter at the governors' meeting of 6 September and was totally taken aback by the strong feelings this elicited from Councillor Pat Corrigan and Gus John who appeared at the meeting unexpectedly. A stormy session followed at which Betty Hales was fiercely supported by a parent governor and a local primary head, who complained forcibly about the way Betty Hales was being treated by the LEA.

The next day Gus John sent by courier a five-page letter of complaint to Betty Hales, in which he claimed that he had discussed both the logistical and the financial implications of the issue fully with Betty Hales and Daphne Gould the previous term, had stressed the importance of recruiting a large intake the following year (1995/6) and the importance of using the year without a Year

7 to consolidate the school's recovery. In his view the matter had been settled. In retrospect Betty Hales believes that Gus John probably did discuss the issue with Daphne Gould at one of their confidential meetings, though she herself was never told of the conversation.

The Director complained that Betty's paper had been prepared without consulting the chair of governors, and that before he himself had been able to respond, Betty had unilaterally published her newsletter to parents soliciting applications for Year 7 places.

He was particularly angry about the effect the change of policy might have on other Hackney schools, especially Homerton House, where he assumed many of the Year 7 boys displaced from Hackney Downs would have gone. (In fact, the Homerton House intake did not increase dramatically that September. The displaced Hackney Downs intake seems to have gone elsewhere.) Betty Hales' actions were, he said, 'utterly incredible', he demanded a full explanation, especially for 'blatantly wasting my time and that of senior officers', and he instructed her to write to parents immediately informing them that she had the authority of neither the governors nor the LEA to reinstate Year 7.

Betty Hales was deeply upset by the personal tone of the Director's letter and by what she considered to be inaccuracies in his account of what had happened. She seriously considered taking out a grievance procedure against the LEA at this stage but was eventually persuaded that this would not be in her own or the school's long-term interests. However, she remains convinced that her treatment was not what should be expected by a newly appointed acting headteacher carrying the burden of running a school which was attempting to fight its way out of a period of serious crisis. Neither personally nor professionally did she feel that Hackney was offering her or Hackney Downs the support they needed at this time.

However, it was at this point that the school gained increasing support from an existing ally. Dr Tony Burgess, a governor and an academic from the London University Institute of Education, became increasingly involved with the school where he was hoping to set up a research project on the progress of pupils who had learned English as a second language. Tony Burgess was keen to help sort out the 'misunderstandings' which seemed to be developing between the school and the LEA and requested that Gus John's letter to Betty Hales be raised as an agenda item at the special governors' meeting arranged to approve the Action Plan on 4 October.

The LEA in the meantime seemed to be trying to clarify its own position. Betty Hales met the deputy director, Danny Silverstone, at his request, at the education offices on 26 September. She gave him a paper outlining what she felt were inaccuracies and misconceptions in Gus John's letter to her, which Mr Silverstone promised to pass on to Gus John and respond to. By this time Betty Hales was beginning to feel distinctly threatened by comments being made to her about 'consequences' and 'legal implications' which she did not fully understand.

On the day of the scheduled special governors' meeting, it became clear. She was telephoned unexpectedly by the chair of governors, Councillor Pat Corrigan, and told to 'clear her desk' because he would be arriving with a senior personnel officer to suspend her for 'gross misconduct'. He said that she had been accused of tape-recording the previous governors' meeting at which she and Gus John had clashed over the Year 7 issue. This was the meeting at which Betty had been accused of lying to governors about her letter to Gus John about the admission of Year 7 pupils. This new accusation followed a jovial conversation the previous evening with a middle-ranking education officer while waiting for an exclusion appeal meeting to continue. Another teacher had joked that both she and Betty Hales 'moonlighted' as undercover agents and tape-recorded everything, including governors' meetings. It is an indication of the level of suspicion in Hackney that this was taken seriously.

An emergency meeting followed at which Gus John met Tony Burgess and Betty Hales' union representative. Betty Hales herself was not invited. They agreed a compromise by which the suspension of the acting head would not be pursued and Tony Burgess would recommend that the governors should agree not to admit any more Year 7 boys.

Tony Burgess and others persuaded themselves at the time that this deal was in the interests of the school, whose future depended upon the head and governors being able to work with the LEA. With hindsight, they now wonder whether it was not a compromise too far and whether a public airing of the dispute might not have been preferable at that time. Investigations into the allegation of misconduct apparently took place but Betty was never officially informed of the result of the inquiry.

Progress on the Action Plan

While all this was going on, the Action Plan, now ready for governors' approval, was meeting a warm reception from Daphne Gould and the Ofsted Registered Inspector who had been responsible for the May inspection. It was also being vigorously implemented even as it went through the official process of approval. Betty Hales felt at this stage in the school's history they had at last achieved a hard-working and united staff who were beginning to make progress. Even the long-term sickness problem which had caused such disruption over the previous few years appeared to have disappeared. Staff absence had never been lower. Morale was high and there was a sense of real optimism among staff, pupils and parents.

But the acrimony generated by the Year 7 issue marked a turning point in the relationship between Hackney Downs' governors and Gus John. At the first of two meetings in September and October, the governors took serious exception to Mr John's tone in rebuking Mrs Hales. At a special meeting two weeks later they accepted unanimously that she had acted in good faith and in line with their wishes on Year 7 admissions after receiving the copy of the letter to the LEA from the DfE on the legality issue. A proposal that a decision should be deferred while further clarification on the legal position was obtained from the DfE was defeated on the chair's casting vote.

The governors decided at this point to re-advertise the post of headteacher after the abortive efforts to fill the post the previous term. The decision was taken on 6 September, and the advertisement appeared in the *TES* at the end of the month. The advertisement sparked off another round of unpleasant anonymous letters, allegedly from parents, accusing Betty Hales of, among other things, incompetence and racism. They were typed rather than handwritten, and sprinkled with such similar words and phrases that it did not take Hercule Poirot to work out that they could only have been part of a concerted campaign.

Fortunately Betty Hales was buoyed up many times during the subsequent months by a steady stream of heartfelt letters from real parents thanking her and many of her staff for the efforts they had made on their sons' behalf. This letter was typical:

> Considering that English is not his native language, he has progressed in leaps and bounds due entirely to the teaching staff at Hackney Downs. There is no racial disharmony at Hackney Downs because black, brown, yellow and mixed race are treated equally and when they grow up to be responsible adults we will more than probably find that racial tension and hatred is at an end. I would attribute a large measure of this to the teaching staff and environment of Hackney Downs School and to yourself.

External pressures

Meanwhile, external events were beginning to impinge on the school's hopes for the future. Although the school's own financial position was sound – the 1993/4 closing balance showed the school more than £62,000 in the black – Betty Hales had advised her heads of department to spend the minimum necessary to keep the school running at the beginning of the autumn term. But the Borough of Hackney's financial situation was becoming desperate. The Education and Leisure Services Committee was told at the beginning of September that the 'budget gap' for 1995/6 was likely to be £10.5 million. Savings of more than £4 million might be required in education and leisure alone.

The school staff were also becoming increasingly restive, not about their ability to pull the school round, but about what they saw as the increasingly difficult relationship between the school's management and the LEA. An NUT meeting at the end of September heard the teacher governors raise concerns about the lack of information from the LEA about its own Action Plan, a general lack of co-ordination over the supposedly joint response to Ofsted, and what they saw as an increasingly dismissive attitude towards the school from LEA officers.

The NUT's members at Hackney Downs clearly felt threatened by this stage and decided to seek advice nationally on their situation. They backed the acting head in her efforts to recruit a Year 7 intake, aware that this was a governors' decision which had been over-ruled by the LEA earlier in the year, and they questioned what they saw as a serious conflict of interest between the roles of chair of governors and chair of education held by Pat Corrigan. They put their concerns in writing in a letter to Mr Corrigan on 30 September which called formally for his resignation.

Meanwhile the life of the school went on. Betty Hales had not waited until the school's Action Plan was due at the DfE before setting to work to implement improvements. The DfE was given a note of progress when the documents were submitted on 10 October. Behaviour around the school had already noticeably improved and Year 11 (the top year) boys were taking on extra responsibilities, assisting in the running of the school. The School Council had begun to meet under Wendy Brooks' leadership.

In addition, the newly formed Parent-Teacher Association had held two meetings and was organizing a social event for later in the autumn term. A Parents' Newsletter had been established and was being sent home weekly. Some parents were coming into school to observe and assist with lessons.

Within the subject departments, initial preparations had begun for departmental development plans to be drawn up. In-service training days to clarify the roles of form tutors and heads of year had been held at the end of the summer term and at the beginning of the autumn term. The English and special needs departments were working together on plans to raise levels of literacy.

Ofsted had already commented on the fact that staff morale was remarkably buoyant given the school's problems. The management and staff were confident that they could maintain this momentum and implement their Action Plan successfully, provided the LEA left them alone to get on with the job without further distraction and, crucially, began to offer the necessary support. They reckoned that the immediate cost to the school would be about £20,430 that financial year.

On 30 September, Betty Hales also wrote to the deputy director responsible for pupils with special needs, stating that one of the biggest problems Hackney Downs still faced, and with which it still urgently needed LEA support, was the overwhelming number of pupils who were waiting to be seen by an educational psychologist. Until they had been assessed it was impossible to issue Statements of Special Educational Need and work out the appropriate action to help these boys. The school estimated that about 40 additional days of EP time would be needed to clear the existing backlog.

But of course the cost of turning Hackney Downs back into a successful school would be much higher than that. The school's own Action Plan estimated that eleven out of the fourteen targets Ofsted had identified required some input from the LEA: most seriously, an assault on the backlog of building problems which plagued the school and which had led the Ofsted inspectors to raise serious concerns about Health and Safety.

LEA action

The full financial implications of improving Hackney Downs became clear when the LEA's own Action Plan, also required under the 'special measures' procedures instigated by Ofsted, finally emerged in draft at the second September governors' meeting. It was shorter on specifics than the school's own plan but it also starts from the key points for action outlined by Ofsted and quotes approvingly from *Effective Management in Schools*, the report of Ofsted's Management Task Force, on the importance of senior managers in schools 'modelling desired behaviours and attributes such as mutual support and team-work' and behaving with 'modesty and integrity in straight-forward and non-devious ways'.

That quotation signals the first of many ironies which emerged over the autumn term, not least at a school where for four years successive headteachers had struggled with a divided staff and an ineffective governing body, both split by the black faction which the LEA had been repeatedly asked to deal with, but had failed. By the time of the publication of the Action Plans the staff was united for the first time and the governors strengthened and beginning to take their role very seriously.

The LEA was due to present its final Action Plan to the governors at their meeting on 4 October, after they had seen the school's draft, and prior to a meeting arranged at the DfE to present both plans in draft on 7 October. In the event this important document did not appear – an event reminiscent of previous occasions when unwelcome messages from the LEA to the school had simply not materialized when promised.

At the meeting at the DfE three days later, the school's representatives met, among other senior officials, the HMI, who had visited the school previously, and one of the officers who was to be an important link with the DfE in the months that followed. After the school and the LEA had presented their plans and been advised on useful amendments, Gus John requested the opportunity to make a confidential verbal report to the DfE officials.

Betty Hales had been consulted just once early in the term over the preparation of the LEA plan, but, as the new chair of governors was to complain to the DfE later, he and his colleagues were consulted for only part of the meeting two days before the plan was due to go to the DfE, and had still not had the final version delivered to them by November.

Superficially Hackney's Action Plan appeared to propose a rapid remedy for the neglect of the previous five years. They proposed to appoint a permanent headteacher to:

- manage a programme of development and change;
- review and rationalize the school's staffing on a permanent basis;
- involve the governing body in monitoring and evaluation;
- establish a behaviour policy for pupils;
- raise the expectations of staff and establish clear criteria for success;
- help improve the staff's professional strategies;
- help implement clear strategies for classroom management and for monitoring and evaluation of new initiatives;
- establish a climate of co-operation, integrity and trust;
- ensure the school's accommodation supported the effective teaching of the National Curriculum;
- emphasize the need to positively and overtly praise all improvements which were made.

The LEA proposed that action would be taken under five headings: improving pupil behaviour, rationalizing staffing, raising achievement by improving the quality of teaching and by improving the quality of learning, and by supporting the governing body. The plan would be initiated, overseen and monitored by a steering group of six senior LEA officers and members of the school's senior management team, the special needs co-ordinator and the head of the Section 11 team.

In the light of subsequent events it is impossible to read the LEA's Action Plan for Hackney Downs without a sense of unreality creeping in. Yet it is impossible to imagine that such a detailed document was drawn up without someone from among the officers and members of the LEA believing in its necessity and its practicality.

Taken at face value then, Hackney proposed to launch a rescue plan for Hackney Downs which would, over a three-year period, have cost almost £3 million. The proposals broke down as follows in terms of expenditure for the year 1994/5:

1	Improving pupil behaviour (psychological and special needs services)	£61,700
2	Rationalizing the staffing situation	£25,000
3	Improving the quality of teaching	£90,800
	Plus 1995/6 and 96/7	£40,000
4	Improving the quality of learning	
	Revenue (mainly Health and Safety requirements)	£128,700
	Capital – science facilities	£520,000
5	Support to the Governing Body	£1,000
	Total:	£867,200

The plan also included a schedule of other maintenance and improvement work required at Hackney Downs with a price tag of £2,127,000.

In addition, and to the school's complete surprise, the final document proposed appointing five additional LEA governors and to suspend the school's right to a delegated budget for one year, when there would be a review of progress and improvement. The rationale for this proposal was that the governing body had a recent history of difficulties and in the view of the LEA 'had demonstrated both lack of urgency and lack of proper ownership in respect of the weaknesses of the school'. New governors, it was suggested, would bring with them fresh perspectives and objectivity: this at a time when, as the school was quick to point out, the governing body had already changed its composition substantially and was becoming an effective force for the first time during the years when the LEA could have strengthened it but signally failed to do so.

The loss by the governors of financial control was justified on the grounds that it would be more appropriately exercised by the LEA because of its paramount importance in the short term and because, when full formula funding was achieved, 'difficult and harsh decisions will have to be made about resourcing levels'. Those decisions were evidently ones the LEA wished to take itself. In other words, it appeared that the LEA fully expected their hopefully short-to-medium-term improvement programme for Hackney Downs to be followed by draconian spending cuts which they did not trust the governors to make willingly or without a fuss.

Closure proposals

Much worse was to follow. On 12 October the school submitted its final Action Plan, as required, to the DfE. The following day a confidential meeting of the Community Education Sub-committee, the details of which were almost immediately leaked to the *Hackney Gazette*, noted the intention of the Director of Education (Gus John) to report to the full Education Committee on the future of Hackney Downs School, including its possible closure on the grounds of the quality of teaching and its financial unviability.

This was an astonishing reversal of policy. Only weeks previously both Gus John and the chair of education, Councillor Pat Corrigan, had been writing to Hackney Downs parents assuring them of their personal commitment to the future of the school.

Only a year previously Hackney had undertaken its major review of its secondary education provision and concluded that although it currently had surplus places, the school-age population was rising and it would need all its ten secondary schools in order to meet demand by the year 2000 because

if a reduction in the borough's overall secondary school provision were to be contemplated as a result of closure of one of
the boys' schools (Hackney Downs and Homerton House),
there would be considerable problems in meeting the Authority's future need for secondary school places.

The paper presented to the Community Education Sub-committee on 13 October is a remarkable document, as much for what
it leaves out as for what it includes. It summarized the adverse
inspections of the 1990/92 period, but offered no information or
comment on the headships of Peter Hepburn and Betty Hales, the
impact of Daphne Gould's presence in the school, the Ofsted
inspection report or the school's reaction to it, or the massive disruption caused by the Black Staff and Parents' Group the previous
spring term.

The consequences of LEA actions, implemented without consultation with the governors, in seconding John Douglas to other
duties and in employing Daphne Gould, are regarded as 'costs' generated by the school. This 'doubling up' of headteachers, which had
in both cases been presented to the governors as a *fait accompli*, had
cost the LEA £130,000, the paper complained. Other costs listed
were the transitional funding cushioning Hackney Downs (and
Homerton House) from the full impact of LMS (£200,000 since
1992), the costs of long-term sickness (£30,000) and of the cushioning required to cover the loss of Year 7.

The first of these is a cost which has been routinely borne by
LEAs introducing LMS to avoid unacceptably sharp budget
changes for individual schools; the cost of long-term sickness is routinely covered by insurance in most LEAs; and the third item was
a cost which the school's governors and head had specifically asked
not to have incurred on its behalf.

The paper goes on to discuss the school roll – 'an enormous cause
for concern'. This was certainly true. The loss of Year 7 and of 72
boys during the course of the school year 1993/94 had reduced the
roll in twelve months from 470 to 319. The paper gives no indication that the loss of Year 7 was opposed by the school, or to the fact
that the loss of 72 boys from all years was a direct result of the

disruption caused by the Black Staff and Parents' Group, an event that no one in their worst nightmares expected would be repeated. There was no acknowledgement that parents were still actively seeking places at the school and being sent elsewhere by the LEA.

Far from recognizing this unprecedented series of events, the paper takes the most pessimistic view, without any substantiation, that the haemorrhage of pupils might continue. 'Assuming that this pattern of reductions continues, i.e. the loss of students as they move up a year, one would anticipate that the current total of 319 would reduce even further.'

In its financial forecasts for the school it assumes the reduction in the LMS cushioning of £200,000 a year, which was not unexpected. But it also implies that the cushioning for the loss of Year 7, a loss of pupils which would take five years to work through, was only anticipated to last until April 1995, i.e. two terms after the entry stopped, which is not what the governors or senior staff thought they had been promised when they were persuaded against their will not to admit boys the previous September.

In making forecasts further into the future the paper appears to assume that the roll would remain at 300 indefinitely, regardless of the improvements that Gus John and Pat Corrigan had been commending to the parents so very recently, and regardless of the fact that in the normal course of events, with rising pupil numbers in the borough, the very small upper-year groups would very likely be replaced by larger groups of 11-year-olds as each year went by. It was, in other words, a very brief paper which seemed to put every aspect of the school's future in the worst possible light.

The logical conclusion of the analysis presented to the sub-committee was that Hackney should not continue to pour good money after bad and that on the grounds of 'both poor quality education and financial unviability' members should consider closing the school.

The school's first knowledge of the LEA's proposals arrived by fax at mid-day on 14 October from a reporter at the *Hackney Gazette* who had received the information from an anonymous source. The reporter wanted the school to confirm the rumour! Within minutes the proposed closure seemed to become common knowledge in the borough and staff received a phone call from the local NUT branch confirming the basic facts.

It was not until 18 October that Gus John attended an emergency meeting of governors to inform them officially of the decision to consult on closure. Councillor Pat Corrigan claimed not to have known anything about the proposal until 13 October.

The governors reacted with predictable fury. Councillor Corrigan resigned as chair, on the grounds, already put to him by the NUT, that holding that post as well as that of chair of the Education Committee would face him with an irreconcilable conflict of interest. He was replaced as acting chair by Dr Tony Burgess.

Two days later Gus John wrote to the acting head confirming the details of what he was proposing. Essentially this was to add the closure proposal to the LEA's Action Plan, now due at the DfE, and immediately to suspend the delegation of the school's budget and to appoint five additional governors. This plan was approved by a special meeting of the Education Committee on 31 October. The staff and governors immediately set to work to counteract what they regarded as the very selective information which had been presented to councillors in Gus John's report.

Even as the Action Plans were being presented and, as we now know with hindsight, secret plans were being made to close the school, another scenario was unfolding which added to the pressure on Betty Hales in particular. This was the continuing and by now long-running saga of the appointment of a substantive head to run Hackney Downs – a pre-requisite for successful change in the minds of most people with any knowledge of school improvement.

Betty Hales had been officially appointed as acting head on 1 March 1994 (after two months in the job following Ken Russell's illness). The appointment was a temporary one to run until 31 December 1994. There had already been one abortive attempt at short-listing for the permanent post in July and a re-advertisement in September.

The second short-listing meeting was held on 10 October, the Monday following the meeting at the DfE to submit draft Action Plans and two days before the 'confidential' proposal to close the school. Gus John and Pat Corrigan were present at a meeting at which five candidates were selected for interview. At the end of this long meeting Gus John told those present that he did not believe that the appointment should go ahead because the DfE took the view that an appointment should not be made until they had accepted the Action Plans. Pat Corrigan chaired this meeting and the governors gained the impression that they must accept this DfE advice and duly postponed the interviews which had been provisionally fixed for 18 October.

An extensive correspondence a few weeks later between Tony Burgess, as the chair of governors, and the DfE, established that the DfE's view on the matter was that this was something which should be discussed locally and that the governors retained their right to make an appointment until such time as the LEA took over their delegated powers. Almost inevitably over the subsequent year, no permanent appointment was ever made to the headship of Hackney Downs. Betty Hales remained as acting head for 22 eventful months.

13

A Sense of Betrayal

Deep suspicion

It is hardly surprising that by this stage in the life of Hackney Downs School, its friends were beginning to feel paranoid and grossly betrayed. Looking back, few of those at the school who were closely involved can feel sure that the decision to close was taken as late as the beginning of that autumn term. In retrospect, a whole raft of decisions could now be interpreted as having been part of a much longer-term and secret plan. A deep suspicion of the LEA's motives was perhaps inevitable and came to dominate the relationship between the school's supporters and the LEA for the rest of the school's life.

Small pin-pricks added to the gloom. Artwork by Hackney Downs boys, some of it A★ grade work for GCSE, which had been exhibited at the Town Hall, was thrown away afterwards by cleaners. Colleagues from other schools turned away from Hackney Downs staff in embarrassment. The budget print-out for the previous financial year – which finally arrived in October, six months late – showed a healthy balance but within weeks of the LMS budget being derogated to the LEA the school was being accused of overspending. When Betty Hales investigated this she discovered that no allowance was being made for cushioning the loss of Year 7, as promised to protect the curriculum, and the school was being 'charged' for long-term sick pay and for other additional costs incurred by the LEA's decisions on the headship, i.e. John Douglas' secondment and Daphne Gould's appointment. For the rest of the school's life, she says, neither she nor the chair of governors were ever sure about the state of the school's budget because the information coming from the Education Offices was not consistent once the responsibility passed to the LEA.

The governors' meeting on 18 October soured relationships between Betty Hales, the new chair of governors Tony Burgess and most of the governing body on one side; and on the other, Gus John, who became very angry at accusations of cynicism and betrayal. He justified the LEA's U-turn as his 'professional duty' and said that it was his right to make his recommendations to council members before approaching the governors. There was an angry discussion about where responsibility for high costs at Hackney Downs lay, given that the LEA had been taking decisions against the wishes of governors. The governors felt that there was little chance of turning the school around financially while prospective parents knew that its future was under threat.

There was also great bitterness expressed about the loss of the Year 7 intake, which many governors felt must have been a ploy to seal the school's fate. Officials were not believed when they claimed that the LEA had only just become aware of the school's financial unviability and dramatic reduction in roll. Governors claimed that the problem of a small school under LMS funding had been constantly drawn to the LEA's attention and that LEA actions had made the situation worse. The meeting polarized between LEA officers and Labour councillors who blamed the school's staff and governors for its likely demise, and the rest of the governors, who blamed the LEA.

Gus John wrote to Betty Hales after the meeting, apparently because he had overheard her complain that she felt the staff's considerable efforts in drawing up the school's high-quality Action Plan had been wasted. This was not the case, he argued, because both the school and the LEA were statutorily obliged to complete the plans, regardless of the closure proposal. This seemed to Betty Hales to miss the point entirely: the time had been gladly spent on the assumption that the LEA was behind the school and would provide support and give it a reasonable time to recover. The realization that this was not so was what had led to the massive sense of betrayal among staff and governors.

Gus John went on to say that he wrote his report on the school recommending closure on the afternoon before it was presented to the evening meeting of the sub-committee concerned, having made up his mind only that weekend. The leak to the Press had led inevitably to accusations of bad faith which followed. Drawing the sub-committee's attention to the fact that the school was not financially viable under LMS was no more than his duty, he claimed. He concluded:

> Let me add that, like you, I seek to work in the best interests of the children of Hackney and in support of their life opportunities. It is in recognition of the fact that your students deserve more than most, given the over-representation of black males in a range of negative indicators, that I personally have put so much time and energy over the years in supporting the school and committing the LEA against many odds to do the same. I am now recommending closure to the LEA with the same conviction with which I supported the school unstintingly over the last four years.
>
> On behalf of the LEA and my senior management team, let me thank you most sincerely for leading the school during that most difficult pre-Ofsted period, for working so diligently on the school's Action Plan and for helping to stabilise the learning environment.

Breakdown

In spite of these kind words, it was from this point on that the relationship between LEA officials and the school effectively broke down; and Betty Hales in particular, for the rest of the time she ran the school as acting head, felt the full force of disapproval which could be brought to bear by Hackney Council when it found one of its employees apparently defying it.

She was particularly hurt and angry about this because she had gone to work for Hackney with the best possible intentions and motives in May 1990. Before taking over as head she had long been frustrated by the limited effect that a deputy can have within a school unless the senior management is really working together as a team. Since becoming acting head she had used every ounce of energy and influence to unite staff, parents and pupils to achieving the near impossible and there was evidence that she was succeeding. Why a plan to close the school now? Because it was proving to be successful at last? Had the plan always been to let the school die slowly and naturally? Now it looked as if it might actually live, was action being taken to kill it off? Such thoughts passed through many minds and it is worth considering the facts for a moment.

Through the previous four years whilst the school was floundering from one crisis to another, with constantly changing leadership, with a minority of disaffected staff and a divided governing body, no direct moves to close it were made. But just as all the problems were beginning to be tackled by a coherent and well-considered Action Plan, instead of giving it six months or a year – or preferably the two years Ofsted regarded as standard to come out of special measures – to see if it could improve, an announcement of consultation on closure was made immediately.

At the point when success was within sight and grasp, it was snatched away cruelly, Betty Hales believed. Would not anyone have been angry, let alone 'a spiky Hackney native' as she is proud to have been described by Andy Beckett in his *Sunday Independent* article of 27 November 1994.

Gus John had very little official contact with Hackney Downs after this point. His deputy, Danny Silverstone, was appointed as Betty Hales' 'line manager', with control of the school's budget and staff issues, pay and conditions, discipline and grievance procedures. Betty Hales was instructed to make no financial commitments beyond £300 without permission, and her spending was cash-limited.

The LEA appeared to have two priorities once the Education Committee decided to confirm the closure proposal on 31 October. The first was to get through the statutory consultation procedure and closure process as quickly as possible. The aim at this time seemed to be to close the school by the end of the summer term 1995, eight months ahead, although this assumed an unusually rapid response from the DfE, which normally took about six months to a year to consider objections and ratify a closure once it had been confirmed by the full council, which could not happen much before March 1995.

The second priority appeared to Betty Hales to be to prevent the school from organizing an effective campaign to save itself: this was not to prove so easy. The day after the Education Committee decision, Betty Hales sent the normal weekly newsletter home to parents. On behalf of the whole staff she included a paragraph concerning the proposal to close the school. It explained that the decision so far taken did not mean that the school would definitely close. The proposal first had to go though statutory consultation procedures and then be ratified by the full council and the DfE. All of the staff at the school, she told parents, were determined that the school would continue and that all of the hard work put in to improve it over the last few months would not be wasted. She promised to keep parents informed.

In response to that, she received a letter from Gus John on 15 November informing her about line-management responsibilities now that LMS had been removed. It included the following paragraph: 'You will provide drafts of any publicity or communications with parents or external parties to Daniel Silverstone to agree before they are issued. He will, where possible, turn these round within twenty-four hours.' Betty still wonders what other headteacher would tolerate this interference in home–school relationships and the implied affront to their professional integrity. The practical difficulties that this created were enormous. In practice it often held up letters going to parents for two or three days.

She was encouraged in her determination to fight the closure by external and internal events. The very next day the special needs department launched a corrective reading scheme, as part of the school's drive to improve literacy. The same day a letter arrived from the national Investors in People scheme, which the school had joined. This complimented the school on its 'vastly improved atmosphere since Betty Hales took post', improvements to the school environment, including a welcome absence of vandalism, and positive policy and management responses to the Ofsted Report.

The LEA also instructed the school to have no communication with the Press, who would be dealt with by Hackney Council's Press Office. Over the following months the LEA's attitude towards the anti-closure campaign, which was organized through the Parent-Teachers' Association and the teachers' unions, became increasingly authoritarian.

Before Christmas tension arose over the alleged taping of the formal consultation with staff on closure, a meeting which Danny Silverstone attended. Betty Hales was instructed to investigate but could find no evidence to support the allegation. Another dispute erupted over how the consultation documents and notice of meeting should be delivered to parents, Danny Silverstone preferring to use 'pupil post' which Betty Hales believed, from experience, to be an unreliable way of reaching families. She opted to take up the offer of staff to deliver the documents by hand. It was clear from the ensuing argument that neither side trusted the other, and Betty Hales felt herself under considerable psychological pressure if she questioned what appeared to her to be unreasonable instructions.

The school also continued to suffer severely from its building problems. Just before Christmas, the deputy head, Jeff Davies, found himself in temporary charge of a school which had become virtually uninhabitable during heavy rain. He informed Danny Silverstone:

I have given instructions for the music block to be closed due to serious flooding on the stairwells which meant that I could not guarantee the health and safety of students in that area. Lessons have needed to be relocated.

I have also closed the gym for the same reason.

There are other areas of the school which will constitute health and safety risks if the heavy rain persists. These include classrooms (especially two geography rooms on the top floor of the main block), technical workshops, art studios and the top floor of the science block. The main staircase has only been prevented from becoming a serious health and safety risk as the result of persistent and regular mopping up by the school-keepers.

The school-keepers have also regularly mopped the art/technical block, music block, to no avail, and other areas.

I have relocated some classes for this afternoon but if the bad weather persists, especially overnight, it will be difficult to find sufficient teaching space for all classes or to guarantee the safety of large areas of the site.

It was small wonder, perhaps, that the LEA was desperate to keep the Press out of Hackney Downs.

Internally matters were also complicated throughout this period by increasingly active campaigning by the teacher unions across Hackney over the long-running issue of the abolition of the Inner London supplement. Several half-day strikes over this issue led to further tension throughout the borough's education service as the LEA deducted pay from striking teachers. Hackney politics, particularly the politics of the Labour Party and its edgy relationship with the unions and its own staff, were becoming increasingly volatile.

Angry governors

A special meeting of the governing body was held on 9 November. This was informed that the delegated budget had been suspended and that the LEA was going ahead with the appointment of five new governors. At this stage the governors had not yet received a copy of the LEA's Action Plan for the school, although copies had been requested.

Understandably angry governors complained that their ability to function effectively had been usurped. Due to the difficulties of 1993 very little business had been conducted at a series of traumatic governing body meetings that year which had culminated in the black parents' demonstration. Crucial decisions on the appointment of a permanent head and the admission of a Year 7 had been taken out of their hands. Now that the governing body – which was substantially different in personnel from the body which had experienced such difficulties earlier – needed to use its energies to implement the Action Plan, it complained, it was again being diverted from its proper tasks by the proposal to close the school.

After a heated discussion, the governors approved a motion which affirmed their support for the staff and their ability to implement the Action Plan in spite of the new pressure placed upon them; supported the campaign by parents and staff to keep the school open; sought support from other Hackney governing bodies for the campaign; rejected the 'misrepresentation' of the school and its Ofsted report by the Director of Education to the Education Committee; and put on record the governors' sense of betrayal at the decisions made by the chair and Director of Education despite their assurances that the school would remain open. Councillor Pat Corrigan (still a governor) and another senior Labour Party governor voted against all the clauses of the resolution.

The battle lines were now drawn. Quite apart from the substantive issues, governors were angered by reports that the closure of the school was already being regarded as a *fait accompli* by the LEA. Primary headteachers were already being advised not to recommend Hackney Downs to parents of 11-year-olds and that parents interested in the school should be referred to the education offices for personal advice. It was well known that Hackney Downs and its staff were well respected among local primary heads, who knew from personal experience that it took in many of their most difficult and deprived boys and did its best for them. In these circumstances, it was inevitable that relationships between the school and the LEA would go from bad to worse.

Tony Burgess proved an energetic and knowledgeable chair of governors and remained in office until his role was superseded by the Education Association a year later. He was, from the beginning, very active in fighting what he perceived as, on the kindest interpretation, confusion emanating from the LEA.

One of his first actions was to prepare a document for councillors commenting on the governors' response to the closure plan and explaining why they were so adamantly opposed to it. He ran through the arguments put by Gus John to the Education Sub-committee and refuted them one by one. He complained that the Director of Education had ignored the main thrust of the Ofsted report which was that Hackney Downs was at a turning point. Recovery was possible, he said, and a consultation on closure at this point would destabilize the school just at the time when progress was becoming apparent on many of the Ofsted issues. He asked councillors to defer the move to consultation.

Immediately after his election as chair, Tony Burgess had written to the Department for Education to seek advice on three issues in the light of what he called 'the wavering and uncertain' support which was being offered to the school. (This was the letter in which he had also queried the advice the governors had been given that it was not appropriate to appoint a permanent headteacher.)

He also raised with the DfE the difficulty posed by the LEA's simultaneous production of an Action Plan and a plan for closure and by the removal of the school's delegated budget and the proposal to 'flood' the governing body with new LEA appointees.

What evidence was there, he asked, that the greater powers sought by the authority would not be used to further run down the school, particularly in the light of his view that there was no acceptance by the authority that they were in any way responsible for the problems at Hackney Downs outlined by Ofsted? He suggested, though not in so many words, that the LEA's role as the school's support during the renewal process had effectively been pre-empted by its closure plan and that its greater involvement in the running of the school in the immediate future was therefore fatally compromised.

The DfE merely confirmed that there was no legal impediment to this apparently contradictory stance by the authority. 'Special measures' and a statutory closure procedure could proceed simultaneously.

On 8 November, Dr Burgess wrote again to the DfE in even stronger terms, in a last-ditch attempt to influence the Secretary of State's decision on the two Action Plans, now imminent. He commended the school's 'high quality' Action Plan to the department, and the visible improvements which had already taken place within the school. He complained that governors had been persuaded to connive in the running down of the school by allowing themselves to be persuaded not to admit Year 7 in September 1994, and not to appoint a permanent headteacher. He complained that there had been no sign that the LEA was acting on the key points for action as required by Ofsted, in refurbishing the school, stabilizing the staffing, or acting on the question of mid-term admissions which had proved so harmful.

The governors' consent has been won through an extraordinary combination of *ad hoc* decision-making, juggled meetings, drip-feeding of the authority's plans, at times misleading information and the dual responsibility exercised by a chair of governors who was also chair of the education committee. The chief, but not the only indication of this was that the decision to apply for closure was apparently taken by the director in the fortnight between the school's submission of its action plan and that by the authority, and confirmed at a special meeting of the education committee brought forward from December.

With hindsight, it is ironic that Dr Burgess concludes that such was the dissatisfaction among governors, staff and parents at the way the school had been treated by the authority, that the feeling was growing that the appointment of an Education Association (the so-called 'hit-squad' permitted by the 1993 Education Act to be appointed by the DfE to run 'failing' schools) would be preferable to continuing under Hackney control.

The governors were strengthened in their resolve to save the school by the arrival at the end of November of Ofsted's encouraging response to the Action Plan. The letter complimented the school on producing clear, comprehensive and detailed documentation which addressed all the key issues raised in the Ofsted report. Aims and priorities were regarded as appropriate and the means of measuring progress and time-scales were realistic.

The letter warns that the proposed rate of change is very fast and might not be sustainable. The plan would place a heavy burden on staff and would require new methods of working. They did not baulk at the school's suggestion of a fifteen-month programme but commented that to maintain progress over a longer period the governors would need to review and revise the plan at regular intervals. These comments are in line with Ofsted's published view that a school requiring special measures would normally require two years to improve sufficiently to be taken off the 'at risk' register. Ofsted would, of course, require signs of progress before that and expected to revisit the school in March, the month when Hackney looked likely to be voting on the proposal to close the school.

The DfE also wrote to Tony Burgess at this time, suggesting that his response to the monitoring visit should be combined with an LEA response in a single submission, noting any changes in policy which they felt might need to be made in response to HMI comments. If anyone felt schizophrenic on receipt of these communications, they were too wary to say so.

14

'Save Our School'

Consultation on closure

Hackney Downs School and its parents became deeply unhappy about the way in which the statutory closure procedures were conducted around Christmas 1994. The first meeting for parents was scheduled for 12 December, which the school felt was far too close to Christmas to produce a full turnout. Even so, STOP, the campaign to save the school, had already got itself under way. The first lobby of the Town Hall, where the full council was meeting, was organized by the teacher unions and parents for 23 November. Petitions and a parental letter campaign had started. On 27 November a sympathetic article appeared in the *Independent on Sunday* which picked up the wider issues succinctly and painted a depressing picture of a community in turmoil.

> A modern ritual of education politics seems to be in motion: from tabloid decryings to damning inspections to shut-down, with the school sliding to its end along rails set up and greased by Conservative education reforms. But there's going to be a fight: teachers have until February to save their school. In the staff-room two days after the council's decision, flyers and petitions are piled up for distribution to parents. There's an air of defiance and resentment against the council; teachers say it's been neglecting Hackney Downs for years, deliberately running it down, and now, stung by the tabloids, wants to look tough by closing it down.

The *Independent*'s journalist, Andy Beckett, got a real flavour of student and teacher loyalty and of the rumour factory which Hackney had now become. Pupils and teachers commented on the improvements that Betty Hales had implemented. One young teacher told him: 'When I came to the school in the spring I thought "This is tough". But since then the behaviour of the kids has got remarkably better, the atmosphere is much more positive – or it was before the council meeting.' The boys Beckett interviewed agreed: 'Behaviour is improving a lot. The new head's quite good'. Praise indeed from a 15-year-old. Boys told Beckett that there were about 50 disruptive pupils who made life difficult for everyone, but on the whole they wanted to talk about more positive things – the English lessons, the school sport, the relatively easy race relations, Turkish boys who had special English lessons 'and after a couple of months they start talking'.

Even the former vice-chair of governors, who had removed her son at the height of the turmoil over the Black Staff and Parents' Group campaign, conceded that 'some of the teachers were excellent' and that her son had liked the school. Stephanie Taylor, a recently elected parent-governor and now a leading member of the STOP campaign, told the newspaper that she had met nothing but dedication from the school staff.

Betty Hales remembers Andy Beckett with warmth, although she was unable to talk to him directly as she had been told, under threat of disciplinary action, not to talk to journalists. She invited him to attend a parents and friends of the school meeting as an interested party. She is proud of his comment in the article that she knows and speaks her mind.

But staff were aware that teacher militancy had a long history in Hackney and that they were already being tarred with that brush because of this new defiance. They scented conspiracy and believed that the LEA wanted to sell the school site to ease its parlous financial plight; or it wanted to move the boys to help Homerton House which had let it be known that it might opt-out; or it supported the Black Staff and Parents' Group in their alleged ambition of setting up an all-black school in Hackney. For any or all of these reasons – all officially denied – they reckoned that the LEA was rushing to get the closure through before any improvement in the school could make the task more difficult to justify.

Gus John made no secret of the fact that he was anxious to press ahead with the consultative procedures. The formal consultation period on the closure proposal would last two months, from December 1994 to February 1995.

Growing conflict

The next governors' meeting was held on 6 December when newly-elected parent-governors took office and the five new LEA appointees were due to appear. The meeting got off to a bad start when two of the five failed to turn up. The LEA itself was well represented at this meeting by Gus John, his deputy, Danny Silverstone, with the acting head of the Secondary Schools' Review Team and the senior LEA secondary adviser.

Betty Hales' report to governors concentrated on the progress which was being made on the Action Plan, in spite of the uncertainty which now surrounded the school. She gave details of work on behaviour management and pastoral care, which had been restructured, and on measures to identify and refer pupils in need of a full SEN assessment. (The school's educational psychologist had just identified one boy in Year 8 who, unknown to Hackney Downs, at his primary school had been given a Statement of Special Needs which had been mislaid by the LEA for fifteen months since he changed schools!)

She reported progress on departmental development plans, on building pupils' sense of responsibility through the school council, through assemblies, after-school activities, sport, the Activities Week and the promotion of the school uniform which was now being worn by 95 per cent of the younger pupils.

She reported on progress in school examinations and on preparations for GCSE, links with parents and local industry, the Investors in People scheme, and the Choice programme which aimed to persuade more Hackney pupils into higher education. Attendance and punctuality had improved and staff illness had declined significantly.

Gus John asked about work on pupil SEN profiling and suspensions, and Betty Hales reported progress in both areas. Profiling was proving successful and the school had successfully kept two pupils on the roll who might previously have been excluded.

The meeting agreed that individual governors would take responsibility for monitoring particular areas of the school's progress and visit the school more regularly. The acting head and the governors seemed determined to turn the school around in spite of the threat now hanging over it. But the good news was inevitably tarnished by the closure proposal and the deep resentment that had caused among most governors. At one point Gus John's continued presence at the meeting was openly challenged.

At this meeting the disagreement between Danny Silverstone and Betty Hales over the best way of distributing the consultation documents to parents also surfaced angrily. Betty Hales was questioned because she had not used pupil post to deliver the letters to parents. She explained how unreliable pupil post was – unless it was a letter advising parents about an additional day off for pupils! She said that the staff had considered the consultation document so important that all tutors had volunteered to deliver their own tutor groups' letters by hand. Officials did not appear satisfied with this response.

Tony Burgess was confirmed as chair of governors at this governors' meeting, but in spite of his appeals for respect for differences of opinion the meeting developed into a series of wrangles over its status as part of the formal consultation on closure, over the timing of meetings with staff and parents, and the distribution of documents to parents.

Governors were particularly annoyed that their AGM was being taken over by officials and was apparently being regarded as part of the consultation process on closure. They were also concerned that the timing of the consultation meetings for parents were being scheduled with what appeared to them to be unseemly haste at the end of term and just before Christmas. Parents and pupils were being expected to consider the closure of their school at the same time as presenting an ambitious end-of-term show to which Gus John and other officials and councillors had been invited.

The consultation document

The next day Danny Silverstone wrote to Betty Hales instructing her to distribute the documents and attaching the translations for non-English-speaking families, which would need to be distributed even more urgently for the meeting six days ahead.

A day later he despatched an agenda for their next school management meeting which included

> The results of your inquiry into the report that our meeting with staff was tape-recorded; clarification of which school-level decisions will require my prior agreement; communication with parents; the consultation process (on closure); the claim for substantive headship status [Mrs Hales was now the only acting appointee in the school]; the council's code of conduct and your contacts with the media; and the school's budget position.

These less than educational issues looked set to take up more time than discussion of the Action Plan which was so vital to the school's future.

The LEA's Consultation Paper for public discussion on the future of Hackney Downs was more detailed than the paper put to the Education Committee and had gone back as far as the ILEA's report on the school in 1985 and that of its own inspection in 1991 to justify its contention that the school had been consistently failing on educational grounds. This was particularly galling to staff and senior management, two-thirds of whom, including all the heads of major departments, had been appointed over the previous year.

The paper quoted four critical conclusions from Ofsted in 1994 on under-achievement, poor behaviour and truancy, unsatisfactory teaching, and poor class control. No mention was made of Ofsted's more encouraging comments or on whether or not the school had improved since the inspection the previous May.

The document reopened the argument on the provision of school places for boys in the borough which had been dealt with in the July 1993 review of secondary education, just over a year previously. That review had proposed the retention of ten schools, including

Hackney Downs reconstituted as a mixed school. The whole discussion ignored the fact, revealed at a meeting of secondary heads and chairs at the end of November, that there were at that time 94 pupils, mainly boys, currently without school places in Hackney. It seemed that the parents of these boys were not apparently being informed by the LEA that Hackney Downs had spare capacity, even though the closure proposal was still in its earliest stages.

The LEA now stated that projections of need for boys' places had been over-estimated and revised them downwards by some 53 immediately (though by only sixteen by the year 2000, the end of the planning cycle). These figures were fiercely disputed throughout the consultations which followed. But the argument was complicated by the fact that more boys than expected were opting for mixed schools than boys' schools, and large numbers of boys were going out of the borough. Hackney's response seemed to be to accept this rather than seek ways of improving boys' education so as to persuade more Hackney parents to choose boys' places in the borough. At this stage there was no information on the financial implications of this approach.

The LEA's conclusion was that the borough could dispense with an all-boys' Hackney Downs, but that to avoid an imbalance of boys and girls in mixed schools in the longer term 'it would have to revisit the secondary review in due course as far as the eventual use of the Hackney Downs campus is concerned, should the public consultation process result in closure'. This is a significant comment in the light of later proposals to sell off the site and use the money to fund improvements at other schools.

The consultation document also notes that the previous autumn, when there had been no intake at Hackney Downs, the intake at the other all-boys' school, Homerton House, had actually dropped slightly. Relations between Hackney Downs and Homerton were complicated from that point on by the belief at Homerton that Hackney Downs had in some way 'poached' substantial numbers of their intake that autumn. In fact only a handful of boys ever entered Hackney Downs' Year 7 in 1994. Wherever the frustrated intake for Hackney Downs went, it was not to the other all-boys' school, another point of some significance in the light of later plans to move Hackney Downs boys *en bloc* to Homerton House.

The third plank in the LEA's case for closure was financial. Its first concern was the rapidly falling roll, down to 319 in September 1994 from 470 the previous year. Funding a school of 300 boys at a level which would offer them a full curriculum would inevitably be expensive. The LEA estimate was that an additional £460,000 would be required in 1996/7.

In addition there would be the cost of implementing the Action Plan: £370,000 of revenue resources and ultimately capital bids of £2,647,000 for refurbishing the buildings, some of which was to come from the government's Regeneration Budget. The point was not made that if the buildings were eventually to be required for another school, the £2.6 million is money Hackney would have to spend anyway. Indeed if the site were to be used for a co-educational school even more investment might be needed to make it suitable. Hackney Downs staff and governors were always convinced that the financial figures were presented in such a way as to make it appear that the least favourable option for the council financially was to support the school's remaining open.

The consultation document concluded that the evidence of the previous two years suggested that despite the school's low roll and high pupil–teacher ratio, the quality of education could not justify that level of expenditure to the detriment of other schools in the borough.

> What is clear is that given the quality of education at Hackney Downs School and parents' lack of confidence in its capacity to deliver effective schooling, the Authority cannot support the school financially over and above its formula allocation.

The governors' response questioned the LEA's interpretation of much of the data at its disposal. In particular it objected to what it regarded as a highly partial interpretation of the evidence of the quality of education at Hackney Downs, relying as it did on Hackney's own inspection findings, some of them now four years old, and a very selective use of the Ofsted report of 1994.

> We must take issue with the impression given by the consultation paper that the areas of concern raised by the LEA

Inspectorate in 1991 are identical with those noted by Ofsted, with the implication of continuing areas of professional weakness which have been left neglected and unaddressed. This is too condemning, and takes insufficient account of progress made under the senior and middle management team since March 1994.

The changes for the better, the governors reminded the authority, had been achieved through LEA support, partly from its advisory service and partly through the appointment of the consultant headteacher who had worked with the school throughout the period. They wondered whether a genuine misunderstanding existed about the depth and substance of the changes that had been taking place. But they wanted placed on record their view that the consultation paper did not reflect recent developments or give a balanced and internally informed analysis of the strengths and weaknesses of the school.

The fundamental issue of quality, the governors argued, was whether the potential existed within the school to make the changes which were needed. Ofsted, they claimed, believed that potential was there. A high quality Action Plan now existed and there was considerable detailed evidence that progress was being made. This progress, they said, was recognized by parents and those who knew the school.

The governors also challenged the LEA on the question of the school roll, reiterating the point that the present low roll was the direct result of the failure to admit Year 7 in September 1994, against the wishes of the acting head and the governors, and the removal of boys as a result of the activities of the Black Staff and Parents' Group. The loss of Year 7, the governors reminded the LEA, had originally been agreed on the basis that the borough could absorb the inevitable costs of the school 'skipping' a year's entry as part of the co-educational reorganization plan. Far from absorbing the necessary transitional costs, the LEA was now holding this loss of pupils against the school in the most damaging way possible. More importantly for the school's future, the governors said, it was unreasonable to look at the school's loss of numbers in 1993/4 in isolation. Before that period the school was holding its own and the assumption that the decline could not be reversed, particularly if the Action Plans were successful in raising standards and improving the physical environment of the school, was not reasonable.

On the financial considerations, the governors commented that prior to 1994 the school had been moving towards viability. This had been delayed initially by the lack of a Year 7 admission in 1994 and would be made worse by the current uncertainty over the school's future. As far as the major costs were concerned, the governors pointed out their inability to estimate how far these were reasonable, except to suggest that the additional costs for education psychology services seemed to be those for the borough as a whole, rather than for Hackney Downs in particular, and that the overdue refurbishment of the buildings had now become unavoidable for health and safety reasons.

In essence the governors argued that there was, on pupil number projections, a continuing need for Hackney Downs School, that there was demand from parents which had been artificially suppressed for a year, and that the current parents and the local community wanted the school kept open and were supportive of the improvements being made.

Contingency plans

On 9 December, Betty Hales attended a meeting with the school's link adviser to discuss 'downsizing' the school in the event that the closure did not go ahead. In the light of the much reduced roll, and the fact that primary heads had already been advised not to recommend the school to pupils about to move up to secondary schools, there seemed little chance that Hackney Downs' roll would increase greatly in September 1995 if the school did remain open. The meeting worked on two scenarios – an intake of 100 Year 7 pupils, or one of 50 pupils. In order to offer the National Curriculum, the school would have to run three parallel forms instead of four, and the staff would be reduced to 23/24 teachers including the head and deputy head. Whatever happened as a result of the consultation now beginning, it seemed that Hackney Downs was going to be in desperate trouble the following September because of decisions taken not by the staff and governors, but by the LEA.

The document produced for parents at their meeting on 12 December followed closely the document presented by Gus John to the Education Committee, but included some more information on the LEA's intentions if the school should close. The site would be retained for educational use, it said. Consideration would be given to helping the staff to find other appointments; otherwise voluntary severance deals, early retirement or redeployment might be considered. As far as pupils were concerned, parents would have the opportunity to consider future provision for their sons. But in order to ensure continuity and progression, discussions were already under way with Homerton House, where some additional building work might be required, and with the Hackney Community College.

Senior education officers met the school staff at the end of school on 12 December and went on to the meeting of parents attended by 60 people at 6.30 p.m. Neither group being consulted was at all happy at the end of the meetings. A part-time member of staff employed as media resources officer, who was also a lay preacher, wrote to John McCafferty, the leader of the council, immediately afterwards to express his dissatisfaction. It had become apparent, he said, that officers were either unable or unwilling to answer relevant questions. Their determination to discuss the situation for staff after closure, rather than the reasons for closure as the staff desired, seemed to imply 'a determination to process closure even though the public consultation is yet to begin'.

He concluded: 'Whilst I am not qualified to comment on the standard of education on offer at the school, I do know that the last 18 months has seen significant improvement in staff morale and pupil behaviour.'

Parental anger

Reaction to the meeting for parents was equally unhappy. Some parents expressed their determination not to allow their boys to transfer to Homerton House. Another asked Betty Hales to discover whether the consultation was actually legal as so little factual evidence seemed to have been presented to justify the closure. (Mrs Hales passed the query to the NUT's legal department.) And the new parent-governor, Stephanie Taylor, afterwards faxed an open letter to Gus John and the local Press seeking answers to questions which she claimed had failed to gain answers at the meeting.

She asked to know how many children the borough was currently responsible for educating in its secondary schools, how many were being sent out of the borough, what were the average costs of educating children in and out of the borough, how many parents from other boroughs chose Hackney schools, and what revenue that brought to Hackney if any.

> If, as I suspect, a substantial number of parents prefer to trust another borough with the education of their children, despite the inconvenience and cost of additional travel, then we should be looking to rectify the situation, not run from it. This means improving our schools to make them more attractive to these parents, not closing them. This is what Hackney parents want from you, this is what our children need and what residents of Hackney have a right to expect.

School staff were not allowed to attend the parents' consultation meetings, which were eventually held at the school after the LEA had initially refused permission. They were told afterwards by angry parents that they had been told by officials that the standard of teaching at the school was low and that their sons 'needed to be protected' from the teachers. They gained the impression that the school would definitely close and that they were only there to discuss what would happen to their sons afterwards.

The governors had a strong case for calling in the aid of the local community. In January a meeting to discuss the closure had drawn in 107 people, parents and staff, plus the local MP, Diane Abbott. This is in contrast to the fourteen parents who responded to the Ofsted questionnaire less than a year previously. Two councillors and the deputy director of education attended the meeting as observers.

Parents at the meeting said that they had come away from the official consultation meeting the previous month frustrated and angry. They felt that their questions had not been answered and their concerns not addressed. They still had not been advised what their options were if they did not wish their sons to be transferred to Homerton House, as many did not.

The questions from parents at the meeting indicated a high level of dissatisfaction with the council, and anxiety about the future of the school and their children. Persistent questioning had now elicited the information that almost 5,000 children left the borough to attend schools in neighbouring areas, while over 1,000 came in, at a cost to Hackney of some £9 million a year. Speakers expressed strong feelings. Governors said that they had been assured there were no plans to close the school when the short-listing for a head-teacher was postponed for the second time on the grounds that the proposal to take powers away from the governing body precluded an appointment. Two days later the closure plan emerged.

Most of the speakers accepted that harking back to the 'golden age' of Hackney Downs was not relevant to its present problems. But many parents reiterated their belief that the school was now improving, that it was dealing successfully with some very difficult boys whose lives would be disrupted if they were moved, and that it met the needs of the local community. There was a strong feeling expressed that consultation was a sham, that the decision to close the school had already been taken 'in back rooms' and that the needs of the boys were not being made a priority.

Diane Abbott MP made the point directly to Councillor Pat Corrigan, the chair of education, that parents and teachers should not be regarded as the enemy in this sort of dispute and it would be tragic if a Labour-controlled LEA clashed with them. It was clear, she said, that the educational case for closure had not been accepted by the parents and they were owed a proper explanation. 'If local Labour politicians were not in politics to empower people and give working-class boys a break, then what were they in politics for?'

A resolution opposing closure was carried unanimously. The councillors and the deputy director did not vote.

Struggling on

The term continued with Betty Hales feeling increasingly under siege and the staff doggedly continuing with their efforts to fulfil their Action Plan commitments. When school began in January,

Mrs Hales discovered that the LEA (now in control of such details) had inadvertently cancelled the school's oil contract so that there was no effective heating for some days. Planning continued on reduced staffing levels, should the school still be open the following September. The issue of the abolished London supplement and consequent pay freeze for some Hackney Downs staff festered on. Relationships with officials at the LEA deteriorated as the school attempted to gain appropriate help for some of its most difficult boys.

In early January the school's long-serving and highly regarded secretary was taken seriously ill and never returned to school. She was replaced in an acting capacity by Maureen Thurlow, who did a magnificent job of handling personnel and finance work as well as her own responsibilities. The school was expected by the LEA to continue indefinitely with one member of the office staff short, and it even proved impossible to replace a computer, used for school administration, stolen in a burglary the previous August.

The LEA did not seem to be willing to do anything to support the school which would cost money at this stage. As notes on the Action Plan steering group indicate, the school met its planning targets throughout this period. LEA targets were either delayed or 'on hold'. No work was done on the buildings and, even more ominously, Betty Hales was informed that the money from the 'Heart of Hackney' Single Regeneration Funding, earmarked for work at Hackney Downs in the LEA's Action Plan, would be diverted to Homerton House in 1994/5 in view of the school's uncertain future. Hackney Downs would get its share, she was told, in what was evidently regarded as the unlikely event of the school still being open the following year.

In view of the fact that the LEA Action Plan and its closure proposals were being drawn up at the same time the previous autumn, one is left asking what credence should have been given to the LEA's financial promises for that year when the DfE accepted the plan. It must have been clear to DfE officials that with a closure proposal on the table, that money would never be spent during that financial year. This was a point picked up by the governors, who were told by the DfE and Ofsted that they expected the school to be treated 'as normal' until a final decision was made on closure by the DfE.

In February the NUT, whose General Secretary, Doug McAvoy, had recently visited the school, became so concerned about the still deteriorating state of the buildings that a regional official was brought in to make an inspection. He reminded the LEA that the borough had a legal obligation to provide a safe working environment for its employees. His report commented on the general state of disrepair and highlighted hazardous floors in the science labs, water penetration of electrical fittings, dangerous surfaces at the top of flights of stairs, structural damage, and dangerous floors and electrical systems in the swimming pool building.

While the parents were continuing to lobby their local councillors in preparation for the crucial Education Committee meeting in March, the school was trying to draw in bigger guns. Betty Hales sent a dossier of documents about the school to David Blunkett, the Shadow Education Secretary at the House of Commons, pointing out that Diane Abbott was supporting the Hackney Downs campaign. She got no reply.

HMI's return 'Special Measures' visit

Betty Hales was greatly encouraged soon afterwards when HMI returned to the school in the middle of March to judge what progress the school had made since it had been placed under special measures after the original Ofsted inspection. Two inspectors spent two days at the school. They had a long discussion with Betty Hales, met all the heads of department and interviewed ten staff. They went to twenty lessons across the curriculum, attended an assembly and two registration periods, and were given a full range of documentation on how the school had set about implementing its Action Plan.

They gave an immediate verbal report to the acting headteacher and the chair of governors which left both feeling that real progress was being made. They commented on the reduction in the number of pupils gaining five A to C grades at GCSE the previous summer, and the improvement in the number gaining five A to Gs. They accepted that the sample was very small and that six pupils had narrowly missed Cs in one subject.

They found high standards in art, English and drama lessons, and acknowledged evidence of improved achievement. But overall, they concluded, achievement was still below average compared to national norms. The school did not find this surprising given the levels of need the school was now attempting to handle.

The inspectors found that lesson planning had improved considerably and teachers were seen to be working hard. The right policies, processes and procedures were now in place but the 'payback' in pupil performance was not yet evident. They expressed confidence that this would come. The senior management team was praised for having worked extremely hard and for having successfully raised staff morale in extremely difficult circumstance. They displayed good mutual support, HMI said, and there was a climate of openness which showed that the school was ready for further development and improvement.

The inspectors also found that there had been significant progress in improving pupil behaviour and that staff development was going well. There were still some disruptive pupils in classrooms but their activities were being regarded by other pupils with 'disdain'.

Apart from the lack of a substantive headteacher, staffing had become more stable, internal controls of the school's finances were sound and the governors were playing a more constructive part in the school's affairs. However, they noted that the LEA had not yet instituted its programme of maintenance and repair and was not addressing health and safety issues sufficiently.

Understandably the school was greatly encouraged by this report and hoped that it would have some influence on the Education Committee meeting now imminent. Unfortunately the written report was not received in time to be presented at that meeting and no attempt was made to report to the councillors the results of the inspection informally. Betty Hales gained the impression that any attempt on her part to ensure that councillors were in receipt of such information would be regarded by officials as acting against her conditions of service and might attract disciplinary action.

15

Changing Minds

The campaign to save Hackney Downs was having an effect on Hackney's volatile political scene. The easy option for the school's detractors has always been to dismiss its growing number of political friends as well as its teaching staff as 'wild Left-wingers', but this was by no means the case. Of course the school's supporters included members of Left-leaning groups, as is only to be expected in an inner-city borough with such appalling levels of deprivation. But the period when the school staff was dominated by the ultra-Left was long past.

The same was true of Hackney's Labour councillors. It would be more accurate to define the growing split in the ruling Labour Group which ran the council, and faced accusations of corruption and incompetence, as one between a fundamentally authoritarian group of 'new' Labour councillors, who had more or less successfully ousted the hard Left in the 1980s, and a more liberal and consultative group, who were more willing to listen to public opinion on issues like school closure.

By the time the Education Committee met to consider the closure proposal on 21 March, there was increasing unease among some members of the Labour Group. One of the councillor governors appointed to Hackney Downs when the LEA took away its delegated budget was Chris Gardiner, an education official in neighbouring Camden. Having got to know the school and its problems, he became increasingly convinced that the closure proposal was wrong, but found the council's Labour establishment unwilling to listen to his reservations. Other councillors had taken up the school's open invitation to visit and had come to the same conclusion. The Liberal Democrat opposition on the council were also opposed to the proposal.

There was a growing feeling that the whole plan was based on financial considerations, which is not surprising given the parlous state of Hackney's budget under the government's regime of cuts in inner London. Although the official line continued to be that the buildings would be retained for educational use, this would have been almost as expensive as fulfilling the LEA's Action Plan and repairing the buildings for Hackney Downs School. The belief that there was a secret plan to sell the site for redevelopment was widespread.

In school the acting head and staff felt themselves under increasing political pressure as the Education Committee meeting approached. Opposition to closure, now aimed specifically at councillors, had to be carefully channelled through the governors or parents because of the risk of disciplinary action if teachers were seen to be involved. Betty Hales gained the impression that she would be 'looked after' if she co-operated with closure, and would be unlikely to work again as a teacher if she did not. The teacher–governors felt similarly at risk. It was in this demoralizing atmosphere that HMI made their final visit, offering the verbal feedback which sent morale sky-high again and renewed the school's determination to fight on.

The only tangible – and the staff felt, pretty half-hearted – support which the school received from LEA advisers during the run-up to this crucial HMI visit is documented in the school visitors' book and SMT and departmental minutes. The school's link inspector arranged to visit the school and inspect lessons in February and March. No feedback was ever received after the February visit and the March appointment was cancelled without explanation. Gus John's later claims that the school was well supported in implementing its Action Plan was, the school felt, at the least, optimistic. Fortunately for the staff, morale was boosted at this time by Open University and London University tutors who visited the school's PGCE students and licensed teachers regularly and complimented staff on the school's progress. None of the teacher training institutions had suggested removing trainees from Hackney Downs.

The crucial vote

Like many political groups in local government, the Hackney
Labour Party ran a strict whipping system on controversial issues.
Councillor Chris Gardiner became convinced that this was not
appropriate, or possibly even legal, on an issue in which the committee was acting in a semi-judicial capacity. But in spite of
Gardiner's opposition, the Labour Group meeting before the Education Committee met decided in the early hours of the morning
to impose a whip for the Hackney Downs vote. Gardiner complained that the closure was not on the agenda for the group's
private meeting or recorded in the minutes. He was encouraged by
the fact that the vote was a close one, even though it was taken so
late that some elderly councillors known to support the school had
gone home. It was not until after the Education Committee meeting which took the closure decision that he received legal
confirmation that a whip should not have been imposed as it was
against Labour Party rules.

Councillor Gardiner was also deeply unhappy about the consultation process which, with its emphasis on only one option for
Hackney Downs, did not seem to him to have met the guidelines
laid down by the DfEE (formerly DfE) which suggested that a range
of options should be explored and objectors' views taken into
account before a final proposal was formulated.

The proposal which Gus John put to the Education Committee
on 21 March reiterated much of the evidence in favour of closure
which he had outlined in his consultation document four months
earlier. On educational issues he still relied heavily on the early
inspection reports, but he gave a more balanced summary of the
1994 Ofsted report which the school felt so strongly gave grounds
for optimism about pulling the school round.

On the issue of viable numbers he now committed himself to the
figure of 500 pupils as a 'break-even' point for viability under LMS
formula funding. But he saw no prospect of the school, with a current roll of 291, reaching that figure over a reasonable time-scale.
He still failed to mention that the low pupil numbers were a direct
result of the loss of Year 7 and the failure to refer any new pupils to
Hackney Downs as families had moved into the area over the pre-

vious twelve months. In spite of the fact that most families remained remarkably loyal to the school and only about twenty pupils were withdrawn as a result of the closure proposal, the paper reiterated the view that the school had become 'unpopular' with parents and potential parents.

In this paper Gus John also again revised downwards his projections of the need for secondary boys' places in the borough up to the year 2000. Demand could be met, he said, by increasing the intake at Homerton House. His preferred option in the event of closure would be to transfer all the Hackney Downs boys to Homerton House, apart possibly from Year 10, about which Homerton had some reservations. It might therefore be necessary to keep them at Hackney Downs until they had finished their GCSE courses in the summer of 1996. Staff would be offered voluntary redundancy/ early retirement if they qualified. If not, they would be redeployed, although under LMS other jobs in the borough could not be guaranteed.

It is an interesting exercise to look at how radically Hackney LEA trimmed back its predictions of demand for boys' school places in the borough between the time of its secondary review in 1993 and the closure procedures of 1994/5 (see table). The obvious inference has to be that official pessimism about recruitment had been affected by the events of the intervening year when neither the boys who had left Hackney Downs the previous spring nor the 'lost' Year 7 intake had gone in any numbers to the obvious alternative, Homerton House. Indeed, the majority seemed to have left the borough. The LEA's predictions by March 1995 had become deeply pessimistic and implied a further drain of resources from Hackney to its neighbouring boroughs.

How Hackney's boys disappeared:

Projections of boys' places needed in Hackney secondary schools

	1995	1996	1997	1998	1999	2000
1993	690	685	723	789	792	789
1994 (Nov)	637	667	674	701	768	773
1995 (Mch)	602	601	616	668	666	662

On revenue funding, the director's report argued that substantial resources had already been spent on Hackney Downs since the borough took over the school. Further resources to fund the Action Plan and support the school until it reached viability would have to be redirected from other schools. Conversely, other schools would gain if Hackney Downs' funding was redirected and the LMS 'cushioning' ceased to be needed.

And he dismissed the argument that Hackney Downs was now an improving school. 'The pace and trajectory of the improvement process across the total curriculum and within the school's various policies and management practices continue to cause me concern.' This was the first time Betty Hales' management had been criticized by anyone and came only months after Gus John had written thanking her for her efforts and her success in improving the educational environment of the school.

The school site could be retained for educational use, Gus John suggested, which to some extent explains the relatively modest direct savings which would accrue to the borough if Hackney Downs closed. Apart from staff costs, these were estimated at £149,000 for 1995/6, £78,000 for 1996/7 (taking account of maintenance and security at the site and additional pension costs), and £50,000 in 1997/8.

Councillors were given another document by the school to assist them in their deliberations. This made available some of the conclusions of the latest HMI visit a week earlier, which the LEA had not seen fit to pass on to them itself. It also highlighted the long-standing failure of the LEA to address the school's dilapidated state, which had been an issue between headteachers, and first the ILEA and then Hackney Council for ten years.

Buoyed up by the latest comments from HMI, the school argued that the educational case for closure could not stand in the light of the progress being made: a more stable staff with far less sickness; strong and effective management which had raised morale; improvements in the quality of teaching and learning; much better behaviour by pupils; better parental support and involvement. The school flatly rejected Gus John's suggestion of concern over the quality and pace of the improvement process. One of the inspectors who had been in the school on both visits, in July 1994 and

March 1995, had specifically said that he had been impressed with the pace of improvement and described the school as having a completely different climate.

The school also rejected Gus John's concern about 'educational opportunities and entitlements', pointing out that Ofsted had praised the curriculum provision as 'balanced and comprehensive by design' and that there had never been any criticism of the provision of the full National Curriculum.

On the issue of the school's viability, the school pointed out that if it had not been for the 'hate' campaign surrounding the Black Staff and Parents' Group and the LEA's determination not to allow a Year 7 group the previous September, the school would still have a roll well over 400 and probably approaching the vital 500 level.

The school maintains that if it were given encouragement and support and a positive infrastructure it would be able to recover its roll and become financially viable within two years. The LEA's arguments about parental choice are null and void since parents have had no opportunity to choose Hackney Downs School either for Year 7 or as mid-term entrants.

As the roll had been rising until the unprecedented events of 1993/4, there was no evidence to support the LEA's view that it was in an unstoppable spiral of decline.

But the paper raised a real worry that as Hackney Downs was not being recommended to primary school parents as an option for the next September, the roll was likely to be depressed still further. There was no sign that the school was being 'treated as any other school' during the consultation process: quite the reverse. The chances of recruiting an adequate Year 7 should the school *not* close were looking increasingly remote.

Closure confirmed

On 21 March 1995, the Education Committee voted to recommend the closure of Hackney Downs by twelve votes to one. Several councillors, believing the vote to be whipped, left the meeting to avoid voting for closure. It also decided to increase the admission number at Homerton House from 150 to 210. Chris Gardiner is still of the opinion that if there had been a free vote at the meeting, the closure proposal would have been defeated. As it turned out, the dispute over the use of the whip exacerbated the growing split in the Labour Group and precipitated a major Party crisis within weeks.

Bitterly disappointed by the vote, Tony Burgess, the chair of governors, who had presented the school's case with passion and commitment in the council chamber, spoke for most of the campaigners when he told the local Press that he believed the school had been the victim of a determined campaign by the council which included refusing to allow the school to recruit and advising primary heads not to recommend families to opt for the school. Gus John was quoted as denying that there was any malice in the closure decision and as saying that he did not think that anything new had been learned from the latest comments from HMI.

Even at this stage, if those involved had been more direct and had explained sound reasoning as to why the school should be closed, and had treated the senior managers and other staff with respect, Betty Hales believes that the school would have listened and probably co-operated with a dignified closure, if they had been persuaded that this was in the boys' best interests. Instead those who were determined that the school should close appeared to be looking for scapegoats, and the staff and their supporters were determined not to lie down quietly and allow that to happen.

Betty Hales learned two days after the Education Committee meeting just how difficult it was now likely to be for the school to increase its roll to save itself. A letter from a parent described how he had been told by the LEA in February that the only school with vacancies was Homerton House. When he asked whether he could appeal, he was given a list of schools *outside* the borough. Only by being persistent and telephoning Hackney Downs was he able to discover that it had vacancies. He wished to complain, he said, on behalf of himself and other parents who might not have the time, or be able to speak English well, but who were concerned about their sons' education if the school were to close. They were disappointed and angry at the threat to the school and if it closed would not be willing to send their sons to Homerton House. Mindful of the law on open enrolment, Betty Hales offered the boy a place.

Aware of that sort of support in the community, the campaigners planned their next move, which was to make their objections known to the Secretary of State for Education, who would take the final decision. Hackney NUT decided to call for strike action on the issue and eventually held a half-day unofficial strike on 30 March, which was the only industrial action of any kind during the closure dispute. It was quite clear that the battle was not yet over.

The LEA's determination to stifle dissent, which had been covert before the Education Committee decision, became overt after it. Danny Silverstone wrote to Betty Hales spelling out his expectations: requests for use of the school premises had to be referred to him for clearance; the media were not to be given access to the school; media queries were to be referred to the council's press office and 'staff and students are not to be given access to the media on the school site or indeed on Hackney Downs, the open space opposite the school between 8 a.m. and 5 p.m.'

Mr Silverstone went on:

It has come to my attention that Hackney Downs students are being encouraged to join and support anti-closure campaigns being organised within the school. This has to cease immediately. I will take a particularly strong view of any 'events' during school time which involved the attendance and participation of students.

Last Tuesday's committee decision constitutes a formal LEA decision. It is now the policy of Hackney LEA which both of us serve. Accordingly I seek your formal assurance that you have taken the necessary steps to ensure that *none* of the school's facilities are being utilised for *any* anti-closure group – staff, student, parents – associated with the school.

By the same token, I need your formal assurance that no school assemblies nor *any* internal school information materials are used to communicate anti-closure information.

Please confirm your understanding of each of these points and the actions you have taken to operationalise them by return. I would suggest that our diarised meeting next week *should* take place so that we can review these matters. I would also suggest that we discuss best options for decanting and parental contact and an appropriate time for Gus John and myself to attend a whole school assembly to update the student body on the action following the closure decision.

It was quite clear from this that the LEA officers intended to proceed from this point on the assumption that the closure would go ahead at the end of the summer term, although it still had to be ratified by the full council and approved by the DfE after a statutory period of two months for objections.

It was also becoming apparent that the power struggle within the Hackney Labour Party might well result in a shift in the balance of power at the Party's AGM in April. If that happened there was no guarantee that the full council would ratify their Education Committee's closure decision. In the meantime, the school was only too aware that with control over finance and staffing now firmly in the hands of the LEA, by the time a reprieve had been organized politically the school could well be on its knees and virtually past saving.

It was also clear that further campaigning was going to be made as difficult as possible. But while Betty Hales was scrupulous in complying with Danny Silverstone's demands, to protect herself and her staff, others were not so susceptible to pressure.

The school governors met on 28 March. In view of the media interest, they agreed to allow a television film crew into the meeting. Betty Hales prudently withdrew from this discussion. The governors then passed a resolution reiterating their belief that the best interests of the boys would be served by the school's remaining open. And after hearing Betty Hales' report on the implementation of the Action Plan and the positive feedback from the most recent HMI visit, the governors thanked the head and the senior management team for their hard work and dedication and registering their appreciation and delight that they had been responsible for the improvements noted by the inspectors.

On 4 April Gus John and Danny Silverstone came to school to address an assembly about the closure and their plans to move the boys *en bloc* to Homerton House where they would 'receive better teaching'. The school, the boys were told, had to close for 'educational reasons' and it would be wrong for anyone to 'rubbish'

Homerton House which had recently been praised by Ofsted inspectors for its improvements.

All it took to quell the murmurs of dissent when they were told about the proposed move was for Betty Hales to raise a finger to her lips. The boys listened for the rest of the time in total silence, even when the headteacher was addressed as Betty rather than Mrs Hales by Danny Silverstone. They showed a level of self-restraint which, Betty Hales believes, would have been impossible even a year earlier and offered a far more powerful protest than any amount of noise could have made. By this time the pupils' commitment to Hackney Downs appeared total.

16

To the Rescue

Anti-closure campaigns

The fight to save Hackney Downs now broke into three separate, though still closely interlinked, campaigns. There was the school's internal fight for survival; the parents' and governors' efforts to persuade the DfEE to over-rule the LEA through the statutory process or, failing that, by having the decision scrutinized by means of a judicial review; and the increasingly fierce internal struggle within the ruling Hackney Labour Party to have the decision overturned through the local democratic process.

At the same time, Betty Hales and her staff attempted to provide as normal an education as possible for the boys still in the school. Special GCSE study classes were run during the Easter holidays, work experience and parents' evenings continued as normal, parents' newsletters went out as full of optimism as it was possible to be in the circumstances. GCSE and school examinations took place as normal that term, as did the Activities Week in July and regular meetings for parents and the school council. The only unusual feature on the school calendar was the Final Assembly billed for 21 July. Ironically the one bit of building work completed that term involved the construction of the *wrong* type of safety barrier in the swimming pool building.

Regular meetings also continued on the implementation of the school's Action Plan. School progress was routinely on target, while LEA objectives were now routinely 'on hold'. Hackney Downs had to watch as the government funds won for literacy work were diverted to Homerton House.

Betty Hales even found the time and the energy to go through her headteacher's appraisal process, the first stage in the delayed implementation of appraisal in the borough. A very positive appraisal report concluded that during her very difficult time in post, Betty Hales' leadership had been open, approachable and supportive of staff and had maintained staff morale in spite of the school's problems. She had encouraged staff to feel that they ran the school and that they must address problems rather than expect management to do so on their behalf. With the boys she was firm but approachable and non- confrontational. She had improved behaviour and the school's curriculum offer. She was considered by staff and pupils to be a good headteacher. She had achieved a great deal in a short time and improved her management skills. Her appraiser felt that she could look forward to a promising career in education management.

In April both the chair of governors and the LEA reported in writing to the DfEE on the implementation of the Action Plan. It is instructive to compare the two documents. Tony Burgess endorses the comments made by the HMI who visited in March and accepts that the school still has some way to go in improving standards. While pointing out the particular difficulties of the school – the most recent special needs audit identified 90 boys out of 300 (30 per cent) as having difficulties sufficiently serious to enter the first stage of the SEN statementing process – Dr Burgess said that the professional effort was now in place and that the gap between staff effort and return in terms of pupil achievement was closing. Monitoring structures were in place and staff collaboration to meet needs was being promoted.

As far as Ofsted's points for action were concerned, he reported significant progress in improving pupil behaviour with better sanctions and monitoring, sharing of good practice, improved teaching methods, and a sharp fall (from 103 to 38) in the number of exclusions. Apart from the lack of a substantive head, staffing had been stabilized.

Dr Burgess went on to point out that other matters were being hampered by inaction by the LEA. The borough had taken no action on a borough policy on mid-term admissions or on repair and refurbishment, and there was still insufficient input from the LEA to enable all pupils who needed Statements of Special Educational Need to be processed.

Dr Burgess complained about the way the school had been treated during the period since closure was first mooted. The LEA had not met its commitment to treat Hackney Downs as a fully functioning school prior to and during the consultation period. He believed that it had effectively destabilized and run down the school at a time when its future was not yet decided, and 'in neither the spirit nor the letter' had it fulfilled its commitment to an improved quality of education.

In his response to the DfEE, which followed four weeks later, Gus John claimed that the improvement in discipline and behaviour was largely due to the high level of support the LEA had offered in this area. Work on repair and refurbishment had only been promised for 1995/6 and capital approval from the DfE had not been obtained for the science block, but design work had begun which 'will take some time to complete'.

Gus John rejected the school's estimates of the proportion of its pupils with special needs. The audit, he said, so far indicated that between 10 per cent and 20 per cent of the pupils required some form of learning support, 'a profile which would be found in many other schools in Hackney'. And as far as health and safety matters were concerned, he put the onus on the school to rectify most of those out of its own budget.

Gus John went on to say that he regretted that the HMI's recent report had concentrated on matters where the school felt that its needs were not being met rather than acknowledging the support which had been provided by the LEA in terms of INSET and advisory work. He also noted that 60 boys had left the school during the autumn and spring terms and that more parents seemed to wish to move their boys elsewhere. 'This pattern has almost certainly skewed the remaining school population more towards those with learning difficulties and language needs.' He argued that the falling roll had pushed the pupil–teacher ratio to 10:1. 'If indeed the school feels it cannot meet children's needs with a PTR of 10:1 this does not bode well for the future.'

The argument upon which the DfEE had to adjudicate had come down to whether Hackney Downs was uniquely disadvantaged, deserved support and was now improving, or whether, as Gus John argued, it was no worse off than other Hackney schools and had only itself to blame for its problems.

Internal stress

Internally, pressure from LEA officers to wind up the school as quickly as possible intensified and there was little comfort during the summer term either for the staff who would lose their jobs or the boys who were expected to move school. The aim still appeared to have Hackney Downs closed down by the end of July, which meant that none of the normal planning for the start of the September term was done. It was becoming clear that a last-minute reprieve by the council at their June meeting would leave the school very little time to organize itself properly for a fresh start in September. The very tight timetable for closure which the LEA was attempting to implement left the school very close to being damned if it closed and damned if it stayed open.

Staff were understandably in a state of extreme uncertainty and anxiety about their own futures at this time. Under LMS there was no guarantee that they could be redeployed by the LEA to other schools in Hackney, and certainly no likelihood that many, if any, of them could 'follow the pupils' to Homerton House. All but one of the staff were members of the NUT, which went to considerable lengths to send senior officials to negotiate with the LEA about the consequences of the closure decision, but with no very satisfactory results.

The LEA told the NUT that it now had a clear mandate to move the closure on as quickly as possible and that the redundancy notice period for staff had effectively started on 28 March as soon as the Education Committee had taken its decision, an interpretation which the NUT officials disputed. The NUT complained that its officials had found difficulty in making contact with Homerton House, which was currently advertising no fewer than nine vacancies, in order to discuss possible job opportunities there for the Hackney Downs staff.

By the end of April all Hackney heads had been informed of the likely redundancies at Hackney Downs and been urged to do their utmost to help with the redeployment, and staff had been told of their entitlement to voluntary severance and early retirement and to pay until the end of the year if awaiting redeployment. Job advertisements from other schools began to trickle in. By the middle of

May staff had been given their redundancy notices and informed of the terms which would be available if they took voluntary severance. Instability had now become endemic.

The LEA was also pushing hard for parents to take their decisions about their sons' transfer to other schools on the assumption that Hackney Downs would close. The LEA's clear preference was for a mass transfer to Homerton House, including the Year 11 boys coming up to GCSE who had originally been promised classes on the Hackney Downs site. Danny Silverstone wrote directly to parents on 25 May (the school received its copy a day later). He went to some lengths to 'sell' Homerton House to parents while also pointing out their legal right to choose another school. However, there were, he told them, currently no vacancies for boys in any of the other Hackney schools.

Although by this time it was clear that political changes might lead the council to reverse its closure decision, parents were merely informed that the Education Committee would meet in June to 'reaffirm' its previous decision, a choice of words which seemed to supporters of the school to display a misunderstanding of the democratic process. Parents were meanwhile invited to 'choose' Homerton House, or apply to another school, by 23 June.

Tony Burgess was so incensed by this letter that a day later he wrote to parents to inform them that the 8 June meeting of the Education Committee might well reverse the closure decision and that the Save the School campaign was still very much in business. Parent-governor Stephanie Taylor, who worked indefatigably to save the school, had by this time confirmed with the DfEE that there was no legal impediment to prevent the borough from changing its mind about Hackney Downs. The governors and parents were still convinced that there was all to play for.

Financial problems

Although the major responsibility for running the budget now rested with the LEA, the head and governors were also becoming increasingly concerned by budget monitoring forms which indicated that the school was falling further and further into deficit. Betty Hales expected that there would be some overspending, given the unusual circumstances the school found itself in. However, schools were normally funded for a year on January pupil numbers, so the staff in post that April should not have pushed the budget into deficit because their salaries had been built into the calculations.

The financial future, she knew, was infinitely more problematic. As all the staff had now been told to expect redundancy at the end of the summer term, no effort was made by the LEA to work out which staff would be needed if the school was still open in September. A meeting scheduled for 1 March by the LEA to discuss 'downsizing' the school in the event of its remaining open in September had been cancelled and never reconvened. Equally, no arrangements were being made for an intake of Year 7 boys, so if the school were to survive in September it was clear that the pupil-related funding would fall dramatically for the second year in succession.

Mrs Hales was also puzzled to discover that the LEA's current budget figures seemed to include no allowance for the Year 7 protection which the school had been promised in return for missing the previous year's intake. The governors also sought explanations for the apparently alarming budget figures coming from the LEA, but without success.

In spite of this complete lack of interest at LEA level, the senior management team did its best to work out a sensible shadow staffing structure, curriculum offer and timetable for the school in case it should be needed in September. This was the working structure which was eventually adopted by the Education Association when it took over the school.

The chair of governors, Tony Burgess, recalls finding the budget situation incomprehensible once Hackney took over control of the school's finances, but did not find this particularly surprising given Hackney's council's reputation.

The information we were getting was extremely limited but we were certainly never given to understand that we were disastrously over budget or that there was anything we should be doing about the school's finances that we were not doing. We were never treated as if we had, or should have, any purchase on the school's financial problems after Hackney took over the budget. Our only financial responsibility was for ordering materials for very small amounts of money.

In spite of local support, the school staff felt quite isolated at this period while the battle over its future went on elsewhere. By this time Gus John had effectively retired because of ill health, and his deputy Danny Silverstone preferred to communicate by telephone.

Statutory objections

Statutory objections to the closure went to the DfEE from the Hackney Downs governors and from the senior management team, from dozens of parents and from the teacher unions. The documents rehearsed many of the arguments which had already been made during the local consultation period.

Tony Burgess passed on to the DfEE what he called 'concrete evidence' of improvements in the school:

- the changed atmosphere noted by HMI;
- effective whole-school assemblies passing on messages about pupil responsibility;
- the striking reduction in the number of exclusions;
- the well-established school council;
- the revision of old or production of new departmental development plans and systems of monitoring;
- improved parental involvement;
- the introduction of staff appraisal;
- working parties on parental involvement, language, and discipline;
- the completion of the latest SEN audit.

The last of these is important in that it addresses the increasingly common argument coming from those in favour of closure to the effect that Hackney Downs' pupil roll had no greater needs than other schools in the borough. The previous year the SEN audit, endorsed by the school's educational psychologist, had indicated that about 50 per cent of the boys in every class had either learning, language or behavioural problems. The audit completed in the summer of 1995 and accepted by the LEA showed that the situation had actually deteriorated sharply as a result of the turbulent year 1994/5. In almost every class in the school, between two-thirds and three-quarters of the boys had a problem; many had multiple problems.

In addition the school also had on roll at this time 22 boys who had joined Hackney Downs after experiencing difficulties in other schools. Fourteen had transferred from other Hackney schools, the rest from schools in neighbouring boroughs. Most boys who came to the school in these circumstances completed their education there, since the school was unusually successful in modifying their behaviour enough to prevent the need for further exclusion.

There are inherent difficulties over definitions of problems and their severity in this sort of audit, but the LEA's contention that Hackney Downs' students were no more difficult than those at any other school in the borough appears optimistic in the extreme. The 'market' in school places had worked effectively to ensure that many of the boys at Hackney Downs were those who either could not find a place anywhere else or had been ejected – officially or unofficially – by other schools. By the summer of 1995 Hackney Downs had moved from being essentially a secondary modern school almost to the point of becoming a special school. There were very few children without definable problems left there.

In spite of all this the senior management team's submission to the DfEE produced evidence that the school was holding on to boys who had been excluded from other schools and helping them to achieve modest success at GCSE. The team also produced roll projections which suggested that, given positive support from the LEA and enhanced provision for science, as promised in the LEA's Action Plan, the school could be made viable with a roll of 455 by July 1997, much sooner than the LEA was suggesting. They also claimed that the LEA costings for supporting the school if it remained open were inflated. Normal support, they claimed, would not be higher than for any other school. Support for the needs of individual children would be higher, but only because children with special educational needs and language needs were concentrated within one school disproportionately. Those children would still need exactly the same support if they were moved elsewhere.

The school's self-defence did not go uncontested. Gus John wrote to the DfEE on 18 May to answer some of Dr Burgess' points in his last submission. He told the DfEE that building work at the school was never intended to start in the 1994/5 financial year, that action would be taken during the summer half-term holiday and over the long summer break, and that window and roof repairs remained the school's responsibility. He denied that the LEA had in any way used its budget powers to impede the school's development or that the restriction of the head's spending powers had been a matter of contention. He justified the strict control over the school's contact with parents: 'Once the LEA had decided to seek closure, it was clearly neither tenable nor desirable for the school's resources to be used to promulgate anti-closure campaigning.' He also justified the LEA's reluctance to allow the school to recruit more pupils at a time when it might close as not being in the best interests of incoming pupils. He justified his stance in preventing the appointment of a permanent headteacher and strongly denied that the school had lacked advisory and educational psychologist support during the previous difficult months.

There is no way of adjudicating between the LEA officers' view of how much help they had given the school between October, when the LEA proposed closure, and June when the matter would be passed to the DfEE for a final decision. Gus John clearly believed that he had done all he could to help Hackney Downs boys over a period of five years and was continuing to do his best for them. The school remained convinced the LEA had always been stronger on pressure than support, that they had evidence that very little help had been forthcoming once closure had been proposed, and that the Director of Education had effectively washed his hands of them some time during the summer of 1994.

The legal situation had by now been clarified by the DfEE, which accepted that the LEA was within its rights to change its mind on closure. The DfEE also confirmed to Tony Burgess that they would expect a school to move out of 'special measures' some two years after its first inspection given, as in this case, that the school was showing signs of improvement on the inspectors' first return visit. This is the sort of time-scale Ofsted consistently publicizes in its documentation on failing schools.

The battle for the Labour Party

Parents and Labour Party members were already discussing the possibility of a judicial review of everything which had happened so far, but these moves were being kept on hold until the June meeting of the Education Committee, at which it was hoped the closure decision would be reversed.

But the real battle now was for the hearts and minds of Labour councillors following the dramatic change within the Labour Group which had taken place in May. This had led to changes in all the committee chairmanships and a real possibility that the council might be persuaded to keep Hackney Downs open. It was a battle the school appeared to be winning. Ironically one of the most active defenders of the school was now Councillor Chris Gardiner, who had been one of the five LEA nominees added to the board of governors when the LMS budget was removed. Far from supporting the official line, he quickly concluded that the school was improving, despite what he believed to be determined efforts by its 'enemies' to ensure that it didn't. He was also convinced that the Labour whip had been wrongly imposed by Labour's 'old guard' at the original meeting which voted for closure, and that the decision should now be reversed. It soon became clear that the new chair of education, Councillor David Phillips, representing the newly dominant group of councillors, was becoming sympathetic to this point of view and that other councillors were convinced of the school's case. Further support came from the annual borough conference of the Labour Party which passed a resolution calling for the closure decision to be reversed and for the LEA to continue to support the school's recovery.

Other friends of the school were equally persuasive in arguing that the school deserved one last chance, and took their views to the highest possible level. Rob Philipson-Stow, director of operations and administration at Guinness Mahon Holdings PLC in the City of London, a firm which had a long-standing relationship with the school, had become the school's business governor. He was a firm supporter of Betty Hales' administration and expressed some outrage at the way the original decision had been 'railroaded' through the council.

On the ground the battle was being won, but messily and in the teeth of opposition from the LEA's officers. When Betty Hales and Tony Burgess met Danny Silverstone on 22 May – a meeting held because the day-to-day management of the school was becoming increasingly problematic given the number of issues which could not be resolved – they gained the clear impression that officials did not believe that the 8 June meeting of the council would prove decisive. They were also shocked by the news that while Homerton House would take Hackney Downs' pupils the following term, it was unlikely they would take on any of the redundant staff. It was not explained why such a blanket ban might be imposed.

The reason for continuing uncertainty at council level soon became clear. Before the Education Committee finally met on 8 June, officers warned councillors that they might be liable to a surcharge if they changed their minds at this stage and incurred additional expenditure. This produced a flurry of furious exchanges between the school's supporters and the authority. Stephanie Taylor extracted an assurance from the DfEE that there was nothing in the Local Management of Schools legislation which could lead to this conclusion. Any legal issues, the DfEE said, would stem from the Local Government Acts, about which the DfEE could not comment, and that in any case they would have to be tested in court.

The National Union of Teachers was more blunt. The General Secretary, Doug McAvoy, who had been consulted by the Hackney Association, wrote to all councillors on the Education Committee on the day of the meeting. He emphasized the view of the DfEE – though not evidently of Hackney's officers – that the council was fully within its rights to withdraw the closure proposal and was not bound by previous decisions. New evidence would not be required, but in any case existed in the form of the last HMI report, the submissions of objectors and the school's own positive plan for action. The right of the councillors to keep the school open, Mr McAvoy said, should not be undermined by the impact of financial projections made on the assumption that it would close – a decision which could only be made by the Secretary of State in any case.

With conflicting advice about their personal liability, the councillors on the Education Committee decided not to vote on the substantive issue of closure at all. However, they refused to 'reaffirm' the closure proposal, and also refused to endorse Gus John's observations to the DfEE on the objections to the closure proposal.

The full council was due to meet at the end of June, leaving a gap of three weeks before any other vote could be taken. This was unfortunate because the vote of 8 June was immediately interpreted in diametrically opposing ways. The school and the NUT regarded it as a reprieve and demanded that the school should now be regarded as back in business for the following school year.

LEA officers chose to act as if nothing significant had happened. It seemed to the school that LEA officers and the majority of democratically elected councillors were following different agendas as far as Hackney Downs School was concerned. The local NUT secretary wrote to the chair of education, Councillor David Phillips, on 11 June complaining with some outrage that parents were still being pressed to make arrangements to transfer their sons to other schools and that the Director of Education had submitted his comments on the statutory objections to the DfEE regardless of the fact that the committee to which he was responsible had failed to endorse them. 'Given that Members were given the specific opportunity to approve this course of action and refused it, we ask that you as chair of education write to the DfEE making this rejection clear.'

The NUT asked Councillor Phillips to ensure that councillors were provided with additional information before the full council meeting. 'Quite simply, we doubt that the information presently afforded to parents/carers is adequate or accurate to make proper decisions.' The school was threatened with closure and

> such a threat is not only to the present students and parents/carers at Hackney Downs – and to an admirable acting headteacher and her staff who have 'recovered' the school – but also to the integrity of decision-making of both the Secretary of State for education and Hackney Council in this and future instances.
>
> The Hackney Teachers Association accordingly expresses the gravest reservations about the conduct and competence of senior officers throughout this process and asks them to reconsider their position, while asking you, as the new chair of education, to do your best to distance yourself from this unhappy history and seek to rectify it.

In spite of the reservations of the Education Committee, Gus John wrote to Hackney Downs parents on 14 June telling them that as the Education Committee had not voted to reverse or amend the previous decision, it still stood. 'Meanwhile the closure proposal and the LEA's comments on the objections to closure are still being considered by the Secretary of State.'

The meeting of Hackney Council

In the short time between the Education Committee meeting and the meeting of the full council, yet another briefing document was prepared, this time on the future organization of secondary education in the borough. This proposed that the borough should re-submit a plan for another co-educational school in the south of the borough, but that because the DfEE was known to feel that Hackney Downs Boys School did not have 'the ethos or appeal' which would make for the successful integration of girls, this should be achieved by closing it and opening a new school on a refurbished campus.

When the full council finally met on 28 June at a highly charged meeting following another intense pro-school campaign, it voted by 31 votes to 23 to withdraw its proposals to close Hackney Downs School. The new Labour administration and the Liberal Democrats voted in favour, 'old Labour' against. The rationale presented in Councillor Chris Gardiner's resolution to rescind the closure was based on the educational progress made since the Ofsted inspection and report, and the fact that plans to support the school financially while it built up its pupil numbers were allowable under the LEA's existing scheme for financial delegation.

The school and its supporters were understandably delighted by the reprieve. They were immediately inundated with congratulations from all over Hackney and much further afield. A former South African Section 11 teacher at the school, who had taken a special assembly for the boys on the day Nelson Mandela became president of his country, wrote jubilantly from North London: 'The next battle is to get the council to refurbish the school without delay and appoint the tried and tested headteacher who has weathered the storms. You can guess who that is!'

Doug McAvoy, the General Secretary of the NUT, wrote to pass on his congratulations and express his delight that the school was to remain open. The Master of the Grocers' Company sent congratulations, as did the Revd Bill Dowling, a very old boy of the school, whose support had raised the spirits of the staff throughout the campaign. A Hackney Conservative councillor and long-serving governor sent a warm letter of congratulations and support, saying that despite the fact that he had been unable to vote to keep the school open in council, he was aware of the good professional work which had been going on.

But the LEA's officers were evidently much less enthusiastic at having their plans overturned. Gus John, who had not contacted the school personally for months, wrote to Betty Hales the very next day, 29 June, in terms which appeared to call the council's decision into doubt. He drew attention to his recommendation to the council that the LEA should resubmit proposals to the DfEE for a co-educational school on the Hackney Downs site.

> As is their right, members rejected that advice and decided to withdraw the proposals to close Hackney Downs School. This decision will be communicated to the Secretary of State for Education by the Council in due course. It would then be for the Secretary of State to determine whether this is the end of the matter or what action she would take in respect of the Council's new position on the future of the school. Meanwhile, as far as the Council is concerned, Hackney Downs School continues in its present form. I will write to you again if the response from the Secretary of State warrants it.

It soon became clear that nobody at the LEA offices intended to move quickly to help the school to continue in its present form. As it happened, the school staff were spending the weekend of 30 June to 2 July at an in-service training weekend at a hotel. They used the opportunity to begin to plan for the new term which they had not expected to see. The chair of education and the chair of governors also telephoned Betty Hales to discuss future plans.

The Director of Education went on sick leave soon after the 28 June council meeting and was rarely seen in public again until his early retirement was confirmed exactly a year after the final closure of Hackney Downs. No LEA officer chose to write to parents about the school's future. It was left to Tony Burgess and Stephanie Taylor, a parent-governor who had campaigned tirelessly for the school, to pass on to parents the news that the school had been reprieved, that it was recruiting boys for September, and that there was to be a Channel 4 documentary about the fight to save the school appearing soon. The National Union of Teachers' local association also took it upon itself to circulate secondary and primary heads urging them to support the school and to draw the availability of places to parents' attention.

When Betty Hales, Jeff Davies and Tony Burgess went to the school's regular management meeting with Danny Silverstone on 4 July they found that the reason for the LEA's inactivity since the council meeting was the fact that they were waiting for a 'decision' from the DfEE. Tony Burgess had himself received a letter from the DfEE on the day of the management meeting confirming that they had been informed of the council's decision to withdraw the closure proposals. 'In view of the above, all consideration of the proposals by the Secretary of State has been terminated.' After the meeting, Betty Hales faxed a copy of this letter to the Hackney Chief Executive in an effort to ensure that advertisements in the local Press for the new intake of boys could go ahead at the earliest possible moment. Despite ensuring that Hackney officers were aware of this decision, parents were still being informed by Hackney admissions office that no places for boys were available in the borough and being given details of out-of-borough schools when they requested places for September.

The school representatives were unhappy to learn at that same meeting with the deputy director that the capital programme, upon which the school's refurbishment hopes depended, could only be altered by a decision of council members. In fact the 1995/6 budget had already been frozen. Apart from that, they were assured that work would start on the school's forward budget and on a staffing plan for the next school year, that health and safety matters would be attended to and that the appointment of a permanent head-teacher would follow as soon as possible. They were encouraged by discussion of a closer relationship with Homerton House School, and the possibility that both could grow together now that the future had become more settled.

Even after the arrival of the letter from the DfEE, officers seemed to be dragging their feet over the urgent problem of recruitment for the new school year. Vacancy lists were still going out to families moving into the area or whose appeals for places at other schools had failed without places at Hackney Downs being mentioned. Betty Hales complained in writing to the chair of governors, Tony Burgess, that a meeting with the relevant official was being delayed.

Betty Hales was disturbed to learn that several councillors who had supported the school had received an anonymous and offensive letter about her, allegedly from a parent at the school. The typography and layout were similar to that used in other anonymous communications at the time she had been short-listed for the headship and to that used in letters and leaflets at the time of the disruption caused by the Black Staff and Parents' Group.

Fortunately for the morale of the school, evidence continued to arrive that some things were going well. The moderator's report on art and design course-work arrived at the beginning of July offering enthusiastic praise. 'The exhibition was a pleasure to moderate and the product of creative teamwork', she said, also commenting favourably upon the way the work reflected the cultural diversity of the school. A day later a young Australian teacher who had been working for qualified teacher status in the UK received a glowing report from his assessor. Parents and governors were now getting posters advertising the school put up in local shops, and requests for places in September were beginning to come in.

For his part, Tony Burgess was so outraged at the way Betty Hales was being treated by fellow-professionals that he complained formally to the Borough Council about it. It was becoming clear that relationships between the school and LEA officers, though not elected members, and with some of the other secondary schools, had been seriously damaged by the successful fight to save the school. Hackney's volatile politics were taking their toll.

Within a few days, arrangements were beginning to be made, however reluctantly, to get Hackney Downs up and running again. Danny Silverstone and Councillor David Phillips visited the school. Arrangements were made to discuss the school's budget for the new school year. GCSE options, which had been put on hold, were revived for Year 9 pupils. A health and safety inspection was carried out. Advertisements for pupils appeared in the local Press. Arrangements went ahead for the Activities Week at the end of term and for a trip to Alton Towers.

Government intervention

Continuing unease about the relationship between the victorious school and the defeated councillors and officials did not prepare the school for the bomb-shell which hit them on 13 July. Betty Hales was out of school at a consultative meeting also attended by Gus John and Danny Silverstone. While she was there Jeff Davies received a fax from the Press, from which he learned to his astonishment that the Secretary of State 'was minded' to set up an Education Association to take over the running of Hackney Downs from the LEA.

The following day Betty Hales, Jeff Davies and Councillor Chris Gardiner, representing the governors, met with two DfEE officials at the school. The meeting had been requested by the DfEE earlier in the month. The meeting took place as the school representatives tried to absorb the latest dramatic turn in their fortunes and the fact that the Secretary of State apparently had four grounds for her renewed concern about the school:

- poor GCSE performance;
- variable quality of lessons;
- poor pupil attendance;
- a significant minority of pupils displaying unsatisfactory attitudes to work.

These were all concerns drawn directly from the Ofsted report of the previous August. As was now becoming routine, the more positive aspects of the Ofsted report, and the encouraging conclusions of the HMI visit in March, just four months earlier, were apparently being discounted.

The option of setting up an Education Association (EA) had been included in John Patten's 1993 Education Act. It enabled the

Secretary of State to replace the LEA and school governors with a nominated body specifically to run a school under the aegis of the Funding Agency for Schools, responsible for financing grant-maintained schools. It had always been assumed that these draconian powers would only be used after a sensible period had elapsed to allow a school to draw up its Action Plan and implement it. Ofsted had spoken consistently of allowing at least two years for progress to be measured.

The Education Association powers had never been used and it was widely believed in educational circles that the government was looking for an opportunity to flex this untried muscle. A school taken over by an EA could be closed or have its character changed, for instance to a technology school. It would not be returned to LEA control. If it were to survive the process it would eventually become a grant-maintained school: a status which had proved signally unappealing to parents in inner-city areas like Hackney.

The two DfEE officials who were at Hackney Downs on the day the announcement was made denied that their presence was anything more than a coincidence and assured Betty Hales that the school's future had not been pre-judged. They did let slip, however, that they believed that LEA representatives had visited the DfEE to discuss the school after the vote in council to allow it to remain open. They anticipated that the Secretary of State would come to a conclusion about the desirability of an EA by the end of July and that if one were imposed, it would take over the school in September. The meeting then went on to discuss issues to do with the school's Action Plan, its roll, funding and staffing.

Reaction to the Secretary of State's proposal ranged from suspicion from the NUT in Hackney, which was particularly outraged that staff, parents and pupils should be thrown once more into a state of uncertainty about their future, to a cautious welcome from business governor, Rob Philipson-Stow, of Guinness Mahon Holdings Ltd. He expressed disappointment with the recent conduct of the LEA and saw an EA as offering an opportunity for a period of stability to the senior management and staff, in whom he expressed his fullest confidence.

A parents' meeting was held just before the end of term at which families seemed bemused and beleaguered. Most found it hard to comprehend what was happening and even harder to know what they should now do to defend their sons' school from yet more uncertainty and disruption. They were deeply disappointed that their hard-fought and successful campaign to save the school seemed to have been trampled underfoot by procedures they did not understand.

Unfortunately the difficult relationship which now existed between the school and LEA officers, though not with all elected members, made a coherent official response to the Secretary of State difficult. An LEA response was presented to the school governors on 20 July and rejected on the grounds that it contained too many factual inaccuracies, errors and generalizations to enable it to be passed on to the Secretary of State. In a letter of explanation to the chief executive, Tony Burgess expressed the governors' discontent and listed nine major points the governors felt unable to endorse. He put on record his sadness at this *impasse* as the governors expressed their continuing desire for the school to remain with the LEA. Senior staff then made a massive effort to draft a revised response for the chief executive, which was submitted to the DfEE on 24 July with the approval of the chair of education, David Phillips.

On 27 July the school was informed that it would immediately come under the control of the North East London Education Association, established by Statutory Instrument according to the provisions of the 1993 Education Act. The decision seized the imagination of the Press, already exercised by stories of falling educational standards and failing schools. On 28 July Professor Michael Barber, one of the EA members, published an article in the *Independent* welcoming 'a new start for pupils sold short by Council policies'.

Once again Hackney Downs found itself in the headlines, pilloried as 'possibly the worst school in Britain'. Its 'history' of Left-wing militancy in the 1980s and 'race riots' in the 1990s was rehearsed again. Its illustrious grammar school past was disinterred to illustrate just how the mighty had fallen. Negative quotations from the Ofsted report (but not the more encouraging news from the return HMI visit) were recalled.

Not all the coverage was entirely negative. Simon Jenkins in *The*

Times wondered what evidence there was to support the idea that central control would be more effective than local control. A *Guardian* leader, more realistically, justified the intervention on the grounds that the swings and roundabouts of Hackney politics were not the best determinant of the school's future, but also made the crucial point that if the school was to be turned around then extra cash was a crucial element in the equation. Not for the first time, the staff noticed that those reporters who took the trouble to visit the school and talk to teachers, pupils and parents, went away with a much more favourable impression than those who relied on old cuttings and hearsay.

George Low, the editor of *Education* magazine, wondered why, when there were currently 80 schools 'at risk', Hackney Downs had been selected as the sacrificial lamb at a time when its performance was actually on the mend. It was, he commented, a long and necessarily expensive business to turn a school around and although the Conservative government might be hoping to prove a point by succeeding where a Labour authority had failed, success was not guaranteed.

Hackney Downs was now inextricably caught up in political games at a high level which had very little to do with the education of severely deprived boys in the poorest borough in the country. Political reaction to the Education Association decision was mixed. Locally the Labour Party opposed the take-over, claiming that the borough had a record of turning failing schools around and could do it again. Nationally the Labour Party did not appear unhappy with the Secretary of State's decision, which, given the continuance of the 'name and shame' culture after its election victory in May 1997, is perhaps not surprising.

By this time the boys had gone home for their summer holidays. There was to be no respite from work that summer for the senior staff or from uncertainty for any of the teachers whose futures were once again on the line.

17

The 'Hit Squad'

The Education Association takes over

Betty Hales and the senior staff were particularly angry about the turn events had now taken because, as she describes it:

We had nearly achieved the impossible and at the point when it was within our grasp it was snatched away by the big guns who were playing by different rules. We were proud of our achievements over the past year since our Ofsted inspection and before that.

We had sorted out many staffing problems. The staff group in place in September 1995 had good potential, given support, adequate resources and good working conditions. Yet they were to be judged in isolation from considerations of what they had recently been living through. A few staff and governors had previously caused immense problems but this was now behind us. Pupils had been generally disaffected but they were now far more motivated and felt themselves to be valued as part of a community. Achievement was being raised and parents were now far more willing to be involved in the school.

Our relationship with the LEA could have become more positive. We might have got our finance and buildings difficulties sorted out, given time.

But despite our frustrations we realized that there really was no point in crying over spilt milk and that although the odds were against us our only chance now of survival was to co-operate fully with the EA, in the hope that they intended to behave honourably.

The Education Association was led by Richard Painter, a senior executive with ADT, an electronic security services giant and a former chief executive of Medway District Council. He was chief executive of the company trust which developed the ADT Technology College in Putney. He was supported by Michael Barber, the former chair of Hackney's Education Committee who had appointed Gus John as Director of Education. Barber was now a professor at Keele University (soon to move to the Institute of Education in London) and an adviser to the Labour Party nationally. Other members were Bryan Bass, recently retired head of the City of London School for Boys, a selective independent school, not far from Hackney Downs geographically but a million miles in every other respect; James Aston, education group manager of the accountants Kidsons Impey; and Richard Davies, former chief education officer of the London Borough of Merton. The secretary was Joan Farelly, former chief inspector in Hammersmith and Fulham. If a gap could be identified in the EA's expertise, it was that they had little experience of schools in a seriously deprived inner-city area. One member confessed that he had never met a child with special educational needs.

Betty Hales and her senior staff co-operated fully with the EA during the whole of August as the take-over was put into effect. This included a meeting between Painter, Farelly and the senior management team at which the latter, in the belief that the EA members were there to support them, were totally frank and honest about the school, warts and all.

Arrangements were made to take over the payroll, contract out services such as school meals and cleaning, arrange staffing for the new term, and decide whether and how to recruit more pupils. James Aston took charge of the school's finances, and Richard Painter, through Joan Farrelly, requested extensive documentation on all aspects of the school's policies and administrative arrangements. The staff were yet again expected to provide reams of paperwork to enable the EA to take control. The only acknowledgement that staff received during the summer holiday was a brief letter from Hackney telling them that they were now employed by the North East London Education Association and that all queries regarding their contracts should now be addressed to the EA. There was no word of thanks for services to Hackney or best wishes for the future, as was usual when staff left the borough in more normal circumstances. The letter was signed by a middle-ranking education officer.

The EA met formally for the first time in the middle of August and received a detailed report from the senior management team. Michael Barber was not present at this meeting, as he was abroad. The only decision of that meeting to which Betty Hales took serious exception was that there should be no further recruitment of pupils until the future of the school was settled. She was horrified to see what she took to be a repeat performance of the previous autumn's freeze on new pupils, with all the financial and educational problems that had brought. The decision, which over-rode the normal guarantees of parental choice, was eventually confirmed by the Secretary of State. Offers of places made before the end of the summer term were honoured, but after that the EA decided that boys were only to be admitted in exceptional circumstances.

However, Betty Hales felt reasonably reassured over the summer that the EA was approaching its task constructively and was looking at the three options for the school which they had spelled out – its continuation in its present form, its continuation in another form, possibly as a technology or 'magnet' school, or its closure – with a relatively open mind.

By the third week in August James Aston had issued a financial policy statement for the school and the exam results had come out. The A–C grades were disappointing, showing no improvement on the previous year. More encouragingly, the proportion of boys leaving without any qualification had dropped for the fourth year in succession. In his analysis of the results presented to the EA meeting in September, Jeff Davies pointed out that only four of the cohort of 61 who had taken the examinations had been assessed as Band 1 ability. The rest were split evenly between Band 2 and Band 3. Leaving aside the language and behavioural difficulties of the majority of the boys, the school was still running in terms of ability levels effectively as a secondary modern school, but with a substantial special school subsumed within it.

At the beginning of September Betty Hales began to feel more uneasy about the presence of the EA members, some of whom were in and out of the school on a regular basis, and about other straws in the wind. The demeanour of those members who did visit the school – and attendance by some members was intermittent – seemed less open and friendly and an atmosphere of 'us and them' seemed to the senior staff to be developing.

The atmosphere in the school was not improved early in the term when Betty Hales was assaulted, physically as well as verbally, by the parent of a particularly difficult boy. The single parent with extremely difficult social circumstances was reported to the police and cautioned. The EA's solicitor also wrote warning against any future intimidatory behaviour.

The LEA continued to niggle about the details of the takeover. The authority, the school and the EA argued about invoices incurred before the takeover during August. At the beginning of September in a letter to Richard Painter it was made clear that Hackney Downs would not be welcome at the annual secondary school exhibition put on for prospective parents. Hackney Downs teachers were also forbidden to use the borough's teachers' centre.

By the middle of September the EA was being told that the amount of educational psychologist support available from the LEA would not continue after November. There was also a dispute over the funding of teacher support for pupils with Statements of Special Educational Need. Rather than pay for this, a senior official at the LEA had apparently insisted that the cost be set against the school's deficit.

Former colleagues were also abandoning Hackney Downs. On 22 September, a five-line note from the chair of the Hackney Secondary Heads and Chairs of Governors Forum advised Richard Painter that the consensus among its members was that the school should be closed. At least one Hackney head contacted the EA individually later in the term making similar points, without paying Betty Hales the courtesy of copying the letter to her. Not all the feedback coming in was so bleak. Guinness Mahon were still seeking to maintain and extend their business links with the school, and the revitalized old boys' association, the Clove Club, was beginning to press the school's case with the EA and elsewhere with increasing vigour.

With so many people now trying to take on board so many

complex procedures very quickly and beginning to 'evaluate' what was going on in the school, the scope for misunderstandings increased as the term went on. Betty Hales was annoyed by comments committed to paper on the school's exclusion policy. There were misinterpretations, she felt, which could easily have been cleared up by a moment's discussion. She was particularly angry that it was assumed that drug incidents were not reported to the police when it was school policy that they always should be.

Early in the term, Michael Barber and Bryan Bass also wrote to staff spelling out their intention to act as 'well-informed governors' as they took on the role of overseeing educational quality in the school. They proposed to study the school's working documents, hold discussions with teachers and pupils, and look at exclusions, class sizes and special educational needs. Bryan Bass undertook a series of classroom visits, although Michael Barber's day-to-day involvement was much more limited.

The staff became seriously concerned that classroom observation was now being undertaken by people without Ofsted training or experience, and without the objective criteria laid down for Ofsted inspections. Some staff complained that verbal feedback offered confirmed their fears. Teachers complained that it was couched in general terms, offered little constructive advice and sometimes seemed subjective.

The EA also announced that three Ofsted-registered inspectors would visit the school later in the term on the EA's behalf. This visit would be in place of the scheduled HMI follow-up review visit which had already been planned for the end of October. The staff were very concerned that, whereas the HMI would have provided a written, public report of their visit, this would apparently not be the case with the privately commissioned inspectors. The three registered inspectors arrived in mid-September and each spent three days in the school. Their brief was to evaluate the quality of teaching and the pupils' response 'to complement the work being done as governors by Michael Barber and Bryan Bass, and to evaluate aspects of the curriculum as potential areas of specialisation'. Only oral feedback would be provided for the staff and headteacher. The outcome would form part of the evidence for preparing the EA's report to the Secretary of State on the school's future.

Staffing had by this time become very difficult. Hackney Downs staff have often been discussed as if they were all militant Left-wingers who had been at the school since the stormy days of industrial action in the mid-1980s. By September 1995 the majority of the staff had been in the school for three years or less. No fewer than five heads of department had left in the previous three years. Betty Hales herself had been at the school only six years. She was supported by a core of no more than six long-serving teachers with between twelve and twenty years' service at the school. They included the highly regarded heads of art and English. Witch-hunters seeking out militants at this point in the school's history would have found no one more threatening than a Left-leaning union officer, an assertive teacher-governor and an outstanding young Australian teacher who claimed to be an anarchist. What is astonishing is that throughout the battle to save the school there was only one half-day of unofficial union action, yet allegations and rumours of militancy persisted.

Still there were staffing anxieties. Technology was still in the hands of a young teacher with only a year's experience who had come to the school as a supply teacher and had taken over the role of the head of department who was taken ill. The geography co-ordinator had also gone and been replaced temporarily on a supply basis. The Section 11 staff, so vital for language support for boys who did not speak English fluently, had not been replaced by the EA when they had taken over, since their contracts were with Hackney not the school governing body. The school ran without specialist Section 11 support until it closed, including during the visit of the three inspectors.

An encouraging report

Betty Hales was told that the Ofsted inspectors commissioned by the EA would not be producing written reports on their visits to the school, but in fact one report was no doubt accidentally left in school after the inspectors left. The same inspector also wrote to the school after the visit to thank them for their co-operation and to wish them well when, he hoped, they would be able to settle down in a less troubled world.

The senior staff who saw the report were greatly encouraged. The inspector had looked at English, physical education and religious education. He found that the quality of teaching in English ranged from good to very good right across the school and that the English department sustained a culture of high expectations. Drama continued to be one of the school's great strengths. If there were weaknesses in the English department it was in the satisfactory integration of boys with special needs. Given the lack of specialist help now available from Section 11 teachers and to support pupils with Statements, the staff did not find the latter comments very surprising.

The inspector also praised the work of the PE department, which he said was well organized and offered boys a well-planned and structured opportunity to develop a sound level of skills in a range of activities. Swimming was handled, he said, in an exemplary manner. Religious education, however, he felt was poorly taught, with insignificant assessment and serious under-achievement. This was an area of concern the senior management had already shared with the EA in August.

But in spite of this encouraging report, which they were not supposed to have seen, as October wore on the senior staff increasingly came to believe that the EA was determined on closure. Members came into the school much less frequently and seemed to be avoiding the senior management team. At the formal meeting of the EA on 18 October Betty Hales felt that the proceedings were extremely rushed and that reports she and others, including pupils, had been asked to prepare for the meeting were of little interest to the members. It was in her report to this meeting that Betty had suggested the school could become a centre for research to look at the academic progress that could be made in a socially deprived area if a full-time education social worker was employed to relieve senior managers of the heavy burden of pastoral work which inevitably came their way. Proposals were made to analyse the cost-effectiveness of this approach with a view to improving value for money in similar schools. By the end of this meeting Betty Hales and Jeff Davies were convinced that a decision to close the school had probably already been taken.

On 29 October, Betty Hales was heartened by the reunion of

Clove Club members which she attended. She had been invited by the secretary the previous March when the first closure proposal was under discussion. She was overwhelmed with enthusiastic offers of help and support from the old boys present. The following day one of the old boys wrote to Richard Painter in glowing terms, a letter which he cannot have expected:

> If the word 'spirit' has any meaning the foundations of Hackney Downs must be bursting with it. That spirit has clearly and firmly seeped into the soul of Betty Hales. Yesterday she addressed our gathering, some 200 strong . . . It was obvious from her address and in talking to her separately, that her dedication to the school and the boys is unquestioned. If that is Mrs Hales' attitude now, in the face of unsurmountable odds, one can only guess at what would be possible from her were she to be given – to use a much-worn phrase – a level playing field. If the school is allowed to continue, unfettered by whatever political manipulations, that lady will clearly stay there every bit as long as some of her illustrious predecessors.

Betty Hales came away from a meeting at the DfEE after the EA was appointed with the impression that there would be at least a six-week consultation period if the decision was to recommend closure. She was shocked when it was eventually announced that there would be only a ten-day consultation on the EA proposals. With hindsight it seems likely that had either Hackney or the Education Association been serious about keeping Hackney Downs open, there was an influential group of former pupils out there whose goodwill and interest could have been of enormous benefit to the school. Unfortunately the possibilities became clear very late in the day.

The EA report

By 31 October Betty Hales and Jeff Davies had learned from the Press that the EA's report was to be published later in the day. Early in the afternoon they met the vice-chairman Richard Davies. The school came together that afternoon for a farewell assembly for a teacher who had taught at Hackney Downs for seventeen years. She was a popular member of staff and the occasion was a happy one until Betty Hales interrupted the proceedings, on EA instructions, to announce that the Association had recommended that the school should close at the end of term. The announcement was met with boos from the boys and some left the hall in tears.

One boy, aged 16, who had struggled for four years to improve his literacy skills with some success, told the *Guardian* how he felt. 'It's all being mucked about. It's been brilliant here. The teachers are really nice. Now everything I've worked for is gone.' Other boys expressed their reluctance to move to Homerton House, which they regarded as a 'rival' school.

The EA had submitted its report to the Secretary of State for Education on 26 October. It unanimously recommended the closure of the school, the offer of places at Homerton House to all the boys, with special help being offered to the Year 11 GCSE candidates, immediate issue of redundancy notices to all the Hackney Downs staff, additional financial help for Homerton House, and the meeting of other costs from the sale of the Hackney Downs site.

They gave three reasons for their conclusion: general management and financial issues, the quality of education, and the school's position in the context of Hackney's overall provision.

In some respects the EA report was a surprising one. It contains the first-ever suggestion that the school's financial management had been at fault. The EA reported a cumulative deficit of approximately £160,000 for the year 1994/5 and the first four months of 1995/6, which would rise to £292,000 by the following March as a result of its own decision to maintain the staffing level it inherited. If the school were to remain open and to become grant-maintained (the EA process precludes the return of a school to its local education authority) it would take its deficit with it and 'it seems unlikely that even with generous terms from the Funding Agency for Schools the school could recover from this budgetary setback'. Only if the school closed and reopened as a new institution could the deficit be left behind. If it closed, the EA suggested, the deficit could be offset against the proceeds of the sale of the school site.

The report criticized financial management by the school prior to October 1994 and by the borough after that date. They found that neither strategic budget planning nor financial control had been properly established and there was no evidence of a strategic plan for 1994/5 or 1995/6. They also criticized the in-school financial management and control over expenditure, despite these having been found 'sound' by the Ofsted inspection and LEA audit.

The EA had been appalled by the neglect and dilapidation of the school site, and during their short period in control reported that they had made some immediate repairs on health and safety grounds. They concluded that the state of the buildings had important implications for the future of the school.

> To provide adequate curriculum facilities especially in science and technology, complete remodelling would be required. To provide an aesthetically pleasing environment which would be conducive to learning the whole site would need upgrading. Our best estimate suggests that at least £3 million would be necessary if HDS were to approach the standards set by most of the other Hackney secondary schools.

To make its judgements on the quality of education the Education Association reported that it took as its starting point the Ofsted inspection of 1994. In addition it based its views on a variety of sources: pupils' work and documented school policies, its own members' observations of 48 lessons, meetings, assemblies and other gatherings, discussions and interviews with staff and pupils, and the observations of three independent inspectors brought in to observe 46 lessons and all the subjects of the curriculum.

They concluded that :

1   Those teachers who combined careful preparation, skilful teaching, passion for the subject matter, high expectations and force of personality, were able to manage their classes.
2   The dominant, overall impression was of a pervasively low standard of achievement and, crucially, that some staff had come to accept that what each of them does in his or her own classroom is the norm.
3   Teacher expectations, teaching strategies, learning outcomes and classroom management are all in urgent need of attention.

4   The boys at HDS are being short-changed in terms of the quality of education provided and the school environment. One consequence of this is that even boys who have reached a reasonable standard already and show some motivation to learn are constantly held back.
5   There is low morale and lack of motivation among the boys, unlikely to be removed under the present arrangements.

The report went on the criticize the 'culture' of the school which, it suggested, was now too weak after all it had been through to face the demanding challenge of successfully educating its pupils.

Four features of the school's culture disturbed the EA:

1   that the difficulties of the school's population, which they claimed were not unique to Hackney Downs, were being used to excuse under-performance;
2   the widespread belief among staff that the school was under-resourced when the pupil–teacher ratio was now extremely generous (as of course it would be given that the loss of Year 7 intakes for two years had cost the school at least 200 pupils);
3   the view among staff that they should be left to 'get on and teach' when in the EA's view precisely the opposite was required because staff appeared isolated and out of touch with what was possible in inner-city schools;
4   the strong belief that the school had improved since the Ofsted inspection, a view for which there was some evidence but which left out of account how far there still was to go.

The EA also criticized:

•   the school's management systems and in particular the lack of central records of academic progress;
•   the lack of teacher appraisal;
•   the lack of a system to bring together all the teachers of a particular class for discussion;
•   the effectiveness of monitoring systems.

Good written policies, they suggested, were not always being implemented and the acting head and deputy were spending too much time on detail and on crisis management.

On the basis of their evidence, the EA concluded that the inadequacies they found were fundamental and of very long standing and that the school was unlikely to be capable of the massive improvements needed to remain open. 'We are therefore forced to conclude that the educational argument dictates that HDS should close and its pupils should be allocated to places at schools which do not have such intractable problems.'

The EA went on to consider the planning issues which would arise from the closure of Hackney Downs and concluded that Homerton House could accommodate the current roll from Hackney Downs and be able to admit annually another form of entry in addition to those currently being admitted to both schools. Neighbouring boroughs had indicated that the closure of Hackney Downs would cause them no problems. The other schools in the borough all appeared to be improving and could be destabilized by the establishment of a new school which 'the borough manifestly does not need and which would draw further funds away from their budgets'. The EA concluded therefore that on planning and general educational grounds Hackney Downs should close.

Public reaction to the school's plight was rather different. During the meagre ten days allowed for consultation a major protest was organized outside the DfEE's Sanctuary Buildings for Wednesday 1 November, which was reported widely in the Press. The school appeared on national and local television news and Betty Hales was inundated with requests to speak to reporters, to the point where it was impossible to ignore them or to even keep them out of the school building.

On 1 November four or five reporters found their way into school assembly, and as a result of this extremely positive and sympathetic articles appeared in the *Independent* and, across a whole page, in the *Evening Standard*. Simon Perry and Geraint Smith in the *Standard* quoted Betty Hales' address to the boys. 'My expectations are as high as they are of any boy who attends the most prestigious public school and whose parents are paying thousands of pounds for their education.' She praised the staff, 'as competent a group of teachers as I have ever worked with. They have behaved professionally through a prolonged period of extreme difficulty.' She said that it had been painful to read the report the previous night. 'It did not describe the school we know and love.'

Betty Hales will always be grateful to all the reporters who bothered to come to find out for themselves about the school and then wrote sympathetic articles about it. The *Guardian* of Saturday 4 November gave the whole of the front of its Outlook section to the story. A well-researched article by Dave Hill and John Carvel concluded that the lessons of Hackney Downs might have a wider resonance. 'When a hit squad next moves into another failing school it should check the patient for signs of life and hope before switching off the life-support machine.'

Rapid closure

Once the report was published, events began to move very fast. On 31 October Betty Hales received a letter from the DfEE, informing her that the Secretary of State was 'minded to use her powers under S.225 of the 1993 Education Act to discontinue Hackney Downs School with effect from 31 December.' The letter was also sent to the LEA, local MPs and the Funding Agency for Schools. The letter gave until Friday 10 November for 'any comments you or other interested parties have on the proposal' – a total of eight working days.

On 9 November the senior management team wrote to the Secretary of State noting that 'along with many others we feel that the ten-day consultation is insufficient for all interested parties, particularly parents, to present a cogent response'. The letter also said that 'anybody involved in education agrees that the transfer of Year 11 boys at this stage in their school career represents educational insanity – and we do not use that phrase lightly'. The letter also put on record the SMT's concerns with the functioning of the EA itself.

On the same day as the letter was sent to the DfEE, Richard Painter, chair of the EA, wrote to all Hackney Downs staff telling them that 'as a redundancy situation arises at the school' there would be a meeting for them on Thursday 16 November. On 14 November, he wrote again spelling out that the objective was to make all staff redundant on 31 December when the school would officially close. 'Following consultations with the Funding Agency for Schools and the DfEE, the Education Association is not proposing to make redundancy payments in excess of those due to be paid under the Employment Protection (Consolidation) Act 1978.' In other words, an attempt would be made to over-ride the normal period of notice for serving teachers and to over-ride the staff's understanding when the EA took over that their terms of employment, including redundancy arrangements, would be no worse than they would be as employees of Hackney LEA.

On 14 November, the DfEE wrote again to Betty Hales to confirm the Secretary of State's decision that the closure would become effective on 31 December. The letter passed on the Secretary of State's conclusion that it would be more detrimental to the Year 11 boys to remain at Hackney Downs than it would be to move them a few months before their GCSE examinations. The letter also said that the Secretary of State would be inviting Homerton House, the Hackney LEA and the Education Association to put up proposals for additional educational provision for Homerton House and for financial resources to be made available for the refurbishment and development of that school.

This was the letter which confirmed in Betty Hales' mind her suspicion, based on a handwritten note which a cleaner had found in the Education Association's room and handed to her, that the EA had been discussing the detail of its recommendations with the LEA and Homerton House even before their report was published. The next day, on 15 November, the head of strategic support services at Hackney Council wrote to Betty Hales to keep her informed 'of steps being taken following the Secretary of State's decision'. She said 'an information pack has been sent to all parents of Hackney Downs boys, including an information booklet on Homerton House, a letter from Gus John and one from Geoffrey Dale (head of Homerton House) and an invitation to an open day at the school on 27 November'. In view of the unprecedented speed and efficiency with which these arrangements fell into place, some people at the school concluded that officers had been working on the assumption that the brief consultation period was a mere formality and that the EA must have made the decision to close the school some time before the formal annoucement.

The EA pushed the transfer hard, to the extent of deciding at their 16 November meeting to provide parents of boys transferring with a voucher to buy a blazer, tie, badge, calculator and dictionary. But the process was not a smooth one. The arrangements for the end-of-term concert and drama performance had to be cancelled because the performers, often the most motivated pupils in the school, would not be available because they were already leaving, finding alternative schools. Reaction to the second closure announcement from the parents and others had been instant, angry and emotional. One parent wrote passionately to Gillian Shephard asking her to stop the closure: 'Hackney Downs School has a glorious past history and we parents do not want the school to die. With your authority, with your power and with your help, Hackney Downs can remain open. Please save the school from the gallows, please save it from closure.'

The school was inundated with letters of support from all over the country, often from people with no connection with the school. Many of the writers were teachers who were obviously deeply angered by what was happening to Hackney Downs and did not believe in the good faith of the EA or the government. A former head of a large socially deprived school in the North of England wrote to ask how the 'so-called experts' of the EA behaved while they were at Hackney Downs.

> What sort of timetable did they each teach? Were they able to keep reasonable discipline? Given a free hand would you have employed any of them on a permanent basis? What sort of rapport did they establish with the students? Were you happy with their teaching records? Of course, I realise it would be wrong to condemn them on just six weeks' efforts.

A teacher who had once worked at the school for six years wrote from the West Midlands that she had been watching the Hackney Downs 'demolition job' with increasing concern.

> Colleagues in this part of the world can see this for what it is. Ofsted and the government need a sacrifice. What do 200+ inner-city kids matter, or 30 teachers. A price worth paying?

Stick to it! It's education that matters and this decision has nothing to do with education.

Letters from people who had close links with the school expressed outrage and support for Betty Hales and the staff in equal measure. One of Betty Hales' tutors on her headship training course wrote: 'I was hugely impressed by you both as a highly competent senior manager and a person. I hope very much that you will get through the closure intact and be able to move on to better things.'

A university lecturer who had worked with Hackney Downs boys on motivational workshops to help working-class schools improve entry to higher education wrote:

I think it's disgraceful and demoralizing to find out that this good start to turning around their fortunes could so easily be wasted. What kind of future do they really have, when they are being uprooted to another school in which they have no involvement? To remove pupils from a school whilst studying for their GCSEs is deplorable.

A former Hackney Labour councillor who had been an SEN support teacher at the school, wrote:

It's hard to know what to say. Sorry seems inadequate. The good news is that the hard work and effort you have all put into the struggle to keep the school open will not be forgotten. It's very clear to anyone who knows about the history of what happened that the people who were primarily responsible for closure are not the current members of staff.

And a parent wrote to Betty Hales on 13 November to say that she was transferring her son to a school in Tower Hamlets 'with regret and sadness'.

Our decision to move him next week bears no reflection whatsoever on the teaching standards at Hackney Downs. (My son) has been very happy at Hackney Downs but is currently finding the situation too stressful. We congratulate all the teachers on their hard efforts and professionalism throughout these difficult circumstances. We would also like to take this opportunity of thanking you personally for all your time, patience and teaching skills you have given to A.

This mother had succeeded in placing her son in a school in a neighbouring borough. Others who tried to buck the strenuous efforts of the LEA and the EA to persuade all the families to transfer their boys to Homerton House were not so lucky. The parents of one boy took him for an interview at Cardinal Pole Roman Catholic School in Hackney and were offered a place there on 21 November. The next day the headteacher wrote to say that regretfully he had to change his mind. 'This decision has been taken as a direct result of advice received from Hackney LEA in terms of numbers on roll and financial implications.' Exactly the same thing happened to another family, whose son was accepted at Cardinal Pole on 21 November and then rejected on 23 November.

Betty Hales believed that the LEA must have told the school that funding for additional pupils would be unavailable if the school chose to exceed its 180 admissions limit. This is an unusual interpretation of the LMS rules, under which funding follows the pupils. Schools frequently exceed their admissions limits when pupils are allocated to them on appeal, and in such cases funding is automatic. Parents do not recall being informed of their legal right to appeal against the rejection of their applications.

If the DfEE and the LEA hoped that the school would even now lie down and die quietly, they were very quickly disabused. The National Union of Teachers' members at the school were disappointed to discover that the union nationally was by now only interested in negotiating better redundancy terms for them rather than in continuing their previous support for keeping the school open. But they determined to fight on. The teachers were particularly incensed at the implication in the EA report of financial irregularities at the school and some explored the possibility of taking action for defamation against the EA.

Court action

Other groups were also still willing to fight. The Clove Club, the newly revitalized old boys' association, in the person of its chair, Willy Watkins, and Professor Josh Silver, an eminent physicist at Oxford University, became the mainstays of a legal challenge to the closure decision. They had visited the school, met Betty Hales and her senior staff and became convinced that the school should have a future. They were joined by Professor Sally Tomlinson of Goldsmith's College, London. She had known the school in a research context for many years and telephoned Betty Hales on 20 November to volunteer her services as an independent educational adviser.

Together with a group of Hackney Downs parents, the Clove Club representatives approached Jack Rabinowitz, a solicitor known for his support for disadvantaged families. On 15 November they made an application for legal aid on behalf of two pupils and two parents in order to seek a judicial review. The application was refused and an appeal against the refusal lodged the following day, 16 November.

That same day the school had been instructed by the LEA to begin the transfer of Year 7 and 8 boys to Homerton House 'in order to acclimatise them'. For the boys the beginning of the end of Hackney Downs was coming with breakneck speed, although Jeff Davies did not feel that the liaison between the two schools was going at all smoothly.

Most ominously, a series of timetabled meetings between heads of department and heads of year at the two schools, which Jeff Davies regarded as a crucial opportunity to discuss academic and pastoral issues and to pass on information about transferring pupils, never happened, to the disappointment of Hackney Downs staff and the embarrassment of Peter Osborne, a retired head who had recently joined the EA and who had been instrumental in arranging it. In general, relationships between the EA members and staff had now degenerated into mutual suspicion.

The future of many of the boys was still unclear. After several meetings had been arranged at Homerton House for prospective parents, the EA meeting on 12 December was told that only 67 boys had definitely signed up there. It is not clear whether the majority of parents were at this stage still hoping that the High Court action would reprieve the school yet again, were not able or willing to attend meetings or sign forms, or simply did not want their sons to make the transfer and were looking for other schools. But three days before the end of the Hackney Downs term, the majority of the boys had no settled future arranged for them.

In spite of the best efforts of Hackney Downs staff to collate all the relevant material, the mechanics of the transfer also went badly. Course-work and records went astray, which meant that Homerton House staff, already in a difficult position, found themselves working in the dark with pupils coming up to GCSE examinations.

The pressure on the senior staff and the headteacher at Hackney Downs was now acute. All were suffering from the same financial anxieties as the rest of the employees of the EA: uncertainty about the redundancy payments which were due, and the legality of the month's notice which they had all been given. All the staff also required references to ease their search for new jobs. The task of providing them fell mainly on Betty Hales, but her request for additional secretarial assistance to help her through the paperwork inherent in the closure was turned down by the EA.

In fact the minimum redundancy terms, particularly harsh for teachers who had long service at the school, were all that the staff were being offered at this stage: a loss for some of thousands of pounds on what they would have received if the school had remained with the LEA. The staff found the confusion particularly stressful since it was just a few days before Christmas. Many of them put off buying Christmas presents because they could not know when they would work again and had no expectation of receiving more than few hundred pounds in redundancy. A number of staff subsequently took the Education Association to an industrial tribunal to attempt to recover the full pay in lieu of notice that they would have received from Hackney under the TUPE regulations. The non-teaching staff only received one month's pay in lieu of notice, and many of these, unlike the teachers, found great difficulty in finding new jobs.

The calculations in the EA report which assumed that the Hackney Downs site could be sold off to help fund other Hackney schools, and in particular Homerton House, proved to be based on a false premise. When Professor Josh Silver, one of the Clove Club stalwarts who had become involved in the legal challenge to the EA report, approached the Grocers' Company, the original founders of the school, he discovered that it had been handed over to the London County Council in 1902 (and thence eventually to Hackney LEA) with restrictive covenants on the use of the site. Far from being available as an asset which could be sold on the open market, the site and buildings had to be reserved for educational purposes. With one simple inquiry which could have been made by anyone during the three years the school's future was under discussion, Professor Silver demolished the basis of the Education Association's financial calculations about what could or should happen when Hackney Downs School closed its doors.

Closing down

While the legal arguments rumbled ponderously on, the staff had to continue to run a highly volatile school for 200 boys until 15 December, which was the date now fixed for the end of term. They also had to organize all the transfer arrangements for the boys, passing on academic profiles, other records, and completed assessments and course-work for the Year 10 and 11 boys who had begun their GCSE courses. At the same time arrangements had to be made for the disposal of all the school's property, which would revert to Hackney LEA: Homerton House was to have first option on usable books and equipment, equipment which had been provided by the local TVEI scheme had to be returned, the future of computing equipment caused administrative problems, and precautions had to be taken to ensure the security of the buildings and their contents until safe transfers had been arranged. The EA insisted that the buildings must be vacated by 21 December, although this gave the staff very little time to remove their own belongings before the security guards took over on behalf of Hackney Council.

The atmosphere between the EA members and the senior staff was now understandably tense. Senior managers and many of the rest of the staff were grateful for the arrangement the EA made to bring in consultants to advise teachers on job-search strategies, although as the EA would cease to exist at the end of the year this was a very short-term measure and yet another pressure on time, which was a very scarce resource by now.

Staff spirits were raised by the First Sight TV programme, produced by Michael Gooding, which appeared on BBC2. The programme asked whether closure was in the best interests of pupils or whether there was another answer. It was followed by a phone-in which demonstrated a lot of public support for the school. Both pupils and staff came into school the following day, the last day for the pupils, buoyed up by the feeling that they were not alone, an impression confirmed by the twenty television cameras which joined them for assembly.

There is some evidence that the EA began to feel somewhat exposed on the issue of references and redeployment. They had by now realized that the very public rubbishing of the school and its staff, in which sections of the Press had again joined with gusto, might expose them to legal challenge. On 14 December, long after most references had been completed, Richard Painter wrote to Betty Hales insisting that a statement from the EA should be included with all staff references. This was to read:

> Prospective employers may be aware of comments in the national press critical of the education provided at Hackney Downs School. The comments give the impression that these criticisms apply equally to all members of staff. The Education Association wishes to confirm that this impression is seriously misleading – such criticisms by no means apply to all teachers, some of whom are experienced, able and caring. The Education Association expresses the hope that in assessing applications from members of Hackney Downs School staff, prospective employers will discount such press reports and judge each applicant on his or her individual merits.

Even the EA now realized that once the 'worst school in Britain' genie was let out of its bottle, it was quite impossible to control.

But the mass rubbishing of a school-full of teachers put the EA in a double bind. They might be liable to legal challenge if competent teachers felt defamed. Equally they did not want to risk recommending potentially less than competent teachers too enthusiastically to other schools. The letter went on to warn Mrs Hales about the risks of either 'exaggerating merits or glossing over weaknesses' in references in case there were legal consequences 'if it was found that a misleading impression had been given to a subsequent employer'.

The closure process became increasingly fraught. The day following a meeting between the staff and Doug McAvoy of the NUT, which had clashed with a meeting with staff from Homerton House, Betty Hales and Jeff Davies and office staff were working flat out to complete the remaining references, having been told that all computers and word processors would be removed at the end of that day. At 11.50 a.m. they were summoned to a meeting with three members of the EA. They were told that they were to hand copies of all references to Bryan Bass. They were also criticized for allowing the clash of meetings.

Betty Hales made the point that staff had been working until 8 p.m. under extreme pressure during the last two weeks, even bringing 'mock' exams forward so that they could be completed and marked before the boys left. It was inevitable, she said, when people are working under such pressures of time and stress that mistakes would be made. She was told 'that's what professionals do'.

Betty Hales was particularly angered by this since she had attempted to bring to the EA's attention weeks earlier that there simply was not enough time to complete all of the tasks which would need to be done to close a school in the remaining few weeks left to her. When she had asked for it to be considered that some staff, including herself and the school secretary, be employed for a period after the school had closed to complete essential paperwork, the suggestion had been rejected. As if to illustrate her point, notification was received at the school that day from the LEA that a Year 9 pupil would be entitled to free school dinners in January! Who was going to sort out this clerical mess, she asked.

This meeting was the last time that any members of the EA would visit the school, apart from James Aston who called in for a short time on the morning of 20 December, the last day the school was open, to finalize financial matters. He left at lunch-time and took with him the school's petty cash, stamps and franking machine. Hence, when the references had finally all been completed Betty

Hales had to leave them in the school office ready for collection. In fact the Borough of Hackney has always denied that they received these and since the school closed Betty has needed to process in excess of 50 duplicate references at her own expense. Hackney Downs' confidential personnel files have proved impossible to track down since the school closed.

The only member of staff who did not receive a usable reference when the school closed was Betty Hales herself, since the EA provided her with a reference which simply stated that all enquiries should be referred to Gus John. However, all staff received a short letter from Richard Painter dated 22 December which ended 'We would like to express our appreciation to those members of staff who have maintained their professional commitment during this difficult time. We very much hope that you will enjoy a happy Christmas.'

Throughout this period, staff believed that the EA members were treating them as 'loony' Left-wingers with a 'deficit model' towards disadvantaged pupils. This was generally unfair and Betty Hales resented it particularly because her background is rooted in traditional values alongside a commitment to a fair and just society for all. In Betty's own words:

At the same time as the EA was attempting to write me and the other staff off as weak and woolly left-wingers during December 1995 I was proud to attend two family events. My eldest son, Robert, was presented with his Queen's Scout award at the Guildhall and my father, Ken Sanders, received his OBE from the Queen at Buckingham Palace in recognition of very many years' devoted and loyal service to social provision for the elderly and mentally handicapped through charity work and as a Labour councillor.

The legal challenge

The legal system, which was swift enough to turn the application for legal aid down, was to prove much slower to hear a challenge to the decision. The appeal hearing for legal aid was set for a date, 5 December, only two weeks before the end of term. Attempts to bring this date forward were rejected.

On 5 December legal aid was granted for the case to go ahead and a barrister was retained. The same day, the Secretary of State issued a Press release attacking the Labour Party's control of Hackney Council 'where even a pupil teacher ratio of 8:1 could not improve Hackney Downs'. The artificially low pupil population was now being used by the government itself to attack the school, without even a passing attempt to put it into context. The myth of the low school roll had become accepted wisdom, and the fatal effect of the denial of a Year 7 intake for two years was now fully apparent. The full flavour of the political opportunism which would from then on be used to rubbish the school immediately became all too clear.

On Friday 8 December, leave to move for a judicial review was sought before Mr Justice Popplewell and granted. When they heard the news, the parents thought they had won the case. They had to be gently told that this was only the first stage in the long legal process.

Professor Sally Tomlinson of Goldsmith's College and Michael Stark of the DfEE both produced affidavits for this hearing. Professor Tomlinson, for the boys and parents, argued that the consultation on the EA report had been too short, the effect on pupils, especially Year 11, would be damaging, and that the report relied on 'inaccurate and selective presentation of evidence'.

The DfEE said that after anxious consideration extra time had been offered for consultation, although this was not a statutory provision. Many of the 96 responses received had opposed closure. Two, including one from all the other secondary heads in the borough, had favoured early closure.

Sally Tomlinson emphasized in her affidavit that it was the loss of Year 7 which had led to the very favourable pupil–teacher ratios in the school. She wanted to counter the impression, she said, given in the EA report and in subsequent newspaper articles by Michael Barber, that the school was functioning in highly favourable conditions without improvement at great expense which 'amounted to daylight robbery of other Hackney pupils'. At the time of the Ofsted inspection, group sizes stood at 18.5 and expenditure was in line with that at other Hackney schools, she pointed out.

The school protesters had two days to prepare their substantive case for the judicial review which was set for the following Monday morning, 11 December. Normally a period of about 56 days elapses between leave being granted for a review and the hearing. The intervening weekend was one of frantic activity for the school's supporters and their lawyers.

On the Monday, before Mr Justice Popplewell, Philip Engleman argued the case for the closure decision to be reversed on six grounds:

1   That the EA had no powers to make a report to the Secretary of State as it did, and that this was an unlawful report.
2   That there was not sufficient consultation before they made the report.
3   The decision to close the school was thus flawed.
4   The Secretary of State did not allow enough time for consultation.
5   The decision was unreasonable because of the disruption to the boys.
6   The EA's report contained inaccuracies and there had been no disclosure of the report of the inspectors engaged by the EA which was relied on by the EA for its report.

The judge rejected each of these arguments in turn. He quoted extensively from the EA report and its conclusions that the school had weak management and poor teaching, low standards and poor behaviour, and concluded that the EA had a duty to act and to report back rather than 'simply sit on their hands, report back to nobody and allow the school to disintegrate'.

He concluded that there was no statutory obligation on the EA or the Secretary of State to consult prior to closure. 'The absence of statutory obligation was very marked.' But he was satisfied in any case that there was adequate and sufficient consultation to enable the Secretary of State to consider the matter.

He also rejected the argument that it was unreasonable to close the school because of the needs of the boys coming up to GCSE, and rejected Sally Tomlinson's argument that Homerton House was on a par with Hackney Downs.

In the end I come back to this. Every professional who has had dealings with this particular school is satisfied that it is failing to give its pupils an acceptable standard of education. That is

Ofsted, the officer of the LEA, the Association and the Secretary of State. In my judgement it is not possible now to challenge this decision of the Secretary of State which seems to me to accord with the professional view.

He therefore refused to grant the judicial review. Leave to appeal was granted. The appeal was heard on 18 December and judgement given on 21 December upholding Mr Justice Popplewell's decision. The appeal judges questioned whether the Education Association's report was suitable for the judicial review process as it was really 'unreviewable ministerial advice'. They saw no reason to question the EA's good faith. 'The members are of the highest repute, as well as great expertise, and had no interests to serve but those of education.'

Professor Sally Tomlinson's suggestion that the report had been selective with the truth, one of the judges commented, had been put 'immoderately high' and the report had not been demolished as a worthwhile advisory document. Lord Justice Simon Brown expressed some surprise that the legislation made no provision for consultation, but felt that the previous five periods of consultation had elicited a wealth of material and allowed time for opposition to the closure to be marshalled.

The challenge on the grounds that it was unreasonable to expect Year 11 boys to change school so close to their examinations was also dismissed.

For the boys, Hackney Downs had already closed on 15 December at an emotional final assembly. This was followed by a party for the staff and supporters, who were still hoping that the appeal court would decide in the school's favour. It was not to be.

Fortunately, Hackney Downs was not to be forgotten. Most of the documentation, minutes, letters and inspection reports relating to the whole affair were still in the hands of former staff, governors and councillors in Hackney who responded enthusiastically to requests for assistance from the authors of this book. Crucially, the authors discovered among files brought out of the school before it was boarded up, EA documentation in a school folder which included the written reports of the three Ofsted-registered inspectors who had visited the school in its final term.

18

Picking up the Pieces

The aftermath

The reverberations of what happened to Hackney Downs School were still being felt in the borough years later. The school itself was standing empty and deteriorating in the wind and rain four years after the last boys departed. The Grocers' Company covenant on the buildings had so far prevented the sale that the Education Association had certainly, and the LEA had possibly, anticipated. Various schemes to keep the premises in educational use had been mooted and fallen through, the Clove Club continued to discuss whether or not the Grocers' Company might re-invest in education in Hackney in some way, while the £2–3 million price tag for refurbishment of the dilapidated property went on rising. By the end of 1997 Hackney had completed yet another review of its secondary school provision and concluded that the Hackney Downs buildings should be refurbished and a new co-educational school opened there in the year 2000. But when Richard Painter led another 'hit squad' to inspect the LEA's performance, which the chief inspector of schools had condemned as 'setting new standards in disorganisation and bureaucratic waste', this plan was quickly rejected.

The cost of the closure had been high. An estimated £800,000 was spent on redundancy and retirement payments to teachers. A further £1 million was authorized by the DfEE for improvements at Homerton House which took many of the boys displaced from Hackney Downs. Total costs are therefore not far off the estimated cost of keeping the school open and putting it back into reasonable repair.

Given that the acting headteacher and the staff had been rubbished by large sections of the media and were given little support when the school closed, they have experienced a remarkable rehabilitation, although in some cases the personal cost has been high. Betty Hales went immediately to the headship of a special school for EBD children in Camden and had her skills as a manager reendorsed by Ofsted inspectors within months of her arrival.

Her deputy Jeff Davies spent some time at Homerton House working with the Hackney Downs boys who had moved there. He then moved to a new job as a deputy head outside London and has been selected for headship training. Almost all the other staff who wanted jobs (a few decided to retire or work part-time) have found new jobs and report no problems in integrating into schools which are patently not 'failing'.

As one teacher put it:

> Since leaving Hackney Downs I have been regarded with nothing but respect by fellow professionals. Two local schools have told me that they considered themselves lucky to have me step in to see them through awkward periods and I am now temporary head of a department which is bigger than anything I have ever led before. (And I was going to take it easy as I can now afford to work part-time!)

Another said:

> I did fear that having been a member of staff at Hackney Downs might have been a problem for my future career. But I have a job now in which I am well respected. After being there for only a few months I was promoted to head of department. I think the head deliberately sought me out because of what happened at Hackney Downs and the experience we had there with Ofsted. I feel I'm valued professionally.

Some teachers carry scars which they say will always be with them. One, a highly regarded and competent member of Hackney Downs' staff whose work was praised by HMI, wrote a year later:

I felt I was held in contempt and that as the school was rubbished, so was I. I am left still feeling fairly inadequate and almost unwilling to apply for jobs because I feel that I must be such a terrible teacher and no one would want me. I am now working full-time but on a supply salary which is very difficult.

She has now also obtained a permanent appointment.

How the pupils fared is a problematic question. In the end 121 of them transferred to Homerton House, in spite of their parents' misgivings about the capacity of a school, which had long been regarded by boys as a rival, to handle them, and the inevitable risks of any move to pupils about to take their GCSEs only five months after the closure. Homerton House had received a critical Ofsted report in 1994 but with a new head had been regarded as an improving school during the period of Hackney Downs' inspection and closure, a perception which the Hackney Downs side attempted to refute during the judicial review.

Reports in the Press that the influx of many boys with severe problems was causing disciplinary difficulties soon after the move were strongly denied by the school. Publicly it was claimed that special arrangements were being made for the boys who had made the move, which included additional classes after school, as the EA had recommended. According to Michael Barber, writing in January 1996, this would offer the boys a much better chance of success than they would otherwise have had.

However, Homerton House's examination results at the end of the school year when Hackney Downs' Year 11 boys took their GCSEs (1996) at their new school were not encouraging: they were, by a considerable percentage, the worst in the borough. And while most Hackney schools had improved slightly on the previous year, Homerton House's proportion of boys gaining five good GCSEs remained at 11 per cent, precisely the same proportion as both it and Hackney Downs had achieved the year before. Hackney Downs staff were working on the assumption that the Year 11 cohort would perform better than this, but there is a possibility that the most ambitious families sent their sons to schools outside the borough, so lowering the likely average performance of those who moved to Homerton.

Even worse, the proportion of boys leaving school without any qualifications at Homerton House actually rose sharply to 19 per cent. This was considerably worse than the 11 per cent (which did not take account of the boys who had left prematurely) who had ended their school life at Hackney Downs without qualifications the previous year, and much worse than Homerton House's own 1995 performance which saw the school achieving the remarkable feat, according to the league table statistics, of seeing every 16-year-old gain a qualification. Whatever the long-term consequences may be for boys' education in Hackney of Hackney Downs' closure, the immediate result, in terms of examination performance at least, provided them with no measurable improvement, and some deterioration.

There were unforeseen political consequences to the closure row as well. Control of Hackney Council slipped from the Labour Party's grasp in 1996 as a result of the expulsion of some Labour members of the council by the National Executive Committee of the Labour Party, following a series of splits, including that over Hackney Downs. The Labour rebels, variously castigated as Left-wingers or ambitious populists, then chose to ally with the Liberal Democrats to take control of the council. The council was still 'hung' after the 1998 elections.

Gus John never fully resumed his duties as Director of Education after the closure of Hackney Downs. After several months on sick leave he opted for early retirement in the summer of 1996. At the same time he took the council to an industrial tribunal for failing to protect him from racial abuse and harassment.

Gus John's assessment of what went wrong over Hackney Downs, as he explained to the *Independent on Sunday* when he retired, continued to be that the switch of council control in 1995, which led to the council's change of mind over the school closure, was a lurch to the Left. His opponents, he argued, did not accept his argument that the only true liberation for black children is through high-quality education and that because that was not being provided at Hackney Downs the school had to close.

There was a certain inevitability – and some comfort for Hackney's critics – in the fact that the new Labour government which took office in 1997 made Hackney the subject of its first inspection of an LEA. The borough was still firmly at the bottom of the league tables, two of its primary schools had been named by the new government as amongst the worst in the country, a reorganization of the management structure appeared likely to down-grade the post of Director of Education, and complaints about mismanagement continued. It was two years before the council appointed a new Director of Education. A year later the government decided to put some council services in Hackney out to tender. The argument that problems in Hackney schools generally, and at Hackney Downs in particular, were simply the result of incompetent teachers was beginning to look very thin.

Continuing debate

In the Press, at education conferences and in books about improving schools, the Hackney Downs war continued to be waged with great ferocity long after the school doors shut for the last time. The accolade of 'worst school in Britain', so beloved of the popular Press, passed on to other institutions, some of them, like The Ridings School in West Yorkshire, evidently in worse shape in terms of academic results than Hackney Downs was before its numbers were reduced to the pathetic and evidently untenable levels of its final term.

In a remarkable series of articles and letters in the *Times Educational Supplement*, Professor Michael Barber and Professor Sally Tomlinson continued to slug it out, each justifying their convictions that the school should, or should not, have been closed. There has probably never been a school which generated so much heat and which continues to generate debate so long after its closure.

Professor Barber continues to use the school as an example of the worst that can happen, to the fury of many of those who were involved, who still believe that the school could have been turned round, given adequate support and commitment from the LEA after the Ofsted inspection.

In his book *The Learning Game*, published in the summer of 1996, Professor Barber used Hackney Downs as an extended example of failure. He castigated the 'far Left' teacher unions and the Socialist Workers' Party and Labour politicians 'happy to play at populist politics to begin their climb up the greasy pole', for supporting the teachers and parents who understandably wanted to keep their school open. He criticized the HMI who had found significant improvement in a number of areas on their return visit for 'questionable judgements'.

> Hackney Downs is an example of the state a school can end up in if it is mismanaged over years and fought over by petty politicians and lobby groups who have forgotten that schools exist for their pupils. Hackney Downs also provides the clearest possible evidence that neither increased funding nor reducing class sizes are, on their own, the solution to this country's educational problems. Unless the management is good and the teaching of high quality even very large sums of money will change nothing. In the autumn of 1995, when the Education Association was preparing its report, Hackney Downs was spending at the rate of £6,489 per pupil per year. This is almost three times the national average expenditure per pupil in secondary education.

This is now a figure which has worked its way into the mythology and one which causes particular distress to those who struggled to turn Hackney Downs around. It is based on an unprecedented situation during the school's last term which it is difficult to regard as working to the advantage of anyone in the school – management, staff or boys. It is worth restating that the school's roll dropped by one-third during the course of 1995 as the closure process was pressed ahead, recruitment was stopped and the Year 11 boys completed their studies and left. There was an intake of only 35 boys in September 1995 – itself remarkable as there had been almost no time to begin recruitment after the school was reprieved. When it took over, the EA prevented further recruitment and the school hit rock-bottom with just 200 boys. Most of those boys had severe language, learning or behavioural difficulties.

During the same period of intense uncertainty the entire staff had been given redundancy notices for the first time by Hackney, and the acting head and LEA had discussed contingency plans to reduce the staffing to the minimum necessary to maintain the curriculum in September if the school should remain open. The LEA, which had control of the budget and staffing, did not attempt to reduce the staffing earlier in the year in order to increase the pupil–teacher ratio, although boys were leaving. Nor did it take urgent action on staffing when the council reprieved the school in June, although plans were drawn up with Betty Hales to cut the teaching force in line with the roll from September 1995. No action was taken to implement this plan when the school was reprieved.

When the Education Association took control of the school, as it says in its report, it deliberately decided to retain the existing staffing level, with the approval of the Funding Agency for Schools, 'as a way of giving some stability for pupils'. The existing staff therefore remained in post as the roll went inexorably down. This did produce an extremely favourable pupil–teacher ratio for the last term of the school's existence. It was not permanent, nor ever intended to be permanent. It happened at a time of extreme uncertainty and instability as the Education Association spent its first weeks assessing the school's future. It was a staff–pupil ratio fully approved by the EA as a temporary measure, but this did not prevent the same EA using it as evidence against the school in public documents and ultimately in court.

It is hardly likely in the circumstances that this short period of very generous funding would have any noticeable effect on the school during the few weeks it took the EA to reach its conclusion on its future. The responsibility for the extraordinary unit cost at Hackney Downs during its last terms of existence therefore lies firmly with the EA and, before their take-over, with Hackney LEA, which between them controlled the finances and staffing of the school for a full fourteen months.

Was the school improving?

The crucial question which divides those who justify the closure of Hackney Downs and those who continue to regard it as an injustice is whether the school was improving during its final terms and had the capacity to build on that improvement. The EA report cited three reasons why the school could not continue: management issues, the quality of education, and the demographic need for two boys' schools in Hackney. Their report was emphatic that the school failed on all three counts.

On educational performance there is a wealth of documentation. Examination results are a crude measure of performance, but they give a snapshot of what is happening. These show quite clearly that the proportion of boys gaining five A to C grades fell in 1994 and remained at the same low (11 per cent) level the following year. But the proportion of boys gaining more appropriate qualifications was improving sharply even while the school was in various sorts of turmoil.

As Charles Bell, of the educational pressure group Article 26, has repeatedly pointed out in letters to newspapers, between 1992 and 1995 the school's percentage of pupils gaining five GCSEs at any grade went up dramatically from 48 per cent to 68 per cent, and the proportion gaining no qualifications went down from 25 per cent to 11 per cent, another significant improvement. He makes the point that in schools where measured ability is very low, there are serious language difficulties and very high levels of special need, these are the statistics which may say more about a school's performance than the bench-mark five A to C grades.

Indeed, when Hackney LEA claimed to be improving its overall examination performance in the mid 1990s, it was the A to G grades at GCSE which had risen most dramatically between 1992 and 1996 (see tables below), bringing them close to the national average, while the five A to C grade measurement has improved only marginally and remained at exactly the same percentage below the national average in 1996 as it was in 1992. If Hackney as a whole could take credit for improving its A to G results, one is left to wonder why Hackney Downs was never allowed to do the same.

The other judgement of the school's quality comes from the inspection reports which followed the initial Ofsted visit which found the school to be failing. Gus John and Michael Barber were both dismissive of the return visit of HMI in March 1995, which reported some improvements, as they became involved in the two successive attempts to close the school. But there is other external evidence to back the claims of the senior management team and the governors that by the time the Action Plan was being implemented at the beginning of the 1994/5 school year, Hackney Downs had turned the corner.

Hackney LEA schools exam results – DfE figures

% 5 A–Cs	1992	1993	1994	1995	1996
Cardinal Pole RC (M inc.VI)	29	34	35	19	33
Clapton School (G)	22	20	21	36	23
Hackney Downs (B)	11	21	11	11	–
Hackney Free & P (M)	11	12	16	17	23
Haggerston (G)	21	24	19	37	39
Homerton House (B)	18	16	20	11	11
Kingsland (M)	17	25	24	18	21
Our Lady's Convent (G inc.VI)	47	41	52	49	51
Skinners' Company (G inc.VI)	16	25	20	25	19
Stoke Newington (M)	17	20	23	23	29
Hackney average	19.3	23.7	22.7	23.9	25.7
National average	38.1	41.1	43.3	43.5	44.5

Notes: Only three schools with sixth forms. No boys' single-sex school with a sixth form.

One or more A–Gs	1992	1993	1994	1995	1996
Cardinal Pole RC (M inc.VI)	84	–	94	95	99
Clapton School (G)	94	–	91	94	95
Hackney Downs (B)	75	–	82	89	–
Hackney Free & P (M)	79	–	95	89	97
Haggerston (G)	94	–	91	98	96
Homerton House (B)	79	–	80	100	81
Kingsland (M)	84	–	88	86	95
Our Lady's Convent (G inc.VI)	98	–	95	99	97
Skinners' Company (G inc.VI)	77	–	91	89	93
Stoke Newington (M)	84	–	95	92	93
Hackney average	81.5	–	88.5	91.3	92.6
National average	91.3	–	92.3	91.9	92.1

The authors of this book have had the advantage of access to documents which the EA left behind in the school before it closed. These documents included the reports from all of the three registered inspectors commissioned by the EA, the EA's working documents on educational issues and on financial and management issues, plus an annotated first draft of the EA's final report. Analysis shows how the evidence presented to the EA was prepared for the public presentation of the case for closure in its final report.

The judgements in the report to the EA of Michael Barber and Bryan Bass, who were the two members charged with assessing the school's educational performance, are largely reproduced in the final EA report. They were highly critical of standards, management and the school's 'culture'.

What has not been within the public domain until now are the judgements of the three inspectors who came to the school at the EA's request in September 1995. Having accidentally seen the largely favourable report on English, physical education and religious education before the publication of the final EA document, the Hackney Downs staff were much encouraged. They would have been even more encouraged had they been able to read the report of the inspector who reported to the EA on art, modern languages, geography, history, information technology and music.

This report concluded that 'the overall quality of teaching is sound in most respects' except for Key Stage 3 French. The teaching of IT to the same age group, the inspector said, showed distinct promise and flair. Almost without exception, he said, planning and preparation were good, the aims of lessons were relevant and clear and the content of lessons was sound if at times rather unexciting. There was some lack of differentiation, although no more than found in most secondary schools, and some under-expectation. But he was particularly struck, he told the EA, by the high degree of commitment from the staff. 'This compares favourably with my earlier experience of bad inner-London schools where commitment to an ideology took massive precedence over care for pupils' interests. The problem with the teaching at Hackney Downs is misdirected endeavour rather than lack of it.'

The inspector commented on the pupils, some of whom, he said, were never anything but volatile, though classroom behaviour appeared to improve as pupils progressed up the school. In Ofsted terms, he said, the actual progress made was often better than the attitudes to learning displayed, a reversal of what quite commonly happens in other schools.

Most significantly, this second report concluded that in the inspector's view there were no problems at Hackney Downs that he considered intractable. 'It is much less a hopeless case than in other former ILEA schools that I have experienced. Fundamentally the pupils want to learn and the teachers want to teach them. Given this personal commitment other obstacles, though serious, are no more than obstacles, not impenetrable barriers.' Much could be addressed, he suggested, without massive cost and in reasonable time. Management could be improved, perhaps at no direct cost.

> My overall view, therefore, is that the school is rescuable, at a cost which is not prohibitive and which, taking a suitably long-term view, would constitute value for money. I do not believe that the present management, for all its commitment, can achieve this rescue without either considerable support or other means of strengthening.

The third report, which looked at maths, science and technology, was the most negative of the three inspection documents, which is hardly surprising as these were the departments which had suffered the greatest disruption and endured the worst accommodation. The teaching in both maths and science, the inspector found, was generally unsatisfactory. Technology was in the hands of a single inexperienced teacher because of the head of department's absence through ill-health. The inspector found the teaching offered by the IT co-ordinator well planned and skilful.

In summary, the three inspectors found weak maths and science departments, poor religious education, a technology department without an experienced head, and the rest of the school functioning satisfactorily or better. Behaviour remained a problem, but staff morale and commitment were high and management weaknesses not insuperable.

It is impossible to know what went on in the report-back meeting between the EA members and the three inspectors before the final report was drawn up. But the notes on that meeting, left behind with the other documents, show that these discussions resulted in very different conclusions being drawn from those in the individual inspection reports: the EA reported that 'expectations regarding behaviour were too low for conformity to be established'; that in science and technology particularly, the school environment was having a damaging effect on teaching and response; that personal and social education, science, modern language and management deficits might be intractable; that only swimming and literature teaching could claim to be 'absolutely' good; and that, therefore, 'improvement would be a long venture and costly'.

Who were the bad managers?

The EA was also alone among those who inspected Hackney Downs in criticizing Betty Hales' management, even though its own management report, when it was found after the school closed, proved to be not entirely unsympathetic to the school team either. It commented:

> The management of Hackney Downs appears to be somewhat like Canute trying to hold back the tide. In this case, however, the tide is represented by the pupils, particularly those with problems, the buildings in their dilapidated state and the day-to-day issues which can reach overwhelming proportions.
>
> In support of the management it can be argued that there are a number of extenuating circumstances over which they have no control.

The document went on to list the problems with which successive heads had sought help from the LEA for the previous four or five years.

Conversely, the document suggested that the school lacked the leadership and sense of direction it needed and that historically neither the governors nor the LEA had acted sufficiently decisively to give the school the support it needed. 'All in all, despite the willingness and co-operation which has been apparent to us all, the overall impression is of a school moving rapidly in a downhill direction.'

The contrast between the EA documents and what Ofsted found a little over a year earlier is stark. Ofsted found Betty Hales' leadership 'effective and thoughtful', believed she had contributed to a greater sense of purpose in the school, improved staff morale and given renewed energy and vigour to the school's management. HMI, on their monitoring visit, were also very favourably impressed by the school's management during a period of great difficulty.

The EA's management working document also raised the issue of financial mismanagement which so incensed the teaching staff when it was repeated in the final EA report. Until Hackney LEA took over the school's budget, there had never been any hint from the LEA, or from Daphne Gould during her time at the school, that financial management at the school was anything other than 'sound', as Ofsted concluded, or that the school had been in deficit.

Ofsted had commented merely that 'the school budget suffers a drain as a result of uncertainties in planning as a result of decisions beyond its control'. Also: 'There is little flexibility within the budget for the acting head to use' and that 'planning for solvency is extremely difficult given the uncertainty about the size of the school in future'. In its last full year in control of its own finances, the school came well within its budget. Gus John is on record as complimenting Betty Hales on her efforts to pull the school round, right up to the point at which the closure decision was taken.

However, the working document prepared by the EA on general management and financial administration is particularly critical of Hackney LEA. Specifically it suggests that the LEA should have taken action on staffing and financial issues:

- by dealing with two disciplinary cases involving Hackney Downs staff which had remained unresolved for more than twelve months;
- by taking action to curtail expenditure and reduce the deficit;
- by dealing with over-staffing and providing a recovery plan and a budget for 1995/6 once it was clear the school would remain open;
- by implementing some strategic financial planning in co-operation with the school.

The EA's management document divides the blame for what it sees as poor financial management between the senior staff, the former governors and the LEA. Expenditure, it suggests, was out of control and there was no proper budgeting being done. Hackney claimed to have held budget meetings for 1995/6 with the head-teacher. She denies such meetings ever took place and Hackney finance department has produced no record of such meetings or any detailed budget for the school.

On the state of the buildings, the management document is also highly critical of the LEA. It notes that the rolling programme of refurbishment promised in the LEA Action Plan for a January 1995 start had never been started. The document confirms that Hackney Downs buildings had been seriously neglected, taken out of use and boarded up, over a period of ten years or more. The governors and staff must, the document suggests, carry some of the blame for not pressing hard enough for money to be spent on the school, but 'the authority must shoulder the main blame for the failure to carry out essential works on the school'.

The unanswered questions

There are a number of questions about what happened to Hackney Downs which remain unanswered. The official line remains that the final shift in LEA policy, the decision to propose the closure of the school, was only made a very short time before it was put to the Education Sub-committee in October 1994. And it is true that officers and councillors were publicly proclaiming their support for the school right through the summer when the two Action Plans were being drawn up.

Many of those involved are not convinced by these protestations. Helen Baxter, the chair of governors who spanned the transfer from the ILEA to Hackney, remains convinced that the school remained unpopular with a number of powerful Labour Party people because of teacher militancy in the 1980s when it was controlled by the ILEA. She also recalls the appointment of a new head in 1989 when, she claims, a strong candidate and potentially tough headteacher was rejected in favour of a less experienced person. 'He would have ruffled a few feathers', she recalls.

Tony Burgess, who was the last chair of governors, and many other supporters of the school, remain convinced that the Ofsted inspection and the appointment of Betty Hales as acting head began to turn the school around, but wonders if this was either expected or wanted by the LEA.

The head and staff are also left asking what precipitated the moves to close the school in the autumn of 1994 and not immediately after the school was put on special measures by Ofsted? What happened in October? Was it an educational judgement that the school could not be turned around? That seems unlikely at the very point at which the senior management was producing a highly professional Action Plan which was accepted by the DfEE; and outside visitors, both professional and from the media, came away convinced that the school was on the mend. It seems more likely that closure became an option when it was realized, very late in the day, that Hackney Downs' decaying buildings had become a financial burden for the borough of quite staggering proportions. Was there pressure at that stage from other schools or borough departments which baulked at the thought of up to £3 million being required to put the fabric back together again at a time of great financial stringency?

Outsiders who came into the fray late were astonished by the volatility of Hackney politics and the evident long-standing neglect not only of the fabric of the school but of internal problems such as that created by the Black Staff and Parents' Group. Hackney Downs was not the only school whose buildings had been seriously neglected by the ILEA and then by Hackney Council. The squeeze on educational spending in London was harsh and the result of quite deliberate Conservative government policy.

But the failure to tackle Hackney Downs' internal difficulties was Hackney's alone, part and parcel of the difficulties of a council besieged by deprivation on a massive scale, by feuds within the ruling Labour Party, by allegations and counter-allegations of corruption, by the still vociferous campaigning of Left-wing groups and pulled this way and that by demands for political correctness.

At Hackney Downs one inexperienced headteacher, appointed as the ILEA was wound up, failed to turn the school around. But instead of moving firmly, Hackney dithered about appointing a permanent, experienced and tough successor, which was clearly what the school needed if it was to have a reasonable chance of survival. All the evidence on school improvement points to the need for strong leadership, a good management team, and high staff morale. What Hackney Downs got was a temporary head, to be succeeded by another temporary head who succumbed to illness and was in turn succeeded by yet another temporary appointment.

By sheer chance that last appointment might have made the difference as Betty Hales proved able to revitalize the management and rebuild teacher morale; but by then the second problem on which the LEA, and its predecessor, the ILEA, had failed to take action for so long, boiled over, putting the school under another form of almost intolerable stress.

There is nothing wrong with a group of teachers seeking to improve the chances of black pupils. There is nothing wrong with their forming a 'pressure group' to seek means of improving teaching and learning for ethnic minority children. There is nothing wrong with black teachers and parents opposing racism or any other unfairness if they perceive that they have grievances. There is everything wrong if that group appears to confront rather than negotiate with management and to exaggerate grievances in order to promote an agenda of its own. And a great deal wrong if the disruption caused actually damages the education of pupils – the vast majority of whom come from one ethnic minority or another.

Political correctness, too, has its place. Hackney Downs had a proud tradition of anti-racism. It had successfully taught the sons of Jewish immigrant families before and after the war, and happily integrated more recent arrivals in the 1970s and 1980s. The school management no more tolerated racism in the 1990s than their predecessors had done. The school took pride in the fact that the inspectors consistently complimented it on its lack of racism and its cultural harmony.

But political correctness becomes destructive if it makes it impossible to criticize members of ethnic minorities. There is evidence that this is what happened during the later days of the Inner London Education Authority, under whose control the Hackney Downs Black Staff and Parents' Group was formed. Hackney Council, certainly in its early days as an education authority, carried a legacy of sometimes destructive political correctness for a time.

If those crucial issues of the dilapidated buildings and the difficult minority of black teachers had been tackled early, then at the point when Hackney Downs found itself, quite inadvertently, in the hands of a strong headteacher it might have survived.

Turning the school around would never have been easy. By the end there was a chasm of perception between the school, which believed, on the basis of its careful special needs audits, that its boys were uniquely disadvantaged, and the LEA which claimed that it was no worse off than other schools.

In fact no other school was taking in the proportion of boys who had been excluded or persuaded to leave other schools for the simple reason that most other Hackney schools were full. Hackney Downs had sunk to the bottom of the 'pecking order' of schools in that part of London, and its problems had become unique. As HMI commented, there were boys in the school who were beyond the remit of any teacher in a mainstream school environment, and as the numbers dropped the concentration of such boys became more acute.

This did not necessarily daunt the staff, young and inexperienced as many of them were. All the reports on the school, apart from the final Education Association report, comment on the high staff morale Betty Hales was able to build up in her short period as head, on the high-quality documentation which had been produced in pursuit of school improvement, on improvements in pupil behaviour and school ethos. The A to C GCSE grades remained fairly dismal, although this was always to be expected at a school with very few able boys. But the proportion of boys gaining A to G grades improved steadily in spite of all the disruption of the school's final years. The final HMI visit suggested that the pay-off would soon come in terms of improved education. The Education Association's own inspectors found only two subject areas with potentially intractable problems. Two out of three of them reported that the school could be turned around. There was promise, if the school had been given the normal two years Ofsted allows to try to fulfil it.

The school was also unique in the level of insecurity it was expected to live with for at least its last three years. Its future was called into question in Hackney's secondary review in 1993 which suggested that it go co-educational. It then went through the trauma of its Ofsted inspection, had the co-educational proposal turned down even as it drew up its Action Plan, and was then faced with a closure proposal almost immediately. It spent the best part of the 1994/95 school year unsure whether it would live or die, and was no sooner reprieved than it was placed under the control of the Education Association which had a remit to consider closure yet again.

Inevitably, during some of this period of violent changes of policy, internal disruption and campaigns to save the school, staffing became unstable, appointments were made on a temporary basis or not at all, stress and ill-health at times became endemic, and only towards the end did staff morale at last begin to improve and signs of educational progress begin to appear. If that experience is not unique, it would be interesting to hear of a school which has suffered greater uncertainty and mismanagement engineered by a malign combination of its own LEA, the inspectorate and the government and, sadly, some of its own staff, over such a prolonged period – and survived. Hackney Downs fought for its future and lost, but there are many people who were involved who hope and believe that it did not fight in vain.

19

The Lessons of Hackney Downs

Naming and shaming

What can we conclude from the Hackney Downs story? At one extreme, the school closure can be likened to the old English custom of hunting with hounds. Seeking out failing schools had, in the 1990s, become a rewarding pastime for politicians and for the media. A quarry run to ground could be publicly savaged and, if necessary, publicly done to death. The media can compete, as they did over other London schools in other boroughs, and in other parts of the country – notably The Ridings School in Halifax – to discover 'the worst school in Britain'.

The Press coverage of failing schools could be negative and derisory, official 'hit lists' distributed responsibility indiscriminately among the teachers, governors, parents and, most damagingly, children who happened to be associated with the school at 'failing time'. Politicians and officials, locally and nationally, competed to be 'tough on failing schools' while wilfully ignoring the effect of their own policy and administrative decisions. Schools not involved in the chase could go to ground as having been reprieved or, as in Hackney, having benefited from the situation. Efforts to explain that some schools do suffer from uniquely difficult circumstances, particularly in a fierce market environment, could be dismissed as special pleading. Through all this, children's education could be ruined and teachers' careers blighted through no fault of their own. Only when a local education authority was exposed as 'failing' over a considerable period of time, as Hackney was, did anyone pause to ask whether the 'naming and shaming' of a single school might not have been more widely shared.

Sadly, 'naming and shaming' schools was a policy introduced by the Conservatives but also taken up and defended by the new Labour government in 1997. Within weeks of taking office, the new administration had 'named and shamed' eighteen schools, including Morningside Primary, a feeder school for Hackney Downs. In November 1997, the Secretary of State, David Blunkett, was still defending the policy of 'naming and shaming' and it was not until October 1998 that the policy was finally abandoned.

The Secretary of State is undoubtedly right to continue to say that parents need to know when a school is in trouble and must be told about improvement, or lack of it. But the Hackney Downs experience casts serious doubt on whether using the distorting megaphones of the tabloid Press is the best, or even an acceptable, way of achieving that end.

Hackney Downs suffered five years of naming and shaming in the media locally and nationally. The effects were wholly negative. Ambitious parents took their sons away, staff were further demoralized and many succumbed to sickness as humiliation was added to the other stresses under which they worked in near slum conditions, and the school's reputation plummeted at a time when it was performing no worse than other schools with a similar intake.

What eventually set it on the road to recovery was not hysterical publicity, but the departure of some disruptive staff, the establishment of a senior management team who raised teacher morale and implemented sound educational policies, and the solid support of an experienced consultant. Given the level of financial and professional support which other failing schools have had – even in Hackney itself – there is no reason why Hackney Downs could not have been turned around much earlier and permanently. Its greatest enemy was its own LEA which in 1997 had disintegrated so completely that it was itself subjected to a DfEE-appointed 'hit squad'.

More generally, the death of Hackney Downs raises questions which have not so far been addressed by those who sought, or acquiesced in, it. Some of these questions are practical and administrative, some more concerned with educational policy and the practice of politics in a culture of 'name and shame'.

School maintenance

The most basic question of all concerns school maintenance. How, in the late twentieth century, can a system for financing schools have been allowed to develop which permits a school campus to deteriorate physically over a period of ten years to the point at which no authority, national or local, can afford to put it right? Reading all the copious documentation, one is driven to the conclusion that perhaps the main reason for closure of the school was the near impossibility of finding the funds to restore and upgrade its squalid buildings to a reasonable state.

Hackney had spent money effectively on other crumbling schools it inherited from the ILEA. The government's restrictions on capital spending, on top of the borough's ongoing revenue crisis which resulted from the fierce squeeze on London local government, almost inevitably meant that the Hackney Downs buildings were a millstone too far. This must carry a grim message for anyone associated with the hundreds of other schools in the UK, whether in out-dated Victorian or shoddy 1960s buildings, which suffer from similar levels of neglect, unless sufficient capital is invested over a long enough period, to catch up on the backlog of repairs and prevent dilapidation occurring on this scale again. It remains to be seen whether the government investment so far planned is sufficient.

Sources of support

One of the ironies of the Hackney Downs saga in particular is that concrete support might have been found for the once-proud Grocers' Company School. Even in its final period of crisis the school attracted support from its well-connected business governor which might have been used to bring in sponsorship or other forms of help. During its final term the school regained the interest of an astonishing array of old boys who were members of the Clove Club and who might have been willing to come to the aid of the school in very practical ways. When Hackney reviewed its secondary provision yet again in the spring of 1997, the Clove Club was still in touch with the LEA about renewing links with education in the borough.

But the Clove Club, like so many other people, ran head first into the incompetence and indifference of Hackney LEA. A letter sent in October in response to the 1996 secondary consultation was mislaid until February. It is unsurprising that when Hackney Downs was sliding ever closer to closure no one had the imagination or possibly the desire to see that this was uniquely a school which could have attracted sufficient support from outside to relaunch it as a major asset for the hard-pressed local community.

Parents' wishes

A related point which could usefully be made here concerns the level of fierce parental support for the school. It is easy to dismiss a parental campaign for a school under threat of closure as merely a knee-jerk emotional reaction of no serious account in making policy. In some cases that might be a fair assessment. But in a neighbourhood where family stresses make any sort of commitment to education rare and difficult, policy-makers may need to give special consideration to the damaging effect of trampling such a tender bloom underfoot with the degree of force that was used at Hackney Downs. There was also little consideration given to the views of pupils. One boy, interviewed after he had been compelled to move school during his GCSE year, was very bitter about that decision which he felt had blighted his life.

When parents and children such as these are made to feel by politicians and administrators that their views are of absolutely no consequence, the possibility of raising standards becomes remote. When many, if not all, of those politicians and administrators claim to have the interests of working-class children at heart, it is difficult to see a way forward for deprived inner-city communities. As that great campaigner for State education Joan Sallis puts it: you cannot do good to people violently. You have to take parents with you.

Accountability

A second major question concerns the relationship between the inspection regimes of both Ofsted and the local authorities, with all their paraphernalia of criteria, check-lists and action plans, and the support which a school needs to implement an improvement plan.

During the period 1989 to 1995 Hackney Downs must have become the most-inspected school in the UK, with regular visits, sometimes at very short notice, by inspectors from Ofsted, HMI and the LEA. Most of these reports reiterated the same points with monotonous regularity.

What the school felt it lacked throughout this process – although of course the LEA disputes this – was sufficient support to help it tackle some of the problems which it faced. There is no doubt that the LEA made some effort to help, but equally there seems to be justice in the school's complaint that what was offered was often too little, too late. On one occasion a headteacher and on two occasions on-site advisers were removed by the LEA at short notice. And of course the inspection process itself, with its demands for endless paperwork, eats up valuable senior management time which a school in difficulties can ill afford.

There may be specific problems – in Hackney Downs' case over building maintenance, the increasingly difficult nature of the intake and the unprofessional behaviour of some teachers – where senior managers and governors need the assistance of the LEA, both financial and administrative, to reach a resolution. This book provides little evidence that Hackney LEA had got the balance between pressure and support right as Hackney Downs School struggled through its final four or five years.

Staffing

Allied to this is the practical question of how schools in desperately deprived areas of our cities, often saddled with the label 'failing', are to attract and keep talented headteachers and other staff. Hackney Downs did not have a permanent headteacher for the last three years of its life. It did not have a head who had previous experience as a head for the last five years of its life. The rest of its staff were mainly young, inexperienced and often employed on temporary contracts. Some older staff were ill. A few preferred to work to an agenda not the school's.

Some of the blame for this must lie with the Hackney LEA and its devastating indecision about the school's future. But some must also lie with the market system which makes it hard for all inner-city schools to compete for and retain the best teachers, and a school funding policy which turned its back on anything which smacked of the 1960s Educational Priority Area policy. It is significant that France, faced with similar inner-city difficulties, launched an EPA policy of its own.

Local education authorities

Another practical question is how LEAs are to be held to account for their stewardship in areas like Hackney where the demands made upon them are so overwhelming. Just as the expectation was that Hackney Downs School should have been able to cope with the problems of the most deprived children in the country, so local government was expected to cope with those same problems at the macro level.

The council, the Education Committee and its officers were much less strongly criticized in the EA final report than the authors of this book believe they deserved. Even allowing for the fact that they were a new education authority taking over schools in a uniquely deprived area, they seemed to display an ineptness in dealing with Hackney Downs School which did not, apparently, extend to other secondary schools in the borough. However, central government decisions, especially over levels of funding, affect local decisions, and politicians cannot simply shrug off their own responsibilities and blame 'failing local authorities' for problems in isolation. It will be interesting to see whether the proposed Education Action Zones, being promoted as a solution to the problems of areas like Hackney, do improve the standard of administration and educational quality, and how much extra finance this entails.

The timetable for improvement

It is also surely worth considering whether it is reasonable to expect a school to implement an Action Plan for improvement at the same time as it faces the long-drawn-out and inevitably highly emotive procedures for closure. Ofsted has put on record the fact that it expects a school to come out of 'special measures' after a two-year period of improvement, given that its interim inspection is satisfactory, and this has been the case with most 'failing' schools. Fairfax School in Bradford was allowed three years to improve under its new name, Bowling Community College.

Hackney Downs was allowed four months, including the summer holidays, to respond to the Ofsted inspection report, before the LEA effectively pulled the plug by launching the closure procedure. Of course this was not an Ofsted decision, and HMI continued to monitor the school on the assumption that it would remain open. But from that point on, the time and energy of governors, staff, parents and children, which should have been devoted to school improvement, were inevitably sucked into the campaign to save the school. The LEA, meanwhile, began to back-pedal on the promises it had made in its Action Plan for the school's improvement. This seems neither fair nor reasonable if a school is genuinely expected to improve over that crucial two-year time-scale.

'Naming and shaming'

Moving on to more general issues, a major question must be why the failing schools movement developed in England in the 1990s, in a way which allowed some schools, in need of 'special measures' under the 1993 Education Act, to become the target of often vitriolic media and political attack. A second must be why the first Education Association to be appointed under the legislation failed so dismally to help a school, which was improving, to improve further, rather than advising closure – a judgement challenged in the High Court.

The first point requires considerable discussion. The closure of the occasional school is nothing new, particularly when there is a demographic downturn of school-age children and there are surplus places. But the closure of local authority schools on grounds that they are so irretrievably bad that nothing can be done, is a new phenomenon that requires explanation.

The problem of failing schools is not unique to the UK. Many countries are grappling with the phenomenon of poor results, particularly in schools in city neighbourhoods with high levels of deprivation; and most are trying to devise ways of improving such schools' performance. Some are choosing to put in extra resources and staff; others are devising versions of the Education Priority Areas which were used in the UK in the 1960s; most are sharpening methods of monitoring performance. But few seem to have chosen to follow the route of 'naming and shaming' which characterized the treatment of failing schools in the UK in the 1990s. Even after the Labour government announced that it would not continue this policy, schools have continued to be publicly humiliated when they have moved into 'special measures' or threatened with a 'fresh start'. It is necessary to ask why, almost without exception, such schools are situated in highly impoverished and unstable communities where children inevitably take their disadvantages into school with them. How has England in particular reached the stage of school closure by public humiliation which was so graphically illustrated by Hackney Downs?

Educational markets and failure

Failure exists in all school systems. In competitive school systems failure is a necessary part of the structure. In England and Wales the secondary education system set up 50 years ago was premised on the assumption that 80 per cent of students would fail at the age of 11 to indicate any potential for academic learning. This was not initially perceived as a problem by politicians or the general public. In the post-war climate, the priority was to hurry as many young people as possible through their schooling and into the waiting labour market. Far from regarding the 80 per cent of young people, who in the late 1940s never attempted any course that would lead to a school certificate ('O' and 'A' levels from 1951), as a problem, the then Labour government unashamedly set up secondary modern schools to cater for those pupils 'whose future employment will not demand any measure of technical skill or knowledge' as a Ministry of Education pamphlet of 1946 put it. In present-day terms all those secondary modern schools were failing schools.

The comprehensive school movement and the expansion of access to examination courses from the 1960s began to allow larger numbers of young people access to equal opportunities and success. The number leaving school with no examination passes decreased, and by 1990, the 1940s figures were reversed with over

80 per cent of young people attempting and achieving examination passes in academic courses. The number of qualifications gained on vocational courses also increased exponentially.

This success has never been of much interest to most politicians or the media, and has seldom been brought to the attention of the public. Prime Ministers have led the way in holding schools responsible for economic and social ills. In 1976, James Callaghan (then Labour Prime Minister) in the wake of a world recession and the collapse of the youth labour market, blamed schools for their failure to provide the nation with vocationally skilled young people who could lever up the economy. The views of business leaders and employers, consistently negative about the capabilities of school-leavers since they were first sought over a hundred years ago, are regularly offered as evidence of decline. International surveys, particularly in maths and science, are gloomily recounted as evidence of our failure to keep up with our competitors no matter how flawed the survey evidence (see Brown, 1997).

By the late 1980s, dissatisfaction with the whole educational system and its standards had become a routine political pitch with all parties competing to produce solutions. Local education authorities, particularly Labour ones, and their bureaucracies, were targeted as contributors to low standards. Schools and teachers, particularly in urban areas, were also targeted. Disadvantage, migration, second-language speaking, and a public culture that did not value education were all identified as contributing to underachievement. But it was not 'politic' to examine the contribution of lack of resources, crumbling buildings, underpaid teachers and the spread of poverty and unemployment. By the early 1990s, the focus of dissatisfaction had shifted to identifying and pillorying individual schools as emblematic of a whole system 'failing the nation'. This culminated in May 1997 in the new Labour government publishing the names of eighteen 'failing schools', singled out from 300 on the special measures list – the failing amongst the failing, two of them, unsurprisingly, in Hackney.

The Education Acts of 1988, 1992 (Schools) and 1993 effected the transition of UK schools into the marketplace. Funding was linked to enrolment, although local authorities could also allocate funds (if they had any) on the basis of other factors such as deprivation and special educational needs. But they had little control over capital spending allocations. Information to consumers was provided by a new framework for schools inspections. Inspectors' reports were made public, and test and examination results were published annually from 1992 in the form of league tables. Newspapers eagerly published percentages of pupils achieving the five A–C passes at GCSE level required for entry into higher education, and other performance indicators, in rank order. These rankings of league tables encouraged competition rather than co-operation and undermined the opportunity for schools to co-operate and learn from each other.

A 'blame culture' surrounding the treatment of failing schools developed. Schools were treated as if they were separate from any historical, social, economic and political context, and it became acceptable to blame the existing headteacher, staff, governors, parents and pupils. This situation has partly developed because of political and policy-makers' reliance on research into 'what makes for effective schools', carried out in Europe and the USA from the 1970s.

School effectiveness

The failing school can be seen as the obverse of the effective school, and the research into what makes some schools more effective than others has become a political tool. It is important to note that most school effectiveness surveys in the UK were carried out *before* the 1988 Education Act introduced competition between schools and the effects of competitive policies began to take effect. The studies were undertaken from the stance that schools with similar intakes of students in terms of prior attainment, social class and ethnic origin might differ in the extent to which they helped pupils to progress in school. The intention was not to deride or pillory schools that did not appear to be as successful in helping pupils to progress, but to suggest reasons for this and encourage the translation of good practice and co-operation from more to less effective schools.

This, in passing, is the kind of policy the London Borough of Lambeth adopted in 1996–97, where, in the words of Ofsted's Deputy Director 'inspection data (will be used) to identify priorities for action, to target resources where they are most needed, and to identify models of good practice in each school which could serve as models for others to learn from (Mike Tomlinson, *Education Guardian*, 7 January 1997).

But in the 1990s, other politicians and policy-makers do appear to believe in a pathological view of schooling. In particular, politicians and the inspectorate have used evidence which indicated that some schools with similar intakes of students are 'doing better' in GCSE league tables, to castigate less effective schools, without accurate knowledge of the socio-economic background of the pupils. The Ofsted Deputy Director wrote in 1997: 'The mix of socio-economic background of pupils in LEA-maintained schools is not widely different across all schools, the poor schools cannot parade this as an excuse for low standards' (Mike Tomlinson, 1997), just as the Education Association had suggested earlier that Hackney Downs staff were using pupil background as an excuse for low achievement.

However, it must be stated clearly and loudly that reliance on school effectiveness research to discover and isolate failing schools is simplistic and dangerous (Goldstein, 1996). The background factors which were taken into account by school effectiveness researchers in the 1980s are *not* as extreme as those experienced by schools in the 1990s. It is *not* acceptable, educationally, methodologically or politically, to ignore two major differences between the 1980s, when the UK school effectiveness research was carried out, and the 1990s.

External factors

The first difference is the effect of market forces, which have *never* been properly taken into account when labelling 'good' and 'bad' schools, and which do appear to be turning some schools not simply into 'sink' schools, as the media have it, but into *special* schools, with the characteristics and intakes associated with special schooling. The second factor is the rapid increase in poverty, unemployment and deprivation and their effect on families, far in excess of anything taken into account in the 1980s' research, and which now affects particular schools in ways that we are only beginning to be dimly aware of.

Hackney Downs School was a school experiencing these two effects. It was a school included in a major school effectiveness study in the 1980s (Smith and Tomlinson, 1989). In 1986, the students achieved higher grade examination passes on a par with the London schools studied, and higher than five Midlands schools in the research. Yet already the school was experiencing staff, resource and maintenance problems and the increased effects of a socially deprived intake. By the 1990s, it was no longer acceptable to assume that it was serving a disadvantaged clientele similar to other schools. In the education market, the school had become a school for 'losers'. Almost two-thirds of the pupils were officially regarded as having special educational needs, particularly learning and behavioural difficulties, the school had taken in large numbers of boys excluded from other schools and was close to becoming a *de facto* special school, although it still had pupils who performed well academically. Although this was put to the Education Association, together with the suggestion that the school could become a designated special school, they chose to ignore the information.

In his 1996 book, Michael Barber discusses Hackney Downs as a failing school which deserved to be closed, and Haywood High School, a school in the Potteries, Stoke-on-Trent, as an improved school deserving of praise. Although the latter school serves two council estates, there is no way in which the intake or the historical, social, economic and cultural circumstances of the schools can be fairly compared. Neither could the ethnic mix or the numbers of children with special needs: 'The good news is that there are many more schools like Hayward High School than Hackney Downs' (p. 122).

That may be true, but the comparison is an unreasonable one. Haywood High's regeneration was described in detail in the National Commission for Education's book *Success Against the Odds* (1996). This makes it quite clear that the school has had the support of its LEA over a period of years, including the investment of a considerable amount of extra funds.

> The physical environment had clearly received a good deal of attention during the past five years. The new buildings provided a superb learning environment and some excellent new

facilities such as a drama studio . . . there were carpets in place
. . . the surroundings have clearly been transformed by the
investment the LEA has made in new buildings. (p. 181)

The contrast with the buildings at Hackney Downs makes it
shameful to contrast the two schools as 'failing' and 'successful'.
Haywood High's experience was much closer to that of Hackney
Free and Parochial's treatment by the Hackney LEA where, in contrast to Hackney Downs, help was given to restructure the staff and
upgrade the buildings while the most disruptive pupils were simply
excluded.

The school effectiveness and improvement literature also stresses
strong leadership and management of schools if they are to be
regarded as successful. Indeed, the enormous amount of literature
on effective school leadership has led to assumptions by policy-
makers that 'strong' leadership of schools is *the* major solution to
educational, and by extension, economic problems. Although the
Hackney Downs leadership had not been criticized up to autumn
1995 – indeed had been praised by Ofsted and HMI – the EA, as
we have noted, did introduce criticism of the head and senior management. It was as if there had been a *post-hoc* belief that because
effective schools are supposed to have effective heads, to prove
Hackney Downs was a failing school, it was necessary to criticize
the head.

It has already been noted that in the winners and losers scenario
that the Hackney schools were part of, some of the schools benefited from the Hackney Downs closure and at the end local
secondary heads, in a highly unusual attack on their colleagues,
pressed the EA to close their neighbour down.

Failing schools

The failing schools movement, however, cannot be explained
entirely by the emergence of competition between schools, and the
inevitable creation of 'loser' schools, or by the misuse of the school
effectiveness research. The legislation concerning school failure and
the creation of Education Associations was political in origin and
was designed as a way of making more schools in urban Labour-

controlled authorities go grant-maintained. Prime Minister Thatcher, her successor John Major and Ministers of Education Baker, McGregor, Clarke and John Patten, had all been mystified that there had been no rush for schools to opt out of Labour-controlled authorities into GM status; by 1992 only 337 had actually 'gone GM' (although over 800 more were in the pipeline), and most of these were in Conservative LEAs. Ministers were also concerned that the market was not working as intended and 'poor' schools closing at the intended rate. From her autobiography (Thatcher, 1993), Mrs Thatcher appeared to believe that there was a conspiracy among some Labour-controlled authorities to keep open poor schools. The failing schools legislation, signalled in the 1992 White Paper *Choice and Diversity*, was designed to kill several birds with one stone. Since schools with low levels of achievement *were* largely located in Labour-controlled, disadvantaged, inner-city areas, legislation could be designed to remove schools from the LEA, further weakening their influence, and boost the GM figures without any parental ballots as to whether the school should opt out.

The Education Association was to be the instrument to effect all this. Schools at risk of failure which had not been improved by their governing bodies or the LEA would be put under the management of a body appointed by the Secretary of State, an Education Association which would 'effectively be in the position of a grant-maintained governing body (DfE 1992, pp. 50–51). The EA would receive a grant for maintaining a school they had taken over on the same basis as a grant-maintained school and 'at the end of its stewardship . . . the normal expectation is that the school will become grant-maintained'. An EA was also envisaged as a body controlling 'as many schools in an area, including neighbouring LEAs, as were found to be failing' (p. 50). The EA was to be the mechanism through which central government took more schools in urban Labour-controlled authorities out of LEA control. Legislation was enacted in 1993 to enable all schools to opt for grant-maintained status more easily and also to set up the 'special measures' which would hand over financial and other powers, first to the LEA and then to an EA.

We have seen how this worked in the case of Hackney Downs. The criteria for failing schools set out in the circulars and Ofsted

Handbooks all locate the failure firmly within the school – poor standards of achievement, unsatisfactory teaching, poor management and bad pupil behaviour. The historical circumstances, the political pressures, and excessive social and economic disadvantages were ignored in the legislation and in inspection criteria. Yet the first report on failing schools produced by the DfEE and Ofsted, for an OECD conference in London in 1995, showed that *the* major characteristics of failing schools were that they served areas of socio-economic deprivation (poverty and unemployment) and that they had large numbers of migrant, minority (especially Afro-Caribbean) and second-language speakers. The schools were also almost all former secondary modern schools and had never been 'comprehensive' in admitting pupils of all abilities. Only on this latter point did Hackney Downs differ from the 'typical' failing school in that it had once been a grammar school but, as we have seen, it had by the 1990s ceased to attract more than a handful of high-ability boys in any given year group.

Failing schools (and there were some 300 so designated by 1997) are officially regarded as operating divorced from their specific historical, cultural, political, economic and social circumstances. From the official point of view, heads, teachers and governors in post at 'failing time' bear a heavy responsibility. They are not only held to be personally responsible for failing children who, in the emotive language of the 1992 White Paper 'have only one chance', they are also failing local communities and the whole nation! Basil Bernstein wrote a well-known article in *New Society* in 1970, entitled 'Education cannot compensate for society'. In the 1990s the message appeared to be 'if your school cannot compensate for society it will go under and you will be personally blamed'. This is what happened in the case of Hackney Downs.

There were signs that this situation was worrying some influential people. At the North of England Conference in January 1997, Sir Bryan Nicholson, President of the Confederation for British Industry, argued that persistent criticisms of teachers and teaching was counter-productive. He said, 'We need to stop expecting teachers to do the impossible. They can't cure all the ills of our society' (Carvel, 1997). When Hackney Downs' teachers attempted the impossible, they were publicly and persistently criticized and, indeed, vilified.

But it appears that no one has taken on board the lessons which should be learned from the closure of Hackney Downs, and public reservations, such as Sir Bryan's, about the policies which made it possible. One of the ironies of educational policy in the 1990s must be the way in which a New Labour government took over a policy which had been designed to embarrass Labour councils and boost the flagging grant-maintained schools policy, and which had the effect of targeting the poor and disadvantaged. The 1997 Labour White Paper *Excellence in Schools* (DfEE, 1997) simply noted that 300 schools had been identified by Ofsted as failing, recommended a Fresh Start by closure and reopening of the school on the same site, or 'in some cases the most sensible course will be the closure and transfer of pupils to nearby successful schools' . . . and 'the government intends to remove some of the legal and administrative barriers to force an LEA to close a failing school where that is the best course'. The Unit charged with carrying out these policies was the new Standards and Effectiveness Unit at the DfEE. Its newly appointed head was Michael Barber, a member of the Education Association which recommended the closure of Hackney Downs School.

The Education Association

The activities of the first, and so far, the only Education Association to be appointed under the 1993 legislation were not auspicious. Indeed, the fact that the advice of this EA to the Secretary of State ended up being challenged in the High Court, rather than being accepted as reasonable by parents, staff and governors, suggests that the Association had in some senses 'failed'.

We have seen that the Secretary of State indicated on 4 July 1995 that she had no further interest in Hackney Downs School, but that just over a week later, on 13 July, she notified the LEA that she was 'minded to set up an Education Association'. It still remains an unknown question as to what happened between the 4 and 13 July to change her mind. It is known that relations between the LEA officers and DfEE officials had been close during the Ofsted visits.

It is noteworthy that the Association was set up as the North-East London Education Association (NELEA), thus fulfilling the intentions of the 1993 legislation that an Association would have scope to take in other failing schools in the LEA and in neighbouring boroughs if necessary. In 1996, Langham School, in the neighbouring borough of Haringey, was threatened with take-over by the same EA but was reprieved. A writer in the *TES* noted that 'The decision by Education Minister Robin Squire *not* to send an Education Association into the Langham School has been interpreted as a government climb-down. Haringey Council had been threatening to seek a judicial review.'

However, the NELEA could be said to have been 'successful' in that it carried out the agenda of the Hackney education officers, some council members, some other Hackney headteachers and, presumably, the Secretary of State, in recommending closure on the grounds that the school was irretrievably failing. This happened despite the judgement of HMI that the school was improving, despite the contrary advice of Ofsted inspectors invited in during the school's final term, and against the wishes of the democratically elected council, the parents, pupils, teachers and many other supporters.

There were no rules of conduct for this or for any other association – a situation noted by the High Court Judge in his summing up of the judicial review. There was, for example, no bar to members of the Association publishing articles in the press *while* they were carrying out their task. Indeed, one member published an article in the *Independent* the day after he was appointed to the EA ('New start for pupils sold short by Council', Barber, M., the *Independent*, 28 July 1995) in which he voiced the view that all schools in Hackney would suffer if Hackney Downs remained open, and that in wanting the school to stay open, the council had 'ignored the strongly-worded advice of the Council's Chief Education Officer'. Three days after the Secretary of State decided to close the school on the advice of the EA, Michael Barber defended the decision robustly in the *TES* ('The school that had to die', Barber, M., *TES*, 17 November 1995). Some people formed the impression that some members of the Association appeared committed to closure from the outset.

This impression was reinforced by the use and interpretation of evidence in the final report of the EA. One of us ('Hit squad needs new set of rules', Tomlinson, *TES*, 22 December 1995) has already commented that 'Historians of Education may well look back to 1995 as a year when the first Education Association to be appointed by a Secretary of State for Education recommended the closure of a school in a report that was distinctly selective with the evidence.' We have already shown that aspects of such selectivity included: –

- The continued assertions, which have now achieved mythological status, that the school was functioning at such a high unit cost that it 'amounted to daylight robbery from other Hackney pupils'. In fact, the high level of expenditure, which was only in operation for the final few months in the school's existence, was entirely the responsibility of the LEA and then the EA itself.

- The assertion in the EA report that the school the boys were to be transferred to against their wishes was a significantly more effective school, despite evidence in 1995 that its examination results were no better than Hackney Downs' – a situation repeated again in 1996.

- The assertion in the report (repeated in a *TES* letter by M. Barber on 5 January 1996) that consultation undertaken by the EA had resulted in support for closure. Scrutiny of *Appendix 2* to the EA report indicates that of 43 responses received by the EA, only fourteen preferred closure, two-thirds wanting the school to remain open in some form. Even when the EA was in charge, there was no overwhelming support in the borough for closure.

- The failure to accept evidence that the school was improving, both from the HMI visit in March 1995 and from the EA's own independent Ofsted inspectors, two out of the three of whom concluded that the school could be rescued, with some support. One commented: 'It is much less a hopeless case than in other former ILEA schools that I have experienced. Fundamentally the pupils want to learn and the teachers want to teach them. Given this personal commitment other obstacles, though serious, are no more than obstacles, not impenetrable barriers.' These reports were not referred to in the final EA report nor in the DfEE's evidence in the High Court.

- The unsupported allegations made against the staff and headteacher over management issues and the presentation of

opinion as evidence. For example, page 4 of the report casti-
gates 'weak management and poor teaching', and 'Even more
serious is our sense that many teachers and boys at the school
have come to accept low standards as the norm and thus low
expectations.'

Professor Sally Tomlinson's counter-opinion after visiting the
school several times in the autumn of 1995 was that teachers
had high expectations of students for whom learning did not
come easily. This view was shared by other outsiders, such as
Professor Josh Silver of Oxford University and a Clove Club
campaigner who visited the school during its final months. The
view that the teachers wanted to teach and pupils wanted to
learn was confirmed by a report to the EA by an Ofsted inspector, which was not at that time available.

- The EA's criticism of teachers, especially the comment that
'they have forgotten what is possible in terms of standards in
inner-city education'. As two-thirds of the teachers at Hackney
Downs in autumn 1995 had less than three years' teaching
experience this comment appears extraneous. It could be held
that the teachers had done well to begin to learn, let alone for-
get, about standards in inner-city or any schools.

All in all, it appears to the authors of this book that the first Education Association to be appointed was not a success, either in terms
of the original intention of the legislation, in its standards of report-
ing, or in terms of the challenge to its advice in the High Court.

The aftermath

In the year following the closure of Hackney Downs there was no
let-up in the castigation of Hackney Downs as a failing school,
although the accolade of 'worst school in Britain' passed quickly to
The Ridings School in Halifax. This school, with many similar problems to Hackney Downs, was not improving, as Hackney Downs
was at closure, and staff there were simply refusing to teach difficult children. The Ridings eventually received plaudits for having
been 'turned around', although in 1998 only 3 per cent of its pupils
achieved five or more higher-grade GCSEs.

By 1997 however, the focus had moved from failing schools to failing LEAs. The 1997 Education Act empowered Ofsted, assisted by the Audit Commission, to inspect LEAs on a regular cycle, starting in January 1998. Hackney was be one of the first to be so inspected. The Ofsted Report accepted that Hackney school standards were rising at or above the national level (thanks perhaps to the heads and teachers rather than the LEA). But it noted that the LEA's development plan was poorly designed and that budgeting was not yet right. It also commented that support for weak schools was 'vague and fitful', two-thirds of school staff needed new contracts, and the borough was uniquely unsuccessful in its IT development.

Even before this, an 'improvement team' (again labelled a 'hit squad' by the Press) had been appointed by the government to report on Hackney's education service. The chair of this team was none other than Richard Painter, chair of the EA which had closed Hackney Downs. The final report of this team in July 1998 criticized Hackney's plans for school reorganization and financing, including a plan to reopen a school on the Hackney Downs site. This had been a pledge made by the local Labour Party in the run-up to the 1998 council elections. The report suggested that all 72 schools in Hackney should be split into two Education Action Zones – Action Zones being an important plank in the new Labour government's policy for helping underperforming schools in areas with high levels of disadvantage (DfEE, 1997). Richard Painter was reported as saying that 'under present circumstances in Hackney, only the private sector would be in an effective position to prepare a bid' for such zones (Barnard, *TES*, 24 July 1998).

However, by 1999 the LEA had decided to spearhead its own plan for an EAZ, embracing all Hackney schools and encouraging them to have an input into the bid and work together co-operatively. The bid was supported by and largely based on the ideas in the visionary publication by the Royal Society of Arts *Redefining Schools* (RSA, 1998). Whether a reopened Hackney Downs would be included in this or any other plan is still a matter for conjecture in 1999. But in the spring of that year the Secretary of State intervened again to ensure that Hackney put some of its services out to private tender.

Failing or failed school?

Hackney Downs has achieved unwarranted notoriety as the first UK school to be closed because it was failing. The intention of this book has been to show that it was in fact, a 'failed school'. Failed, as we noted at the outset, by market forces created by government policies, by near-criminal resourcing for buildings and maintenance over a long period, and by local council political in-fighting, bureaucratic incompetence and vacillation by the local education authority, unprofessionalism by some teachers (though not those in post in 1995) and lack of support from some other Hackney schools.

It was *not* failed by the head, senior staff, teachers, parents and boys at the school at the time it was designated as failing. Most of the staff went on to other posts where they are proving themselves to be competent, caring and capable teachers. We hope that this book has adequately demonstrated that misuse of research findings, politically motivated legislation and politicians' desires for 'zero tolerance of school underperformance' (Blair, 1996) are *not* the solutions for the new kind of *dispossessed school* (in the sense of dispossessed = deprived of rights, hopes, expectations, *Chambers 20th Century Dictionary*) that has been created in the 1990s.

Ultimately, we would conclude that the failures experienced by this school led it inexorably towards some kind of closure. The obvious solution by 1995 would have been a decent, planned amalgamation with Homerton House School, being completed at the end of the school year in 1996, with co-operation and involvement of staff, students and parents of both schools.

This was not to be. The High Court judgement confirming the correctness of *procedures* surrounding the closure did not and could not take into account the appalling history and circumstances surrounding the closure which we have narrated. Perhaps the school will stand as a metaphor for our time. A time at the end of the twentieth century when a society grown desperately unequal tried to assuage its guilt by finding demons to blame in the form of failing schools.

Hackney Downs dared to fight the victimization, the blame and the demonizing, but in the end it was indeed a school that 'had to die'. Those who knew it hope that in death it will ultimately contribute more to the struggle for high-quality education and equal opportunities for working-class and disadvantaged children than it could have done by staying alive.

Note

The legislation pertaining to failing schools is set out in the Education Act 1993 (Chapters 1 and 11 of Part V) and DfE Circular 17/93 *Schools requiring special measures*.

Bibliography

Barber, M. (1992) *Education in the Capital*, London: Cassell.

Barber, M. (1995) 'New start for pupils sold short by Council policies', *Independent*, 28 July.

Barber, M. (1995) 'The school that had to die', *Times Educational Supplement*, 17 November.

Barber, M. (1996) *The Learning Game*, London: Gollancz.

Barnard, N. (1998) 'Hackney hit squad's double blow', *Times Educational Supplement*, 24 July, p. 9.

Bernstein, B. (1970) 'Education cannot compensate for society', *New Society*, 26 July.

Blair, A. (1996) 'Twentieth anniversary lecture', Ruskin College, Oxford, 16 December.

Bowen, H. (1876) *Studies in English*.

Brown, M. (1997) 'The Tyranny of the International Horse Race', in Slee, R., Tomlinson, S. and Weiner, G. (eds) *Effective for Whom?*, Falmer Press.

Carvel, J. (1997) 'Business leader attacks School Inspection Service', *Guardian*, 3 January.

Carvel, J. (1997) 'Name and shame policy goes on, says Blunkett', *Guardian*, 11 November.

Clark, P. (1998) *Back from the Brink: Transforming The Ridings School*, London: Metro Books.

DfE (1992) *Choice and Diversity: A New Framework for Our Schools*, White Paper, London: DfE.

DfEE (1997) *Excellence in Schools*, White Paper, London: HM Stationery Office

Gardiner, J. (1996) 'Hit squad's target wins reprieve in climbdown', *Times Educational Supplement*, 26 July.

Goldstein, H. (1996) *The Methodology of School Effectiveness Research*, London: Institute of Education.

Kemp, J. (1991) *The Last Thirty Years*.

London's Ethnic Minorities (1994) Commission for Racial Equality.

National Commission on Education (1996) *Success Against the Odds*, London: Routledge.

Pool, K. (1996) 'Hard lessons of schools caught in the spotlight', *Guardian*, 16 November.

Rafferty, F. (1998) 'Labour gives up shaming schools', *TES*, 2 October, p. 1.

Royal Society of Arts (1998) *Redefining Schools*, London: RSA.

Smith, D. J. and Tomlinson, S. (1989) *The School Effect – A Study of Multiracial Comprehensives*, London: Policy Studies Institute.

Social Atlas of London (1974) Oxford: Clarendon Press.

Thatcher, M. (1993) *The Downing Street Years*.

Tomlinson, M. (1997) 'The devil is in the detail', *Education Guardian*, 7 January.

Tomlinson, S. (1995) 'Hit squad needs new set of rules', *Times Educational Supplement*, 22 December.

Index